BLOOD, SWEAT
and STEEL

BLOOD, SWEAT and STEEL

Frontline accounts from the Gulf, Afghanistan and Iraq

Peter Darman

NEW HOLLAND

Published in 2010 by New Holland Publishers (UK) Ltd
London • Cape Town • Sydney • Auckland
www.newhollandpublishers.com
Garfield House, 86–88 Edgware Road, London W2 2EA, United Kingdom
80 McKenzie Street, Cape Town 8001, South Africa
Unit 1, 66 Gibbes Street, Chatswood, NSW 2067, Australia
218 Lake Road, Northcote, Auckland, New Zealand

10 9 8 7 6 5 4 3 2 1

A catalogue record for this book is available from the British Library

ISBN 978 1 84773 513 3

Publisher: Aruna Vasudevan
Project Editors: Julia Shone/Marilyn Inglis
Editor: Elise Bradbury
Design: 2m design
Illustrator: Stephen Dew
Production: Melanie Dowland

Reproduction by Pica Digital Pte Ltd., Singapore
Printed and bound by Replika Press Pvt. Ltd., India

The paper used to produce this book is sourced from sustainable forests.

Contents

Foreword   6

Introduction   9

The First Gulf War (1990–91)
Iraq – an introduction   19
Operation Desert Shield   21
Liberating Kuwait   37
Prisoners of war   54

Iraq: invasion and occupation (2003–10)
Operation Iraqi Freedom   69
Fighting the insurgency   93
The Battle of Fallujah   118
A long, hard slog   130

Afghanistan (2001–10)
Afghanistan – an introduction   157
Operation Enduring Freedom   159
NATO's war   173
Helmand Province   185
Winning hearts and minds   208

Casualties of war   224

Appendix: Timelines, Glossary, Index   239
Acknowledgements   256

Foreword

Since the August 1990 invasion of Kuwait by the Iraqi Army, the subsequent conflicts known as the Gulf Wars took centre-stage in international politics. The First Gulf War saw the liberation of Kuwait by a United Nations (UN) Coalition of nations. The Second Gulf War in 2003 toppled the regime of the Iraqi dictator, Saddam Hussein, and witnessed the establishment of a US-sponsored democratic government in Iraq, though only after nearly six years of a bloody insurgency.

By this time the West, predominantly the United States and Great Britain, was locked in a global War on Terror against al-Qaeda, the terrorist organization that had destroyed the World Trade Center in New York on 11 September 2001. Al-Qaeda's leader, Osama bin Laden, was based in Afghanistan and protected by the Taliban, the hardline Islamist rulers of the country. By the end of 2001, invading US troops had toppled the Taliban-led government in Afghanistan. However, as in Iraq, NATO troops were locked in a long, vicious war against Taliban insurgents that remained in parts of Afghanistan and the conflict continues to this day.

This book contains a broad cross-section of first-hand accounts from men and women who have taken part in the conflicts in Iraq and Afghanistan over the last 20 years. The stories are predominantly from a Western perspective, though there are also contributions from Afghan and Iraqi individuals. Whatever the nationality, the accounts convey the emotions, actions and observations that are generic to modern warfare: boredom, frustration, terror, courage, humility and humanity. Throughout there is also the sardonic wit that is universal to all soldiers.

Also universal is the youth (some of them still teenagers) of many who have taken part in often brutal battles in Iraqi towns and cities and in the Afghan countryside. Their words convey wisdom often far in advance of their years, as well as hope that they will see their loved ones and families again, and sometimes sadness at what they have witnessed, but never self-pity.

Blood, Sweat and Steel is not about the rights and wrongs of the wars in Iraq and Afghanistan; rather, it is a record of the experiences of ordinary men and women in uniform who are often called upon to do extraordinary things. These are the voices of those who are the best of their generation, and who like their forebears in the twentieth century, were sent to foreign fields to fight for their country. And to die there, thousands of them, with tens of thousands more wounded. Their voices deserve to be heard.

In war people get killed, but many more are wounded. Bullets and bombs inflict terrible injuries, and those who lose limbs face decades of disability. Seeing wounded service personnel at first hand prompted two ordinary individuals, Bryn and Emma Parry, to found the charity Help for Heroes in October 2007. Its aim was simple – to help wounded servicemen and women returning from Afghanistan and Iraq. The response of the British public was also simple and resulted in an avalanche of donations. In just 28 months, Help for Heroes raised a staggering £40 million, and though the country has been gripped by economic recession, there has been no let-up in the torrent of funds being donated. Help for Heroes called upon the British public to 'do their bit' for the wounded; millions took up the call and donated their time and money. The author of this book is but one among many who is proud to do so.

Peter Darman

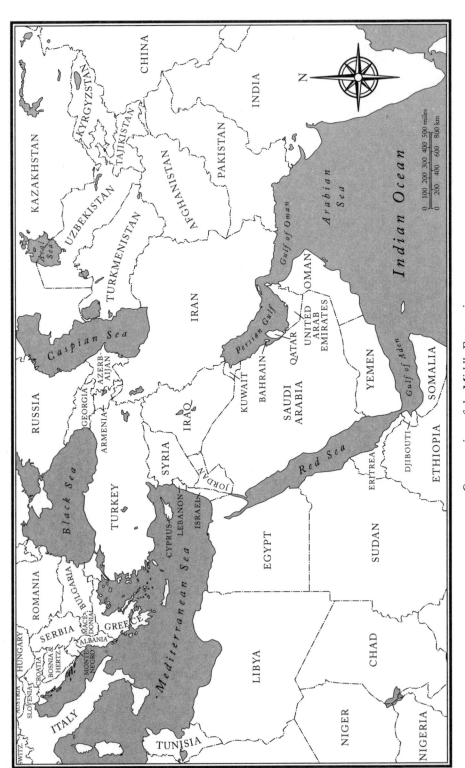

On overview of the Middle East region

Introduction

In August 1990, Iraqi dictator Saddam Hussein (1937–2006; president of Iraq 1979–2003) ordered his army to occupy the oil-rich state of Kuwait. This event would trigger the First Gulf War (called the Persian Gulf War in the US), in which a coalition of states under a United Nations (UN) mandate was authorized to liberate Kuwait using military force. This UN force was assembled in Saudi Arabia in the latter part of 1990 under the codename Operation Desert Shield. It was overwhelmingly American, with sizeable contingents from Britain and France, and also contained troops from Saudi Arabia, Syria, Oman, Morocco and Pakistan, among others. The presence of Muslim forces within this coalition negated Saddam Hussein's rather clumsy attempt to portray the confrontation as a clash between Islam and 'infidels'.

Western Coalition commanders and service personnel were mindful that Saudi Arabia contains two of the Muslim world's holiest sanctuaries: Mecca, the birthplace of the Prophet Muhammad and of Islam itself; and Medina, the Prophet's burial place. Respect for Muslim sensibilities ensured that there were, in general, few cultural clashes between the locals and the tens of thousands of Westerners in their country. That said, Islamic fundamentalists were outraged by the presence of 'infidels' in Saudi Arabia, especially when the Americans maintained a military presence after the war. Islamic militants targeted US personnel in a number of terrorist incidents, such as the June 1996 attack on the US military complex at Khobar Towers, which killed 19 Americans and wounded hundreds more.

The personal accounts in this book from those who participated in Operation Desert Shield highlight cultural differences between themselves and their hosts, the intense heat, the constant fear of Iraqi Scud missile attacks, and the massive logistical problems of deploying hundreds of thousands of troops, thousands of vehicles and hundreds of aircraft to Saudi Arabia. For those who took part in the ground offensive to liberate Kuwait in February 1991 (codenamed Operation Desert Sabre), their experiences recall a battle that pitted overwhelming technical superiority against a demoralized and defeated Iraqi Army that had been subjected to weeks of a merciless Coalition air campaign (codenamed Operation Desert Storm), which had emasculated Iraq's command-and-control network and inflicted serious damage on Iraqi armoured and infantry units. The ground war lasted a mere 100 hours, and when it was over the Iraqi Army had been crushed. The road to Baghdad and regime change lay open, but US President George H. W. Bush (b. 1924; president of the US 1989–93) took the decision that toppling Saddam Hussein was outside the UN remit, which it was, and so the Baghdad regime remained in place. This was to prove a costly decision.

Throughout the 1990s, Saddam Hussein continued to pose problems for the UN, and the US in particular. Despite UN sanctions and the establishment of no-fly zones in the north and south of Iraq (originally established to protect rebellious Iraqi minorities – Kurds in the north and Shi'a Muslims in the south), Saddam Hussein remained a thorn in Washington's side. In particular, Iraq's suspected weapons of mass destruction (WMD) programme caused intense friction between the two countries.

By January 2001, George W. Bush (b. 1946; president of the United States 2001–09 and son of the US leader in the First Gulf War), had been elected president, and he and his Republican advisors were determined to bring Iraq to account. Bush and his administration were convinced that Saddam Hussein was involved in various terrorist activities, and the US State Department listed Iraq as a state sponsor of terrorism. While it is true that Iraq provided headquarters, operating bases, training camps and other support to terrorist groups fighting the governments of neighbouring Turkey and Iran, as well as to hardline Palestinian groups, there is no evidence that Iraq was supplying terrorist groups with weapons of mass destruction. Nonetheless, it appeared that a new confrontation between the US and Iraq was a distinct possibility. This became a certainty when two hijacked airliners slammed into the World Trade Center in New York on 11 September 2001.

The 9/11 terrorist attacks against New York and Washington changed the world. Over 3,000 people were killed in the attacks, which were orchestrated by a previously little-known terrorist organization called al-Qaeda. Al-Qaeda, meaning 'the base', was led by the Saudi exile Osama bin Laden. The latter had issued a declaration of Jihad (holy war) against the US in 1996. Bin Laden condemned the US military presence in Saudi Arabia, criticized the international sanctions against Iraq, and voiced his opposition to US support for Israel. His 'declaration of Jihad' also cited 'massacres in Tajikistan, Burma, Kashmir, Assam, the Philippines, Fatani, Ogaden, Somalia, Eritrea, Chechnya and Bosnia-Herzegovina'. According to bin Laden, this was evidence of a growing war against Islam waged by the US and its allies. In 1998, bin Laden issued a fatwa that claimed the US had made 'a clear declaration of war on God, his messenger and Muslims' through its policies in the Islamic world. The enemy was the 'Zionist-Anglo-Saxon-Protestant coalition'.

The rantings of a Saudi exile would have mattered little had it not been for the 9/11 attacks. In one day, al-Qaeda had cost the US millions of dollars in economic damage and slaughtered thousands of its citizens. In parts of the Muslim world, al-Qaeda and its leader won massive popularity and a following that continues to this day. It also bestowed credibility on al-Qaeda that was, and remains, difficult to suppress.

American vengeance was swift and merciless, and was supported by many governments horrified by the destruction of the World Trade Center. The Taliban regime that ruled Afghanistan according to a brutal interpretation of Islamic Sharia law, and also harboured bin Laden himself, was swiftly defeated in a campaign codenamed Operation Enduring Freedom (the official US government name for the wars in Afghanistan, Iraq and subordinate missions in Africa and the Philippines). But bin Laden and his leading lieutenants escaped, and al-Qaeda continued to wage its religious war against the West. Al-Qaeda wasn't alone in seeing the conflict as a war without boundaries: on 20 September 2001, President Bush had declared a global 'War on Terror'. He explained the principles of the War on Terror in an address to a joint session of Congress and to the American people: 'Our War on Terror begins with al-Qaeda, but it does not end there. It will not end until every terrorist group of global reach has been found, stopped and defeated.'

The World Trade Center attacks signalled the beginning of the end of Saddam Hussein's rule. The Americans, having grown tired of Iraq's brinksmanship regarding UN weapons inspectors and the WMD issue, decided that this was an opportunity to remove him from power. The invasion of Iraq took place in March 2003 and, like the 1991 Gulf War, was an overwhelming US military victory. This time, however, the US did not have the support of a large coalition of nations, but it made no difference on the battlefield. Militarily, the US is a giant among pygmies with its numbers on the battlefield, technological superiority, highly trained and motivated personnel at all levels, superior weapons and equipment, and strategic and tactical excellence.

It took the Americans less than a month to crush the Iraqi Army, and by the end of 2003, Saddam Hussein was in US custody. The accounts of Operation Iraqi Freedom show that though the Iraqis frequently put up ferocious resistance, the end result was never in doubt. So complete was the military victory that a political vacuum was created in Iraq in which a countrywide insurgency soon flourished. This insurgency was waged by a motley collection of former Ba'ath Party members, Sunni Muslims, and foreign fighters, including members of al-Qaeda.

Al-Qaeda believed that it could defeat the US and its allies (predominantly the British) in both Iraq and Afghanistan for several reasons: first, because they believed the Americans could not tolerate casualties; second, that the US government would be demoralized if, despite taking heavy casualties, the insurgents carried on fighting. Additionally, they believed that US high-tech military equipment and firepower could be neutralized by fighting in urban areas at close quarters; and finally, that light weaponry could destroy US helicopters and vehicles in close urban combat.

Al-Qaeda was wrong on all counts. As the events in 2004 and 2005 illustrated, US and British casualties did not dent the Allied will or capacity to take the fight to the insurgents, who suffered heavy casualties themselves. As the accounts in this book from the conflict in Iraq illustrate, the soldiers on the ground were often involved in vicious fighting, but they never lost faith in their equipment, their commanders or the legitimacy of their cause. By 2009, the insurgent war in Iraq had effectively been won by the Americans. There was still the occasional atrocity, such as the 19 August 2009 Baghdad bombings (allegedly committed by either Sunni extremists or al-Qaeda), in which over 100 people were killed, but Iraq had essentially been secured. To maintain this security, the Americans retained a garrison of some 130,000 troops throughout the country.

The Americans and British have also committed substantial forces to the fight in Afghanistan. As Washington recognizes, there is no substitute for boots on the ground. By 2009, NATO (North Atlantic Treaty Organization) troop numbers in Afghanistan stood at nearly 100,000. The largest contingent was American (63,000 soldiers), and the second-largest was British with 9,000 troops. One of NATO's principal aims is to build and train the Afghan National Army (ANA), which will ultimately number around 135,000 soldiers (though many in the US administration want to double this number).

When the Americans first arrived in Afghanistan in 2001, their objective was to topple the Taliban, which was achieved with ease. The emphasis then switched to one of 'nation-building', and with the Taliban gone and al-Qaeda having been (seemingly) likewise eradicated or at least decimated, there were high hopes in Washington and London that the role of NATO forces would be more as police officers than soldiers. In 2006, the then British Defence

Secretary John Reid visited the country, where Britain had more than 3,000 troops deployed and was set to take charge of a NATO-led peacekeeping force. In a bullish mood Reid stated: 'We're in the south [of Afghanistan] to help and protect the Afghan people to reconstruct their economy and democracy. We would be perfectly happy to leave in three years' time without firing one shot.' At the time, it may have seemed a reasonable statement to make, but by August 2009, the British Army was locked in a vicious war against the Taliban in Helmand Province, and its soldiers had fired a staggering 12 million bullets from their assault rifles and machine guns since Reid's statement – an average of 12,000 rounds a day.

Part of the reason for the increased military activity was the decision taken by the new US President Barack Obama (b. 1961; president of the US 2009–), to reinforce troop levels in Afghanistan and launch an offensive against the Taliban. Obama had entered the Oval Office in January 2009, and was keen to make an impact on the War on Terror. Afghanistan thus became Obama's war.

Obama, an astute politician, recognized that the NATO effort in Afghanistan was making slow progress, if any. As a new president he naturally wanted to stamp his authority on the war effort. In February 2009, he stated, 'The Taliban is resurgent in Afghanistan, and al-Qaeda supports the insurgency and threatens America from its safe haven along the Pakistani border.' He said a military surge was necessary in order to 'stabilize a deteriorating situation in Afghanistan, which has not received the strategic attention, direction and resources it urgently requires'. For the troops on the ground, the surge meant the beginning of heavy fighting against the Taliban.

For the British Army fighting in Helmand Province, 2009 brought a major increase in battlefield casualties, as reported by the British Ministry of Defence (MOD): 'As at 25 August 2009, a total of 207 British Forces personnel or MOD civilians have died while serving in Afghanistan since the start of operations in October 2001.' Far from not having to fire a shot, the British Army found itself engaged in a grim battle against a cunning enemy, for now the Taliban were using roadside bombs and booby traps in ever-increasing numbers. As the accounts from soldiers based in Afghanistan in this book indicate, Taliban tactics had moved away from suicidal close-range firefights with NATO force, to trying to kill the enemy using remotely detonated devices. A new, terrifying acronym began to be heard more frequently in the news and in official reports: IED (improvised explosive device). British MOD news bulletins reported soldiers killed in Afghanistan 'as a result of an explosion that happened whilst on a routine foot patrol' with depressing regularity, while back in Britain rarely a week passed without the evening news showing a transport aircraft landing at Royal Air Force (RAF) Lyneham, Oxfordshire, containing yet another coffin holding the remains of a soldier killed in Afghanistan. What follows has sadly become all too familiar.

From the RAF airbase, the hearse (or, more likely, hearses) makes its way to the John Radcliffe Hospital in Oxford, where the body is examined by a coroner before being released to the deceased's family. During the journey, the hearse passes through the small Wiltshire market town of Wootton Bassett. By chance, when the first hearse drove through the town in April 2007, it coincided with the monthly meeting of the local branch of the Royal British Legion, whose members, plus the mayor, stopped what they were doing to pay their respects. Thus began a ceremony, which is now known across the world. When the funeral cortège, accompanied by the toll of St Bartholomew's church bell, makes its way up the High Street and reaches the War Memorial, it is saluted by Legion members. Both sides of the street are always lined with thousands of people, young and old, civilian and military. This simple show of respect for the fallen is deeply moving.

No one knows how long coffins will be coming home from Afghanistan. Politicians talk glibly of the war lasting 'for years', but no politician will ever have to fight the Taliban on the ground. No politician will have to face the enemy on the battlefield, the place where 'the meat meets the metal', and no politician will have to die or suffer severe injuries as a result of Taliban weapons or IEDs. The politicians' role is to send society's best and bravest to die in faraway countries. Their role is also to equip their troops, but British troops in Afghanistan have inadequate equipment, especially helicopters, in their fight against the Taliban. This is the result of successive cuts in the defence budget over the course of the last 13 years of the Labour government.

By its acts, the same government also shirks its responsibility when it comes to the care and rehabilitation of servicemen and women who have been injured in the line of duty. In July 2009, the British MOD attempted to reduce compensation payments paid to wounded soldiers. If, according to the British government, the presence of British forces in Afghanistan is crucial to the security of the British people, then surely those in the front line who are fighting to ensure it deserve the very best in equipment, support and care if they are wounded or disabled in the line of duty.

But the government has neglected its duty of care of the wounded, leaving private charities to take the strain. One of the finest of these, Help for Heroes, established in 2007, has raised millions of pounds to assist those wounded in Iraq and Afghanistan. This includes individuals who have lost limbs and vital organs and will require care and support for the rest of their lives (which may mean for 50 years or more). Every wounded service person should be ensured a decent quality of life.

As well as the physically wounded, many suffer mental traumas as a result of combat. These individuals do not display any signs of injury, but their wounds are just as real. In Britain, the charity Combat Stress specializes in the care of veterans' mental health. In 2009, it had over 4,000 veterans, both male and female, aged between 19 and 90, undergoing treatment at its three centres. It receives around 1,700 referrals a year, though this is set to increase dramatically due to an influx of Iraq and Afghanistan trauma cases.

The legacy of these conflicts will last for years. Ken Lukowiak, a soldier who fought in the 1982 Falklands War in the British Parachute Regiment, wrote in 2009, 'It took me ten years to realize I had a problem and another ten to seek the right treatment for it.' It is certain that the charities involved in aiding soldiers will be dealing with the consequences of the wars in Iraq and Afghanistan for many years.

Obviously, it would be impossible to include accounts from the hundreds of thousands of individuals who have fought in Iraq and Afghanistan since the First Gulf War. This book therefore attempts to present a broad cross-section of experiences from a variety of nationalities and from different services. The wars in Iraq and Afghanistan have cost tens of thousands of lives, hundreds of billions of dollars (by the end of August 2009, the US alone had spent over $900 billion on the War on Terror) and have essentially wrecked the infrastructures of both Iraq and Afghanistan.

At the time of writing, the War on Terror is still being waged, the end date of which is unknown. One thing is certain, though: the legacy of the conflicts in Iraq and Afghanistan will affect those who took part, and indeed the world, for many years to come.

The accounts in this book have been collated from a variety of sources, ranging from official after-action reports to personal diaries, radio broadcasts and individual blogs. Other accounts were the result of author interviews or requests from veterans to submit their stories, which they did, to the eternal gratitude of the author. Particularly poignant were those from individuals who fought in the First Gulf War and who are now suffering the debilitating effects of Gulf War syndrome following their exposure to the toxic chemicals and biological agents that littered the sands of Kuwait and Iraq during the conflict.

Those, and of course the words of the wounded. From the deserts of Arabia to the rocky landscape of Afghanistan, the stories from the men and women who fought in those theatres bring to life the grim reality of modern warfare and the worldwide conflict that is the War on Terror.

The
First Gulf War

(1990–91)

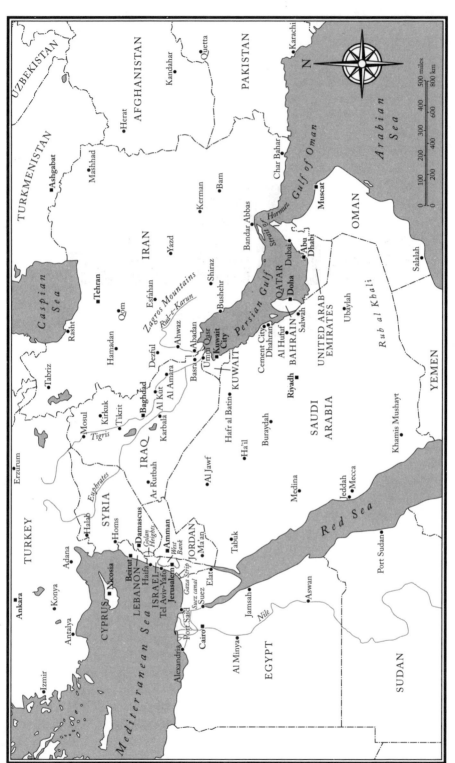

The Gulf region including Iraq and its major towns and cities

Iraq – an introduction

The land occupied by present-day Iraq has been called the 'cradle of civilization' – ancient Sumerian, Babylonian and Persian cultures rose and fell in a region that has known civilization for over 6,000 years. The current population of Iraq is around 30 million, some 80 per cent of whom are Arab-speaking, and over 95 per cent are Muslim in religion. Of the Muslim population, there are twice as many Shi'as as Sunnis. Northeastern Iraq is occupied by Kurds, who are Sunni Muslims.

The two Muslim sects are antagonistic towards each other; their differences date back to the death of the Prophet Muhammad (570–632 CE), and specifically regard the question of who was to take over the leadership of the Muslim nation. The Sunnis agreed with the position taken by many of the Prophet's companions, that the new leader should be elected from among those capable of the task. This is what was done, and the Prophet Muhammad's close friend and advisor Abu Bakr (573–634 CE), became the first caliph of the Islamic nation. The word 'Sunni' in Arabic comes from a word meaning 'one who follows the traditions of the Prophet'.

Other Muslims, however, believed that the leadership should have stayed within the Prophet's own family, among those specifically appointed by him or among imams (Muslim leaders) appointed by Allah. For example, the Shi'a believe that the leadership should have passed directly to Muhammad's cousin and son-in-law Ali. Thus Shi'as have never recognized the authority of elected Muslim leaders, choosing instead to follow a line of imams that they believe have been appointed by the Prophet Muhammad or Allah. The word Shi'a in Arabic means 'a group or supportive party of people'. They are also known as followers of 'Ahl al-Bayt' or 'People of the Household (of the Prophet)'.

Oil accounts for nearly 95 per cent of Iraq's revenues, though the Iran–Iraq War (1980–88), the First Gulf War (1990–91) and the 2003 US and British invasion all seriously affected exports. Today, oil production is around 80 per cent of what it was in 2002.

Iraq's politics have been characterized by violence: in 1958 an army coup led by General Abd al-Karim Kassem (1914–63; premier of Iraq 1958–63) resulted in King Faisal II's death (1935–58; ruled 1953–58), while in 1963 Colonel Arif Abd al-Salam (1921–66; president of Iraq 1963–66) led a coup that overthrew Kassem. The new regime was dominated by members of the Iraqi Ba'ath Party, a socialist group whose aim was Arab unity. Over the next seven years, the Ba'ath Party assumed an iron control over Iraq, partly by murdering its opponents.

Despite the repression, during the 1970s Iraq's oil revenues allowed the government to introduce modernization programmes and improve public services. Although Shi'as made up the majority of the population, Sunnis dominated the government; Shi'as were effectively excluded from politics. In 1979 President Ahmed Hassan al-Bakr (1914–82; president of Iraq 1968–79) resigned and was replaced by Saddam Hussein, who immediately embarked on a purge of his opponents, killing many and forcing the rest into exile. By 1980, rising tensions with neighbouring Shi'a-dominated Iran resulted in the outbreak of war.

Saddam Hussein launched the war in an effort to consolidate Iraq's rising power in the Arab world and to replace Iran as the dominant Persian Gulf state. The conflict can also be seen as another round in the centuries-old Sunni-vs-Shi'a and Arab-vs-Persian religious and ethnic conflicts. More immediate causes were Iraqi claims to territories inhabited by Arabs (such as Khouzestan, an oil-producing province in southwestern Iran), as well as Iraq's rights over the Shatt al-Arab waterway. Iraq and Iran had engaged in border clashes for many years and the dormant Shatt al-Arab waterway dispute had been revived in 1979. Iraq claimed the entire 200 km (125 mile) channel as its territory, while Iran insisted that the official border was the thalweg – a line running down the middle of the waterway – negotiated between the two countries in 1975. Regarding the 1975 treaty as merely a truce not a definitive settlement, the Iraqi Ba'ath leadership under Saddam Hussein launched an invasion of Iran in September 1980 in expectation of a quick victory. An eight-year war of attrition followed, sapping Iraq's human and financial resources.

Operation Desert Shield

On 2 August 1990 over 100,000 Iraqi troops and 1,000 tanks, spearheaded by six divisions of the elite Republican Guard, invaded the oil-rich state of Kuwait. This event would be the catalyst of a major UN-sponsored war to liberate Kuwait and the beginning of a 20-year Western, predominantly American and British, military involvement in Iraq.

By 1988, the end of its eight-year war against the Islamic Republic of Iran, Iraq had accumulated an $80 billion debt. The human cost had also been high: Iraq had suffered 375,000 casualties during the war (the Iranians suffered an estimated 1 million killed or injured). The Iraqi dictator Saddam Hussein believed, with some justification, that he had prevented the spread of Islamic fundamentalism throughout the Middle East and had directly saved the royal families of both Kuwait and Saudi Arabia. This belief was reinforced by the fact that Iraq had received Western backing during the war against Iran.

Far from being grateful, Kuwait immediately demanded repayment of the $65 billion loan Iraq owed. Not only did this alienate Kuwait from the Ba'ath Party regime in Baghdad, Saddam Hussein began to view tiny Kuwait, which had massive financial reserves at home and abroad, as a potential answer to Iraq's financial problems.

Kuwait further incurred Iraq's wrath by extracting oil from the Rumaylah oil field, which extends from Basra, Iraq's second-largest city, south across the border into Kuwait. Rumaylah is the fifth-largest known single reserve of oil in the world, a resource that lay in a disputed tract on the border between the two states. In addition, Kuwait was over-producing oil, which further reduced Iraq's ability to service its debt. Saddam Hussein accused Kuwait and the United Arab Emirates of depriving Iraq of $14 billion of oil revenue.

Aside from the dispute over debts and oil revenues, there were also territorial disputes between Iraq and Kuwait. Both countries had been part of the Ottoman Empire, and the border between the two had never been properly resolved. Indeed, Iraq claimed that Kuwait was, in fact, an integral part of Iraq.

With the financial situation of his country worsening, Saddam Hussein believed that a rapid invasion of Kuwait would result in the latter becoming the 19th province of Iraq, and although in retrospect his actions were extremely foolhardy, at the time they appeared less so. On 17 July 1990, Saddam Hussein had threatened to use force to resolve disputes with his neighbours. On 19 July, the US ambassador in Baghdad, April Glaspie, under orders from Secretary of State James Baker in Washington, informed Baghdad that 'disputes should be settled by peaceful means, not through intimidation'. However, five days later, Glaspie delivered another message from Baker to Saddam Hussein, requesting a peaceful resolution to disputes, but also informing Iraq that the US had 'no opinion on the Arab–Arab conflicts, like your border disagreement with Kuwait'. This was hardly a green light for Saddam Hussein to invade Kuwait but the Iraqi dictator interpreted it as such and ordered an attack.

When Iraqi forces occupied Kuwait, the UN Security Council immediately passed Resolution 660 (2 August 1990), condemning the Iraqi invasion. A trade and financial embargo was placed on Iraq, which was now also threatening to invade Saudi Arabia; Iraqi troops had begun to mass on the Saudi border. Another bold strike would have given Saddam control of Saudi Arabia's oil fields. Of the eight largest oil and gas fields containing more than half of Saudi oil reserves, the two biggest, Ghawar (the world's largest oil field) and Safaniya (the world's largest offshore oil field), are near or in the Persian Gulf itself. Two-thirds of Saudi Arabia's crude oil is exported from the Gulf via the Abqaiq processing facility. Saudi Arabia's two primary oil export terminals are located at Ras Tanura (the world's largest offshore oil transfer facility) and Ras al-Ju'aymah, both in the Gulf as well. Another terminal lies in Yanbu, a port city on the Red Sea.

The possibility of Saddam Hussein controlling most of the world's oil reserves greatly alarmed the US. Therefore, following the agreement of the Saudi ruler King Fahd (1921–2005; ruled 1982–2005), President George H.W. Bush ordered US aircraft and ground forces to Saudi Arabia as part of Operation Desert Shield. In late August 1990, General Norman Schwarzkopf, commanding officer US Central Command CENTCOM (the Gulf region was within the Central Command's area of responsibility), was made UN theatre commander-in-chief and arrived in Riyadh to begin planning the immediate defence of Saudi Arabia.

America's superpower status meant Washington had the ships and aircraft necessary to deploy large numbers of warplanes, troops and military equipment to Saudi Arabia to deter any Iraqi aggression. For example, fixed-wing US

Navy and US Air Force (USAF) combat aircraft were in theatre on 2 August. By the end of the month, the Americans had 700 fighter and attack aircraft in the Gulf region (the Iraqi Air Force at this time had 16 bombers, 390 attack aircraft and 245 fighter aircraft).

The first US ground forces to arrive in Saudi Arabia were two brigades of the 82nd Airborne Division (XVIII Airborne Corps), which provided security for air bases and ports. By early September, Schwarzkopf could call on seven US Army brigades, three aircraft-carrier battle groups, 14 fighter squadrons and 17,000 US Marines in the Gulf, plus a squadron of Boeing B-52 Stratofortress strategic bombers on the Indian Ocean island of Diego Garcia.

By early October, US forces facing Saddam Hussein included XVIII Airborne Corps, consisting of an airborne division, an air-assault division, two heavy divisions, an armoured cavalry regiment (ACR), and the requisite array of combat support and combat service support assets. This translated into over 120,000 troops, 700 tanks, 1,400 armoured fighting vehicles and 600 artillery pieces, plus the 32,000 troops and 400 tanks of local Arab allies and hundreds of US warplanes. In addition, troops and military equipment from over 30 other countries were starting to flow into Saudi Arabia as part of the UN coalition of nations formed to liberate Kuwait. These forces ensured that there would be no Iraqi invasion of Saudi Arabia.

As the weeks passed, more UN forces were transported to Saudi Arabia. The majority were American: 540,000 troops, 6 aircraft carriers, 2,000 tanks, 2,200 armoured personnel carriers, 1,700 helicopters, 100 warships and 1,800 aircraft. Saudi forces numbered 118,000 troops, 550 tanks, 180 combat aircraft and 8 frigates. Other major contributors included France (18,000 troops, 60 combat aircraft, 120 helicopters, 40 tanks, 100 armoured vehicles, 1 missile cruiser, 3 destroyers and 4 frigates) and Great Britain (43,000 troops, 6 destroyers, 4 frigates, 3 minesweepers, 5 support ships, 250 Challenger tanks, 300 other armoured vehicles, plus 70 Tornado and Jaguar combat aircraft). An ironic twist was the contribution to the UN coalition of 300 mujahedeen fighters from Afghanistan. Little did the British and Americans realize that 11 years later they would be fighting their erstwhile allies.

Meanwhile the Iraqi Army held its position in Kuwait. The Iraqis had used four Republican Guard divisions to seize Kuwait, but by early September 1990, these divisions had returned to southeastern Iraq to be replaced by a less capable army division. By late September 1990, Iraq had 22 divisions in Kuwait – 13 light and 9 heavy. As the UN build-up continued, the Iraqis steadily increased the number of divisions they had in Kuwait.

A major concern for UN forces was Iraq's possession of chemical weapons, which Saddam Hussein had shown he was willing to use on his own people. Coalition commanders were extremely worried that the Iraqis might launch chemical attacks, and therefore implemented a large-scale programme of inoculations and issued protective clothing against nuclear, biological and chemical (NBC) threats. These precautions seemed justified when Iraqi Scud surface-to-surface missiles (SSMs) were launched against Saudi Arabia and Israel beginning on 18 January 1991 and continuing until 23 February. In total, 46 missiles were fired at Saudi Arabia and 40 at Israel. Fortunately, none of them had chemical warheads.

The following accounts by professional soldiers, sailors and airmen serving during the Gulf War all share the view that the UN forces possessed a massive technological superiority in the air and on the ground, and none doubted that they would be victorious.

Fred L. Hart

American Lieutenant-Colonel Hart was an advisor to the Kuwaiti Land Forces and witnessed at first hand the Iraqi invasion of Kuwait. He made some interesting assessments about the capability of Iraqi Army units, including the Republican Guard. He wrote this account following the end of the war.

On 1 August 1990, my family and I arrived in Kuwait City. It was over 40°C (104°F) outside at 21.00 hours. Leaving the modern, air-conditioned international terminal and walking outside was literally like walking into a blast furnace. I had arrived to begin serving a two-year accompanied tour. My job was to be an adviser (logistics, maintenance and training) to the Kuwaiti Land Forces and manage foreign military sales (FMS) cases.

By 05.00 hours [on 2 August 1990], we had all been notified telephonically or awakened by low-flying fighter-bombers and the distinct sound of artillery fire. At 05.15 hours I went outside and immediately recognized the smell of cordite in the air and could hear the sounds of war getting closer. Looking to the southwest from my two-story villa rooftop, I could see Kuwait International Airport 5–7 km (3–4 ½ miles) away under bombardment by Iraqi fighter-bombers. Strangely enough, the main highway just to the rear of my quarters appeared normal, complete with the Kuwaiti bus service still operating. Now the whole family was up and Lieutenant-Colonel Tom Funk had telephoned us and confirmed our worst fears; Iraq had invaded. We closed all the curtains and our maid came into our villa. I told my wife and children to remain downstairs close to the centre of the villa, near an interior storage room, for safety in the event of shelling, which was growing louder and closer as each hour went by.

Apparently, when the Iraqi armour/mechanized forces made it to Kuwait City, they decided to push their tanks and tracked vehicles through the city, only to become bogged down, and often, lost. This operational error of not bypassing Kuwait City permitted the bulk of the Kuwaiti 15th Brigade, located south of the city near the al-Ahmadi oil fields, to escape to Saudi Arabia. It also bought time for the southern air base at Ahmed al-Jaber to partially mobilize and actually launch sorties throughout the day. By nightfall, all organized Kuwaiti military resistance had come almost to a standstill.

Lieutenant-Colonel Funk, Chief Forties and I collectively had enough military experience to make some observations of the vaunted Republican Guard during the first week of the invasion. They by no means reflected the discipline of a well-trained, combat-hardened army. In fact, during the first week they reflected the characteristics of a motley force without orders and a total lack of basic tactical skills and discipline. For the most part, Iraqi soldiers milled around, scavenged for food and water and seemed to be generally at a loss for what to do next, often looting and stealing bedding items for their hastily constructed fighting positions, complete with beach umbrellas for overhead protection from the searing summer sun. Without a doubt, Saddam's forces had reached their logistics culminating point and his units would have to live off the land. Fuel was not a problem, but food and water would be scavenged from the locals. Within days of the invasion, Iraqi forces occupied all the major supermarkets in order to procure food stocks. Kuwaitis were permitted entry, but for males this could mean being taken into custody. This was often true for Westerners, too.

On the first day of the invasion, 2 August, our neighbourhood remained quiet until around 13.00 hours, when the Iraqis launched their final assault on the Bayan Palace [the main palace of the Amir of Kuwait] just a few kilometres from our quarters. Their artillery was positioned along the Gulf Road and was now firing directly over our neighbourhood. The Amiri Guards at the Bayan Palace put up a fight all morning. Their return fire often landed in and around our neighbourhood, resulting in many of our Kuwaiti neighbours fleeing the area. By 14.00 hours, the Bayan Palace was captured, and I could see from my rooftop that Iraqi armoured forces had occupied the palace grounds. I spoke by phone to

Colonel Mooneyham several times while the assault on the palace was taking place. He had moved his family to the nearby Japanese Embassy to ensure their safe haven since his neighbourhood was being overrun with Iraqi forces.

By the end of the day things began to quieten down, but from my rooftop I could observe that many of the Kuwaiti governmental buildings were burning or smouldering. The highway (Fahaheel Expressway) was littered with wrecked or shot-up cars. Occasional gunfire could be heard and Iraqi mounted patrols were now enforcing a dusk-to-dawn curfew that had been broadcast both on radio and television. The first TV broadcast the Iraqis began to run was that the invasion was the result of a Kuwaiti coup that had overthrown the ruling family for being corrupt, and the new government had requested the assistance of the Iraqi government. Needless to say, the story did not wash.

The flow of refugees and Westerners to Saudi Arabia, either through the border crossing or across the desert, had all but ceased by 11 August. The Iraqis began sealing the border, trapping those who had not taken advantage of the early confusion following the invasion.[1]

Theresa O. Cantrell

Captain Cantrell was the Accountable Property Officer, 32nd Medical Supply, Optical and Maintenance Battalion, US Army. The battalion provided optical fabrication and medical equipment maintenance support to all forces during Operation Desert Shield. This account is part of a formal debrief carried out by the US Army's Military History Detachment at Fort Bragg, North Carolina.

When the Scud attacks started … the sirens … went off every night, several times a night, until I guess the air-traffic controllers or the radar men became a little bit better at distinguishing what they were really looking for, we would have two or three alarms a night. [I] have never gotten dressed so fast in my life … if anybody wants to test me on putting on a chemical protective garment, we can all do it very quickly. The going joke was, you know, 'What did you do in the war, Mommy?' Well, I got dressed in the middle of the night and jumped in a hole, because we had our bunkers built, and that was our defensive position, because the only defence against a Scud, or against what else might come out of it, was just to be properly dressed. So we spent many nights doing nothing but that, or it seemed like many nights. We had one Scud that actually did get shot down over KKMC [King Khalid Military City]. It was in the middle of the day. It was daylight. [I] had been out to the airfield and I was just driving back in with one of the NCOs [non-commissioned officers], who was driving. And we heard this tremendous explosion, 'POOF', and looked up and ... it looked like someone had set off firecrackers. Fireworks, not a flare ... but fireworks because of all of the small pieces that were burning. And I thought, it didn't click ... it just didn't click. We kind of thought, 'What was it?' Then suddenly, a couple more Patriots went off and we went, 'Oh, no!' ... so we started putting on masks.[2]

John G. Zierdt

Colonel Zierdt was the commander of the US Army's 1st Corps Support Command during Operation Desert Shield. This account is also part of the formal debrief carried out by the US Army's Military History Detachment at Fort Bragg, North Carolina.

We found out quickly in Saudi Arabia that even every piece of the desert was owned by someone, and you couldn't just go set up in the desert and park someplace ... We needed a lot of warehouse space, living space. We were very fortunate. For example, the Dhahran area had all kinds of living space compounds that were empty. [T]hese had been constructed in the late 1970s and early 1980s as Saudi Arabia was going through immense construction projects.

    ... But [these] ended up being in a Shi'a area, which is a very anti-Western area. [O]ur people were in there and started to unload and store in there. But the Shi'as in the local area started complaining every time they saw a female working, or every time they saw soldiers with their jackets off. And so, we just eventually had so many problems in this area that the local prince or general, Saudi general, in charge of that area asked us to please get out of that area because they wanted not to create some religious disturbances in their country. So, we had to then move to another location ...

    They [the soldiers] were working around the clock and in the heat of the day. We found when it was 54° or 60°C (130° or 140°F) over there, you just could hardly work. We forget now how bad it was in August and September, but it was just the worst thing I've ever been in. Especially when you first arrive there, that first week you could hardly do anything in the afternoon. You became lethargic and just couldn't do things ... [W]e actually had tractor trailers driving down the highway [that] had their tires catch fire it got so hot.

We had six million gallons of fuel at Logistical Base Charlie, and they had to keep that filled and keep our ammunition and ... food flowing. All that was being done by host-nation drivers. We were worried at first that those people were going to leave when the war started, but they didn't do that, they stayed with us ... especially when you showed you were taking care of them. I mean, we had in our dining facility in Dhahran, you know, we had a whole group of Pakistanis who were worried about leaving. But we gave them protective masks and CPOGs [chemical protective overgarments] and then they were more than willing to stay. I mean, you wouldn't want to be the only one around without a chemical suit on ... [3]

Dennis G. Morral

Commander Morral was the captain of the guided-missile frigate USS *Nicholas* (FFG-47), operating in the waters of the Persian Gulf and serving as an advanced combat search and rescue platform.

The helicopters, of course, unless it's an unusual circumstance, are only flown at night-time due to the relative slow speeds and vulnerability of the OH-58D [OH-58D Kiowa Warrior, known as the AHIP – Advanced Helicopter Improvement Programme] ... They are, in fact, the ship's eyes at night-time. The mission at the beginning of hostilities for the USS *Nicholas* was to get as far north as we possibly could and try to remain as undetected as possible, so that we could stand by to relieve the pilots who were shot down ... our combat SAR [search-and-rescue] mission was our primary one at the beginning of hostilities. That's why we were so far forward from the rest of the ships.

The ship normally would man at the maximum about 220 people, and that's even with the LAMPS (two detachments) on board. We maxed out at one point at 270 people. So we had taken the furniture out of our lounges and put cots and mattresses in there. We did that prior to deployment, anticipating large numbers of additional people.

There's always some people on watch. With the normal work hours in combat, if you get four to six hours of sleep a night, you're lucky. Therefore one bunk could actually be used by four different people and they would never interfere with each other. Now, we're not going to that extreme.

18 January 1991

We were actually operating with three Kuwaiti naval vessels as well: the [FPB 57-class fast-attack missile craft P-5702] *Istiqlal* and [TNC 45-class fast-attack missile craft P-4505] *Al Sanbouk,* both fast patrol boats, and the landing ship *Salwahil.* So I was in company with them and we were trying to get up into the Dorra oil field area prior to hostilities. So in fact, that's where we were when hostilities started.

Now we went up there the first night, and we were flying helicopters around the [oil] platforms at night and we took some Triple A [anti-aircraft artillery fire] off them, which was somewhat of a surprise since we didn't know there were any people on those platforms at the time. We informed our bosses and they directed us to withdraw to the south, to the east, until they could decide what was the best action to take ....

I asked at that time that we be allowed to go back up there with just my *Nicholas* and the *Istiqlal,* ... and engage and eliminate the enemy forces on these platforms. [T]he following day I was given permission to do that. So I left the *Salwahil* and the *Al Sanbouk* down in the Marjon oil fields, which are about 64 km [40 miles] southeast of the Dorra oil platforms. Under the cover of darkness, the *Nicholas* and the *Istiqlal* were in total EMCON [emissions control], meaning that they had nothing radiating at all. We shut everything down so they couldn't detect us ... Well, before we got up there, we launched the helicopters. Everything was airborne by the time we got up to position to engage the platforms.

I didn't want to fly the AHIPs in between the platforms because I was afraid they'd get caught in crossfire, so I decided to let them take the landward two platforms and to strike those. And then once ... the AHIPs had engaged them, then I was going to have them withdraw to a safe distance where I could then open up my surface-to-surface guns. Also the *Istiqlal,* which has a 76mm and a 40mm gun as well, could open up on the remaining platforms and then take it from there.

So the first volley was in fact from the AHIPs. It was a laser-guided Hellfire missile. We launched three of them. All three of them were direct hits on the bunkers. And I have to say, in retrospect, the weapon of choice against a well-fortified sandbagged bunker, and these were very well fortified, several feet thick, is in fact the Hellfire missile. And I have videos that show that beyond any doubt.

So the idea was to really lay into two of them ... we picked the two on the side that we thought were the most heavily fortified. We thought, perhaps, those were where the radios and the officers, if there were any, were going to be located. In fact that was the case. We were a little concerned that if we gave them too much time they would have the ability to radio back to about 64 km [40 miles] north where the enemy forces were, and then we would be faced with an F-1 Mirage or an Exocet missile threat, or some such thing. So the idea was to lay them as low as we could as early as we could and catch them before they could get to the radios.

The first they knew was the first Hellfire that hit one of the platforms. And then we hit them from the left flank. ... So we caught them in between. And after we pounded them with the guns ... the AHIPs, since they didn't seem to be getting any resistance, actually came back. They came back, reloaded, went out. Came back and reloaded a third time. I believe by the end of the third hop, the guys [pilots] had just about had it and I decided to pull them back a little early and not let them continue.

... I was able to take the first 23 enemy prisoners of war ... I only had to kill five of them [during the battle]. They had heavy armament. If they wanted to, especially in daytime, they could have shot all of my helicopters out of the air. And I took absolutely no casualties. I was able to recover their five bodies and return them, some day, to their families, so at least they'll know what happened to their loved ones, unlike our experience in Vietnam. I don't know what else we could have done better. I mean, we did everything. I took zero casualties. In the words of a dear patron saint, General George S. Patton, the idea is for you to survive and make the other illiterate, illegitimate chap die for his country. [I] think that's what we did. We took no casualties. We didn't take any unnecessary chances.[4]

Gerald R. Harkins

Colonel Harkins was the commander of Dragon Brigade, XVIII Airborne Corps, US Army, and remembers the massive logistical problems that beset US forces in Saudi Arabia.

The thing is, it was tough. I've got a chemical battalion, the 2nd Chemical Battalion out of Fort Hood, Texas. The battalion commander sat around the area. And I told him I wanted him to develop a rear-area chemical defence plan. And, geez, it was like pulling teeth; I mean, he had more valid reasons why somebody else should do it, etc. I think it was on 2 December [1990] when the first Scud was launched. It was Sunday morning. And when that happened, it was really kind of, you know, if you want to thank Saddam for one thing, I really thanked him for that training exercise. Because all of a sudden it was, 'Oh, shit, we'd better get serious about this stuff.'

[T]hat attack by Saddam Hussein really forced us into exercising. We really flat exercised over the next month every damn system, up one side and down the other. So you need to doctrinally define those plans for the rear area. Chemical defence plans in terms of where you're going to decon[taminate], where you're going to refit, where you are going to marshal up before, during and after.

When you're in a city of several hundred thousand people, it just isn't out in the desert. Where are all the automobile car washes in Dhahran (we might as well use them if they're there)? Where are the fire stations where we can get fire hydrants and pressure pumps and stuff like that to help us?

There was, you know, just about every day there were just new things. 'Oh, shoot, I hadn't thought about that.' There are some times you feel very, very smart. But most of the times you feel very, very ignorant because your crystal ball just isn't good enough to look at.

I got a call on a Sunday morning about 05.00 … 'Oh, shoot, oh, dear, we just spotted two Palestinians (there were always Palestinians, PLO members) on the water tower that leads into the British compound and one of our American compounds, and we think we've got problems because we've now tested the water and we've got cyanide in the water.' That's okay. Number one: stop drinking water. I thought that was pretty smart. Number two: get somebody else down there to test it. But number three is, what are the water sources for all 120 compounds? Is this something city-wide? Do we have a means to call up and say, send out the code words, everybody test your water? Do we have a base line on all the water going into these compounds? Do we know and can we test to see if someone is varying it, because, as you know, there was an awful lot of threat of chemical and biological warfare from Saddam Hussein. What happens if he … was able to get in the water system within the rear area and contaminate that? How will we ever know that?

And we didn't have a lot of good answers. We had a lot of people standing around and saying, 'Oh, shoot. Oh, dear.' So we had to then go through a process by which we knew. It took us some time, [but] we figured out where every bit of water came from that everybody drank.

Where all the fruit came from. We figured that out and so forth.

We'd get reports of, there's a car, you know, at a camp taking pictures. That's when we'd call the Saudi police. The Saudi police reacted several times and sometimes we reacted or overreacted on our own. But the Saudis, you know, write in Arabic so, therefore, the license plate on a car is written in Arabic.

We had signs and kind of key phrases, you know, 'Stop, this is an American compound, you may not come close'; written in Korean, Filipino and Arabic. So we thought we targeted the majority of the people that were from Third World countries that would come into our compounds.

We found out that it's really not a smart thing to do to have a female guard outside on the gate. That became a very, very attractive thing for having people come watch and see what the American females were doing.

We had some live fire ranges that we didn't close down, and it caused us some problems. Even down to when I left on 7 May [1991], we had to close those suckers out as well. Because we fired some munitions there that we shouldn't have fired. And what happens if you put cluster bombs into a training area that is not really a dead training area for the rest of its life. Now you're telling nomads that they can't go in there anymore; this is bad, they don't understand. That was a bad situation that we got ourselves into.[5]

Becky L. Morgan

Sergeant Morgan served in the US Marine Corps in the Gulf War and, thereafter, was a member of the Iowa Army National Guard until 1991. She was one of over 40,000 American women who served in the conflict, the first conflict in history in which such large numbers of women served in non-civilian roles.

I was a Staff Sergeant in the Marine Corps with Marine Air Control Group 1 (MACG 1) when we deployed to the Persian Gulf. When the military was first deployed into the Persian Gulf theatre, they were not allowed to take the women of their unit. It was said at that point that to take the women in what the Arabian society considered 'men's roles' would offend them and that would hurt the war effort. I was the only military intelligence specialist in my unit. I donned my gear, my weapons and a very concealing flak jacket. Ten days after the beginning of the war, I was in-country with my fellow Marines. I kept a low profile and did the job that I had trained with my unit for three years to do. I am told that I was one of the first women in-country at that time. This passed without fanfare, without ceremony, and more women came.

Women in combat? There have always been women in combat. Gender does not make a person a hero, no more than the colour of their skin or the amount of money in their pocket. It is what lies within a person's heart and character that makes a hero.[6]

Deborah Gilmore

First Lieutenant Deborah Gilmore served with a US Army reserve unit during the Gulf War. In March 2001 she gave an interview to the American Forces Press Service, some of which is featured below. By this date she was a major with the Army's 94th Regional Support Command.

I remember the astonished looks of the Saudi military as I gave orders. They didn't understand why I was giving orders, but even more, they couldn't comprehend why the men were listening.

Women proved that they were able to work alongside their male counterparts and get the job done. The ability to do this in an extremely different culture that at times was not particularly friendly to women was also a big accomplishment. The Gulf War also showed that combat support and combat service support jobs, such as logistics, can be just as dangerous as the traditional infantry roles.

I am very proud of my service in the Gulf War, and I do believe that I have opened the door for other women to follow me. I believe that the role of women will continue to increase in the military in the future. As the public sees women serving and succeeding in roles, there will be more public acceptance. Today, we see women who are commanders and women who serve in other leadership roles where, in the past, they may have served in strictly support roles or staff positions.[7]

Ray G. Brueland

Lieutenant-Colonel Brueland was the commander of 32nd MEDSOM (32nd Medical Supply, Optical and Maintenance Battalion), US Army. Many people think that the climate of Saudi Arabia is hot during the day and cold at night. For those who served in the Gulf, however, there were a few shocks in store.

Prior to our coming here we were told that it would rain on us three times. We were told to expect about two and a half inches of rain, and that was it. Well, it has rained [on] 10 separate occasions, and on three of those occasions I would say it rained 5 cm [2 in] … We've had some heavy downpours; so bad, in fact, that some of the other sister units in the area have actually been flooded out of their land site. We were blessed or lucky or whatever in that we are kind of on high ground and everything drained off relatively well.

Wind has done us a large amount of damage. We, the brigade, the 44th Medical Brigade, purchased two large warehouse tents from Egypt, and they were constructed and erected. They stood for about four days before the wind blew them down. It was a really windy, bad day, but the tents were just not designed to take the rain or the wind. [I]t rained a day before, and then it got real windy and the steel structures were bent and the tent literally collapsed. And so we had to clear that away and just do without.[8]

Mike Brodie

In the Persian Gulf, the Royal Navy air defence ship HMS *Exeter* was on patrol. On board was Mike Brodie, who kept a diary of each day his ship was on active service in the Gulf.

Saturday, 16 February

Defence watches! It is like night during the day. In fact it has been like that for the last week or so. Constant night-time, when you are in eight-hour defence watches you forget actually when it is day and when it is night. The fires that are ongoing on the Kuwait coastline you can see really clearly, orange just fills the skyline and the air is pungent with thick black oil and death. Silkworms [Chinese-made missiles launched by Iraq] still operational according to the latest BDA [battle damage assessment], so air raids are ordered yet again to blast away the suspected sites. B-52 bombers are tasked to do the job.

They tell us when the raids will be, it's not a problem because you see the aircraft on your radar obviously going inland to do their business. The problem for me is when they have finished. They have a strict set, defined area of the coastline at which they must exit the battle area so we can tell that they are friendly aircraft, but do they do it? NO! Some do but some don't. We are a destroyer and an air defence ship. When we see things coming off land, on occasions, less then 24 km [15 miles] away at speed, you shit yourself.

A couple of times we got to the stage of full alert and locked the target up with our fire-control radar, preparing to shoot it out of the sky. It could have been a missile coming straight for us!! You know what happened ... the decision was made on all those times NOT to fire. Now ... they were friendly aircraft but what if they weren't??? Those bastards flying should have flown according to the rules agreed and exited at the agreed points. If it was a missile we would have, what, 45 seconds to lock it up and get a missile off before it would reach the point where nothing could be done.

A terrible experience this morning when we found three bodies, expected to be Iraqi military from a small boat that got destroyed by one of our helos a couple of days ago. Anyway we found them just floating around, so the sea-boat was sent away to have the unpleasant job of picking the bodies up. The first two came back and were a mess, not a nice sight and I will never forget that, but when they went to the third and tried to pull him into the boat, we could all see that his head had been blown off. The decision was made to have a short service for this poor guy and then we attached a sinker (large concrete weight) to the body and sent him to the bottom. It shook me up and I was standing on the ship, those two guys in the sea-boat were really upset. All in all today we had recovered five bodies. All were put into body bags and sent over to RFA *Argus* where once the war is finished they will be given back to the Iraqis, or so we are told.[9]

Notes

1   US Army War College

2   US Center of Military History interview, 6 June 1991

3   US Center of Military History interview, 10 June 1991

4   ibid, 12 February 1991

5   ibid, 26 August 1991

6   http://userpages.aug.com/captbarb/femvetsds.html

7   Defense Link article, 20 March 2001

8   US Center of Military History interview, 3 March 1991

9   Permission of Mike Brodie

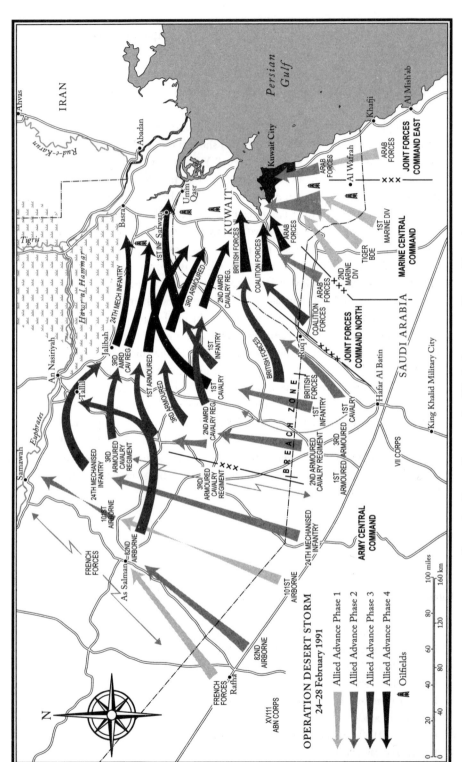

Operation Desert Storm – the Allied advances to liberate Kuwait

Liberating Kuwait

When the UN offensive to free Kuwait was launched on 24 February 1991, there was no doubt that Coalition forces would defeat the Iraqi Army. The only questions were: how long would it take and how much blood would it cost? In fact, the ground war lasted a mere 100 hours. For days before the attack, Iraqi troops had been subjected to merciless air attacks; every possible target was struck. The Coalition offensive had three major prongs: the first aimed at Kuwait City, the second to the west aimed at the Iraqi flanks, and the third targeted the west beyond Iraqi forces that would totally outflank them.

On 24 February, in the largest helicopter invasion ever launched, the US 101st Airborne Division moved 44 km (70 miles) into Iraq and established a support base for future operations. This assault used 300 helicopters carrying 2,000 troops to secure a refuelling base for helicopters on operations near the Iraqi Republican Guard and prevent their re-supply by road. Moving north to supplement the 101st as part of XVIII Airborne Corps was the 24th Mechanized Infantry Division and the 3rd Armored Cavalry Regiment.

The French 6th Armoured and 82nd Airborne Divisions captured the Iraqi city of As Salman, 80 km (50 miles) over the border. The US Marine 1st and 2nd Divisions were successful in their breaching operation and began to take a huge number of Iraqi prisoners, and Saudi tank forces enjoyed similar success in their advance up the Kuwaiti coast.

VII Corps, the main Coalition strike force, moved north into Iraq. It was made up of the US 1st Armored Division, 3rd Armored Division, 2nd Armored Cavalry Regiment, 1st Infantry Division (the Big Red One) and 1st Cavalry Regiment. Joining them in Iraq was the British 1st Armoured Division, including the famous 'Desert Rats' of the 7th Armoured Brigade.

On 25 February, the French 6th Armoured and 82nd Airborne had established a defensive position to prevent the Iraqis from reinforcing their units from Baghdad or the west. To the east of the French, the 24th Mechanized continued to move north, having advanced nearly 160 km

(100 miles). XVIII Airborne Corps deployed to prevent any fleeing Iraqis from returning to Baghdad.

In Kuwait, meanwhile, Saudi and Kuwaiti troops seized the town of Al Zour, 24 km (15 miles) inside Kuwait. The US Marines engaged and defeated the Iraqis at Jaber airfield in central Kuwait, while the M1 Abrams tanks of the US Army's Tiger Brigade (1st Division) shot up Iraqi armour and caused thousands of enemy soldiers to surrender. The main Coalition attack continued with VII Corps moving north to deploy west of the Republican Guard. By the end of the day, 25,000 Iraqis had been taken prisoner, and seven Iraqi divisions had been destroyed.

On 26 February, the US VII Corps moved east to engage the Republican Guard. Once again, Coalition forces captured thousands of demoralized and hungry Iraqis. By the end of the day, soldiers from the 101st Airborne Division were flying over the river, and in the south, Coalition forces had sealed off Kuwait City itself. For diplomatic reasons, it was decided that some of the first troops to liberate Kuwait should be Arab forces instead of US Marines. The 1st Marine Division continued north to a point near the Kuwaiti International Airport, where they once again battled and defeated Iraqi forces.

On the final day of the ground war, 27 February, VII Corps moved east from its positions in Iraq, flanked by XVIII Airborne Corps to the north and US Marines to the south in Kuwait. What followed was a slaughter, as Coalition tanks and ground-attack aircraft destroyed hundreds of Iraqi tanks. By the end of the day, the Republican Guard had been destroyed. The Iraqis had de facto been defeated, and US President George H.W. Bush called a ceasefire. Of Iraq's 545,000 troops in the Kuwait theatre of operations, an estimated 100,000 had been killed and a further 300,000 wounded. American casualties were 148 killed in action and 145 from other causes; 467 wounded in action. Total Coalition losses were 1,800 dead, wounded, missing and captured.

The following accounts record emotions that are common to soldiers once the fighting begins and include boredom, terror, the adrenalin rush of combat and the elation of survival. Although what follows are modern-day accounts, the emotions experienced and reported by these soldiers are the same as those reported from a medieval battle or an American Civil War engagement.

Patrick Haygood

Patrick Haygood served with C Company, 3rd Battalion, 15th Infantry Regiment, 24th Infantry Division, US Army, during the ground war.

I served as a crew member on [a] Bradley fighting vehicle and was in the Gulf from 24 August 1990 [until] 23 March 1991. The 24th was part of the Rapid Deployment Force (RDF), XVIII Airborne Corps. We were the heavy division in the corps, with the 82nd and 101st being the other divisions in the RDF. I fought in the battles of Battle Position 102, Jalibah airfield, the Basra Plain, and the Rumaylah oil fields.

My company lost two killed and [had] 18 wounded in the ground war, all in the battle for Jalibah airfield. The attack on the airfield was rough, and I have vivid memories of seeing the Bradley in front of mine getting hit; I saw the red flash of the round and the burst of smoke on the side of the vehicle as the round penetrated the side armour of the Bradley. The round penetrated into the interior of the vehicle and hit an AT-4 [anti-tank weapon], setting it off, killing one and wounding several others. We charlie miked [continued the mission] and took the airfield, which was defended by two battalions of Iraqi infantry and a battalion of tanks. We also destroyed 25 MiGs [Russian fighter aircraft used by the Iraqis] and helicopters that were on the airfield. Another memory is of the Iraqis in bunkers shooting all their ammo and then surrendering, I wanted to gun them down but didn't; we just pointed them south and let the REMFs [rear-echelon mother-fuckers] handle them. Then, after that, we were moving forward and stopped to refuel. While we were doing this, our SP [self-propelled] artillery moved up behind us and started shelling the Iraqis. Well, after refuelling we were sitting on top of the vehicles watching the shelling when one round sounded funny when it left the barrel; it was a short round and it landed in the middle of Task Force Diamond – it was a DPCIM [dual-purpose conventional improved munition]!!! But luckily no one was hurt; it just scared the hell out of us.

Regardless of what the news reports said, and all the civilians that think the war was easy, the Iraqi Republican Guard tried to fight us, but were just outclassed. I will never forget the smells of burning rubber, diesel fuel or flesh that were everywhere, and the sights of what hot steel does to flesh. I will always hear the artillery and gunfire, and every time I smell diesel fumes it brings back these memories just like it happened yesterday.[1]

Paul Samburg

Paul Samburg served as a crew member in an Abrams tank during Desert Storm, fighting as a member of the 3rd Armored Division, US Army.

I was a crewman on an M1A1 and we had to wait several weeks at this huge apartment complex for our tanks to arrive. My actual combat was three days of racing across the desert just to fight a three-hour battle. Some of the terrain was unbelievable and the one night it rained was probably the worst night of my life. Between trying to refuel, put out these gas detectors, and eat and sleep in the tank, I couldn't wait to kill something.

The main thing I remember is seeing the Air Force pound something just over a crest in what appeared to be a valley, and then our Apaches flying overhead and hitting the same area. A short while later, we headed into this huge valley and began firing as fast as we could load. I remember all the fires looked awesome through the thermal sights and the night-vision. When there was nothing left to fire at, we started moving across the valley floor, and then they called a ceasefire.

After sleeping for a few days, I remember exploring some Republican Guard bunkers and finding some cool stuff. We found Jordanian tobacco, crystal glasses, green shirts and lots of weapons. The biggest challenge was hiding all the AK-47s every time some officer decided to do a weapons search.[2]

Hubert de Laroque la Tour

Colonel de Laroque la Tour was the commander of the 3rd Helicopter Regiment, 6th (French) Light Armoured Division, which was attached to the US XVIII Corps.

On the second day, we arrived with 30 helicopters, 20 in front and 10 in the second line. And when we arrived I was in the centre, in the middle of the formation, and suddenly I see a white cloth, somebody with a white flag.

We fired off two rounds and straight away four people stood up. Behind us they had a Puma [helicopter] for the taking out of casualties. So they landed two Pumas, one of which contained an infantry squad. They [the helicopters] fired again with 20mm guns and straight away another eight [Iraqi soldiers] stood up. The operation was at a place called As Shubakr.

First of all they sent in the gunships and the anti-tank helicopters, and then the infantry were brought in by helicopters to mop up. The first thing they did was to take out the antenna and the anti-aircraft positions. They then sent in the helicopters with the guns to fire on the ground troops, and then they brought in infantry. They landed them just next to the village. The helicopters with the 20mm cannons supported the ground troops at close range, and the ground troops went through the whole village and searched it.

The Iraqis were very surprised. They didn't see us coming in. The first thing they knew about it was when the HOT missiles [high-subsonic optically guided tube-fired missiles] started exploding. The HOT has to be guided in by the same helicopter that fired it, it's not like the Hellfire. It's a good missile, though: it goes into a building and takes it out. Afterwards, the helicopters fired on the armoured hangers at the airport As Salman.[3]

Donald Shawver

Donald Shawver was stationed with the Maintenance Platoon of L Troop, 3rd Squadron, 2nd Armored Cavalry Regiment (ACR), US Army. The 2nd ACR struck the Iraqi Tawakalna Division on a stretch of mostly featureless desert and the engagement became known as the Battle of 73 Easting, after the map reference line of the same name. The engagement started on the afternoon of 26 February.

I am a Bradley mechanic ... 2nd ACR shot into Iraq with lightning speed. We made contact and destroyed many Iraqi OPs [observation posts]. Then we came upon the mighty Republican Guard. I can recall our Bradleys and tankers kicking their ass big time. I saw T–72 and T–64 [tank] turrets get blown clean off. I think one of the contributing factors to our fierce fire upon them was that back in Khafji, before the ground invasion started, US Marines got into a firefight called the Battle of Khafji.

There was this one Marine track [armoured vehicle] that allowed an Iraqi tank to surrender. As the tank approached, flying a white flag, it fired on the Marine vehicle, killing seven Marines. Well, we were told about that and it pissed me and everybody in our unit off. Marines might be jar heads or knuckleheads to an army guy, but in no way does an American stand by and watch another American on the battlefield get killed in such a way. It makes you fire-ass mad as hell. To this day I hate the Iraqi lowlife so-called soldiers for doing that. Don't get me wrong, the Iraqi people I think for the most part just need a new leader. But the other is unacceptable. Well, they paid for that, I think that is clear.

The second day of the ground war a friend of mine from K Troop, Corporal James R. McCoy, was killed. To this day I have not talked about it much. He was killed in action during a firefight. I helped clean up the mess in his track (M113 tank) after they removed his body.[4]

Bill Hobbs

Bill Hobbs was a platoon commander with Charlie Company, 7th Engineers, 1st Marine Division (US). He was convinced that the theatre of operations was contaminated with Iraqi chemical warfare agents.

After the air war started, I went to see Marines with 8th Engineers and saw that a camel had been 'blown up' with some type of anti-tank rocket by the Marine infantry unit guarding the road leading to the 8th Engineers. The chunks of the camel had been pushed to the side of the road with a road grader. On my first trip by the site, I could smell the blood for maybe a quarter mile [0.4 km] before we came to the site. One thing that I recall that was very strange was that there were no flies or other insects feeding on the chunks of camel meat on the side of the road, yet most of the time when we ate our MREs [Meals, Ready-to-Eat], we shook the spoon or blew on our food to dislodge the flies before we shovelled it into our mouths. I passed by the blown-up camel several times and never saw any flies or other insects feeding on the meat alongside of the road.[5]

John Pettit

Sergeant Pettit was serving with C Company, 1st Battalion, 5th Marine Regiment, 1st Marine Division (US), heading towards Kuwait City.

We were moving towards Kuwait City. It was the second or third night after K-Day [the day the Allied Coalition began the offensive], and we had already moved a considerable distance into Kuwait and the blazing oil fields. The rain had been falling nearly all day, and we were in MOP 3 [mission-oriented protective posture suit used in a toxic environment], which consists of coat, pants, rubber boots and gloves. We had incoming artillery earlier in the day, after which the cry of 'Gas! Gas! Gas!' could be heard echoing across the open desert. We quickly donned our masks and prayed that nothing would fall on us and that the all-clear signal would come soon. It was dark by noon with the smoke from the fires ... As the sun went down, we could not see a thing. A huge battle was going on somewhere to our front, and rocket-propelled artillery was flying over our heads. It made for a very eerie and scary situation. We finally stopped for the night and by this time we could not see our armoured personnel carriers that were less than 6 metres [20 ft] behind us. The Iraqis could walk right up on us and we wouldn't know the difference. My sense of hearing has never been as acute as it was that night. We were attempting to dig in with two people per fighting hole across the front. Unfortunately, we hit rock about 5 cm [2 in] below the sand. We had set down our gear while we dug, and could not find it by sight. Once we turned around to find gear, and started crawling around feeling for it, we would lose sense of direction and not know which way was front.

Sometime during the digging, I took off my protective gloves because they were making me sweat so much. The battle that was going on was increasing and so was the artillery going over us. Suddenly we received more incoming artillery, and everyone scrambled for their 'holes', gear and weapons. Through the darkness I heard another cry of 'Gas! Gas! Gas!' echo through the night. I struggled to get my mask on as quickly as possible, but could not find the gloves I had removed. I pulled my hands into the sleeves of my British MOP jacket in an attempt to keep them from being contaminated by whatever may be falling on us.

The night went terribly quiet after this, except for the screaming from my left. One of the younger Marines had lost his bearing, started ripping off his MOP suit and tried to run. The Marines close enough ... tackled him ... trying to calm him down. I was still preoccupied with finding my NBC (nuclear biological chemical) gloves and the explosions to the front of us were increasing and getting closer. This made for one of the scariest nights of my life. We later found out that a member of a tank crew attached to us died that evening of a heart attack. The 9th Marines [Regiment] had encountered a counterattack that was looking for us, ... and the attacking Iraqi forces had dismounted and been literally mowed down by the 9th Marines. They encountered tanks and infantry in the fight. We didn't do any sleeping that night.[6]

David Winkler

David Winklet served as a truck driver with the 1485th Transport Company, an Ohio National Guard unit, US Army.

The next day we were to go with the 1st Cavalry Division to haul their stuff. We got loaded and left in a convoy of 10 trucks, two men to a truck. Don Douglas and I got a forklift, MREs and water.

The 1st Infantry Division was at the line that morning. They opened it and we went through. We stopped and an officer came around that night and said that there were Iraq divisions all around us. We waited around to see if they were going to do something. We were told to get into the war. I was with VII Corps coming from a log base. We left again and got stuck for the fourth time. The five-ton cargo truck didn't pull us out, they kept on going. We were in Iraq by ourselves; we stayed in the truck that night and didn't get any sleep because we saw lights on the ridge line. We didn't know if they were ours or theirs, so we kept watch just in case, our M16s in hand and four clips, 80 rounds, to share between us.

The next morning we tried to dig our truck out, with no luck. We dug a two-man foxhole for cover and stayed in it for a half a day when a convoy came by. We asked them for help, but they couldn't stop; we were there by ourselves again. We got the forklift down and tried to use it to get us out, but it didn't work. We dug until we got to hard sand and finally got out. We broke all of the belts, except for the fan belt. Not knowing where the Cavalry went, but we heard that they were going to Basra, Iraq. So we headed east looking for them.

That afternoon, we ran into three Iraqi troops. One of them was young, about 15 or 19 years old. They needed food and water, so we gave them some MREs. The young one had bad feet, so I told Don to watch them with his gun on them. I washed the young one's feet and gave him a pair of socks. We asked them where Basra was and they pointed east. We took them with us to find help.

We found an MP company and gave them the Iraqis. We asked them if they had seen the Cav. They said no, so we took off again. It was getting dark, and we had to find some place to stay or drive all night.

The next morning we saw what looked liked holes in the ground. We stopped and walked over to the place. We saw a person under a blanket. We didn't know if he was dead or alive, so I fired my M16 at him; he didn't move. I walked over to where the Iraqi was. He was dead all right. One side of his head was gone, what a sight! We walked down into the place. It was a hospital; there was blood on the ground and on the tables. We heard a noise in the wall, so I fired my gun again. The man fell out of the wall, his gun in his hand. He might have been dead already: who knows, who cares? It still gets to me, though.

We needed to find the Cav. We went over to an Iraqi truck to see if there [were] any belts on it. We needed belts bad – ours had broken off when we were trying to get unstuck. The belts on the Iraqi truck weren't any good, though.

We walked back over to the truck. Don said, 'Look down, Dave, don't they look like land mines?' There were three red sticks coming out of the ground, they were all over the place. We walked back in the tracks that were made by tanks or trucks. Boy, that was a hair-raising experience.

We made it back to the truck. Don wanted to drive awhile. I had to take a leak. When I did, Don shut the truck off. I asked him why he shut it off. He said he wanted to see if it would start again. Well, it didn't! We hadn't gotten any sleep, and here we were, stuck again. Out of the blue came a Humvee down the road. There were two GIs in it. We asked if they had any jumpers [jump leads]; they did, they got us running again. We said thanks, and they were gone just like that.

We continued heading east that night until we came upon an artillery unit. We asked them if we could stay with them till morning. We were going to sleep in Iraqi jeeps, but there was blood and glass all over them. We got three hours of sleep. In the morning we asked the First Sergeant if he knew where the 1st Cav was. He said no, so we asked him if he had any belts off the Iraqi jeeps; he didn't. He gave us KEM sticks, two red, two green. We drove on the rest of the day. We saw dead bodies all over the road, on the sand dunes. We drove on; we were getting worried that we were too far north to find the Cav. We came to a dead end, and there were Iraqi troops to my left. There were about 20 of them and two of us. They wanted food and water, but there was no way we were stopping.

We went on down the road and there were about 100 or more Iraqi troops carrying weapons, and tanks, trucks and jeeps which they were fixing. I told Don not to move his head, maybe they wouldn't realize we were Americans. Boy, was I afraid, and Don was, too. We made it through okay. I asked Don if they were Kuwaiti troops across the bridge, and he said they were Iraqis. With nowhere to go, we had to cross the bridge and drove to the gate of a building. Suddenly, two Iraqis jumped onto our truck and put their guns to our heads and said, 'Iraqis bang, Americans.' My heart stopped right there, all I could think about was making my kids daddyless, and Don was praying, too. They got off the truck and opened the door. My M16 was across my lap, but an Iraqi pointed his AK-47 at me. He was going to shoot, when an Iraqi officer came running from the building and grabbed the man's arm. I thought the gun was going to go off. This officer

wanted us to get out and go into this dark little shack. No fucking way were
we getting out. With my foot on the clutch shaking so bad, all I could hear
was Don saying, 'Get us out of here.' I let the clutch out fast, turned the
truck into a jack-knife and we got out. They started firing at us. I could
hear the rounds hitting the truck and trailer. When we got straight, we ran
over some of the Iraqi troops. They chased us down the road, shooting at
us. Don was trying to shoot out his side, and I was trying to shoot and
drive at the same time. I just pointed it [the M16] out of the window and
fired it. I put the pedal to the floor. At the bridge, there was an Iraqi soldier
on the left side of the road with an RPG rocket launcher. I looked him
right in the face, hoping he wouldn't fire – he didn't.

We hit the S-curve too hard and almost turned the truck over; the
forklift was halfway off. We saw helicopters coming from Don's side. I
jumped out, not knowing if I was going to be shot or what. I just wanted
them to land and get us out of there. One landed, the others went around
guarding us from them [the Iraqis]. The lieutenant flying the chopper said
they were two-man choppers and to watch where they were going. We
passed Iraqi troops on the right. I wanted to shoot them, but I didn't, they
weren't worth it. Just shitheads, that's all.

We turned around, went back and made a right-hand turn and ran
smack dab into an APC [armoured personnel carrier] with a 50-calibre
[machine gun] mounted on it. I did a burn-out in reverse, turned around
and ran into the US 1st Infantry Division.[7]

Robert Lewis

Robert Lewis was an intelligence analyst with the 3rd Remotely Piloted
Vehicle Company attached to the 1st SRIG (Surveillance, Reconnaissance,
Intelligence Group), US Marine Corps.

I was 22 years old when I went to the Persian Gulf. The hardest part of
being in the Persian Gulf for me was making decisions on who would live
and who would die. Being in the intelligence field and in a unit that had
not been previously utilized in combat, I had a lot of responsibility that a
person of 22 would not have usually had. When we were flying our
remotely controlled vehicle on a mission, I would have the task of
identifying targets and calling them in for destruction by air. One of my
worst memories was calling in an air strike on several hundred troops in the

open. The targets I called were up to me and I saw this as an opportunity to destroy a large number of 'the enemy' with very little effort. Well, I called in the air, and every one of the 'enemy' soldiers was killed. This was how the war went for me. From the start of the air war to the end of the ground war, my job for 20 of every 24 hours a day was to decide who should live and who should die.

What about the officers in the unit you may ask? Well, in my unit their job was to fly the vehicle, not to do the intelligence. I have respect for every one of them, but the bottom line is that it was my job to decide. You may ask who was the middleman, who called in the strikes; well, let's say more often I sat with a radio in my hand and a fighter pilot on the other end. I was the link. The reason I tell you this is because it has had a direct effect on what I have felt and experienced since I came back from the Gulf War.'[8]

Glenn (Dicko) Dixon

Glen Dixon was a Gunner at FDC (Fire Direction Centre), HQ Battery, 2nd Field Regiment, Royal Artillery, British Army during the Gulf War.

I was a 'flaggy' on the Regimental Command Post, Regimental Command net in one ear, Divisional Artillery net and Technical net in the other. Although commands were given by those on high, the memories of 24 M109s [howitzers] responding to my voice will never [be] eradicate[d].

At about 60 hours into the conflict I received a sitrep [situation report] from a Canadian Forward Observation Officer – India 22 [I22]: 'I am experiencing what appears to be a dug-in company position to my front, on my handheld (night-vision sight). I request Charlie Charlie 1 at priority call to me for the next 45 minutes, 15 rounds HE [high explosive], 5 Rounds WP [white phosphorus], 2 Rounds Illum [illumination], over.'

Suddenly I'm in the chair! I looked to the officer next to me, who was doing the nodding dog through lack of sleep, nudged him, and he replied, 'Yeah,' waving his hand at me in a royal wave fashion.

I then transmitted, 'Hello I22 and CC1, I22 has CC1 at priority call to you for the next 45 minutes; 15 Rounds HE, 5 Rounds WP and 2 Rounds Illum, over.'

The batteries replied, 'I10 Roger, Out,' 'I20 Roger, Out,' 'W30 Roger, Out,' 'I22 Roger, Out.' Then silence.

Fire mission pad poised ready, I was now bolt rigid waiting for the shoot to take place. The OP [observation post] gave the batteries the target location, the target description, the amount and type of rounds he wanted, and they responded as slick as they've never been slicker before. By this point, I was so involved in the fire order process, I was oblivious to the fact that the nodding dog officer next to me was now a sleeping dog, as deaf as a post and unmovable. The delay in the mission was due to there still being a state of 'At My Command' in force, that only he could cancel, and by doing so give the executive order to FIRE!!!!

I knew this, and I knew that I was in no position to give the order myself. The net was silent, the air was still, and 24 guns were poised ready to punch anger into the night ahead.

That which followed will echo in my mind forever, as 24 guns let rip at once, a barrage of Royal Artillery pumping HE and WP rounds towards the soon to be dead, disorientated, demoralized and neutralized enemy. It seemed to last forever, and it was the smoothest mission I'd ever been a part of. Then, suddenly, the OP stopped the shoot. 'Check firing; friendlies wish to dismount, end of mission sitrep to follow.' As he transmitted, the noise in the background was screaming, muffled explosions and the crackling of small-arms fire, and then silence again. A truly deafening silence. The sitrep came through in the most sombre, bereaved manner, as if the OP had lost one of his own. He said, 'Good shooting ... target annihilated ... many enemy dead. Out.'[9]

Tracy Abernathy-Walden

Tracy Abernathy-Walden was a US Marine in Desert Shield and Desert Storm and was assigned to MWSS 273 (Marine Wing Support Squadron 273).

My unit flew out on Christmas Eve and landed in Jubail, Saudi Arabia, on Christmas Day. Of 500 in my unit, 17 were women. Myself and five other women were among the 100 Marines that built the largest/longest mobile runway in the history of organized military worldwide: and we did it twice!

I am now 10 years into a police career, and know a lot of former Marines who give me the credit earned. Still, no one understands that I was there! I captured an Iraqi soldier. I had another Marine die in my arms, from nerve gas poisoning. [But] most [of the] credit only goes to the men. (God bless them, too, though.) [W]e live with hard memories, too, and we are proud, too, and we would do it all over again … On a side note, even though my unit took fire, a lot, we were not afforded the Combat Medal, because women were not 'in combat', so the records show. All 17 of us were bussed south when the IG [Inspector General] came and the unit records were changed to reflect only male Marines. My only hurt is not to have been awarded the Combat Medal, when it was earned.[10]

Lundy Hall

In 1990 Lundy Hall was assigned to HHC 43rd CSG (Headquarters and Headquarters Company, Corps Support Group [since redesignated Combat Support Group]), US Army, at Fort Carson, Colorado. His account illustrates Clausewitz's dictum that 'organization is a necessary evil', and also provides a glimpse into the massive amount of logistical support required to keep modern armies functioning.

My duty assignment was as the unit Prescribed Load List/The Army Maintenance Management System (PLL/TAMMS) clerk, which is army-speak for a parts guy and equipment service scheduler. I did this for my company as well as for the 4th Finance Company and two transportation detachments. This isn't as impressive as it sounds: all told there was only something like 34 trucks (four two-and-a-half-ton cargo vehicles, the rest pick-ups and SUVs [sports utility vehicles]), three generator sets with trailers and four cargo trailers.

On 25 February 1991, my immediate supervisor and I were having supper in our tent after repairing a Water Buffalo [M-149 water trailer], when the first sergeant stepped into the tent and asked for two volunteers. As Gebaurer and myself were the only ones there, we stepped up and said, 'Yes, Top?' 'I need you guys to take this truck a quarter mile down the road to where its drivers are. Now move it.'

Gebaurer and I grabbed our rifles and web gear and piled into an HEMTT tanker, an odd-looking eight-wheeled fuel tanker. We drove three miles down the road to find a line of 75 Czechoslovakian fuel tankers lined up on the side of the road – Czech equipment, US drivers. Driving to the end of the line, we found an M1008a1 and an M1009 (a Chevy pick-up and a Chevy Blazer) at the front of the convoy. This was maybe 18.00 hours.

We found the OIC (officer in charge) in the Blazer, who told us to drive the HEMTT to the third-in-line position and stay until our replacements showed up. Some time close to 19.00 hours, the non-commissioned officer in charge came by and said, 'We're getting ready to roll out and it looks like y'all two are coming with us.' We asked where our replacements were and, if they continued not to show, where were we going … About 20.00 hours, we headed west across the Tapline [Trans-Arabian Pipeline, an oil pipeline from Qaisumah in Saudi Arabia to Sidon in Lebanon]. Sometime later we cut northwest across the desert. Around 02.00 hours we stopped and shut everything down. A sergeant said, 'We're gonna sit here and wait for our escorts.'

I woke up sometime after dawn, looked over and saw Gebaurer was asleep. I peered out and couldn't see the rest of the convoy either ahead or behind. I woke Gebaurer up and asked, 'Where'd they go?' He got a panicked look and then calmed down, saying, 'They're lined up behind us.' I climbed out the door, looked over the top of the truck and saw them all lined up behind and to the left of our position. We switched positions, and I took over driving the rig. It was a while later that our escorts showed up, the protectors of a convoy of 230,000 gallons [870,645 litres] of aviation fuel: three HMMWVs with three MPs in each. Two of them did have an M60 machine gun mounted on a gun ring on top.

We drove off, passing through a berm early in the day. In disbelief, I read the painted plywood sign stating, 'Welcome to Occupied Iraq.' A while later our escorts ran off into the desert to pick up some POWs [prisoners of war]. I never saw them again. Between 15.00 and 18.00 hours we came across a site full of fuel pods and helicopters. Everyone in the convoy pumped their load of fuel into the pods while the helicopters were trying to pump the pods dry. Gebaurer got out, walked around the site and came across one of our transportation detachments. He scrounged some food and a case of water. Once the convoy was 'dry' we headed back south … we had pulled off the side to allow some Brits to move south. I believe they had been the victims of a 'blue-on-blue' incident – a US-on-British attack. That thought still makes me sick … The sun didn't come up the next morning … we were in the smoke from the oil well fires. It was like a cloudy, moonless night. By noon it was like dusk. That's when we heard President Bush had announced the ceasefire. When I later heard someone call it 'The 100-hour War', I replied that I was driving a fuel tanker for 80 hours of it.

I've always said I was the middle of the road. Some troops … stayed in hotels the whole time, some slept in or under their vehicles; I slept in a tent with a plywood floor. I didn't have a combat MOS (military occupation

specialty), but I was in Iraq refuelling helicopters to attack Iraqis in Kuwait
… I spent my fair share of time burning shit, hauling garbage and doing
KP ('kitchen police': don't ask me why 'police' means 'to clean' in the
US Army). The old phrase 'Too many chiefs and not enough Indians'
applied to my unit. I was only able to do my job one day out of four thanks
to the 'worker' shortage. The rest of the time I was on camp police, KP or
guard duty.[11]

Andy Hoskinson

Andy Hoskinson was the commander of Battery C, 3rd Battalion, 82nd Field
Artillery, 1st Cavalry Division, US Army during the occupation of Iraq.

After 28 February 1991

For the next 13 days, we pulled occupation duty in Iraq. This duty was not
pleasant – boring, uncertain and dangerous. There was much uncertainty;
would hostilities resume? When would we pull out of Iraq? When would
we go back home? As is always the case in the interim period between the
end of a war and redeployment, it was a leadership challenge trying to keep
soldiers' morale up. There were four specific problems that sapped soldier
morale: complacency, uncertainty, the anti-climactic nature of the war's
end, and souvenir hunting.

After a war, soldiers tend to let their guard down and become
complacent. However, it was still a dangerous battlefield for us out there in
Iraq. Our occupation sector had previously been the TAA (tactical
assembly area) for the Iraqi Republican Guard Tawakalna Division. As a
result, there were still lots of unexploded surface munitions on the ground:
Iraqi minefields, cluster bomblets from B-52 strikes, and DPICM [dual-
purpose improved conventional munition] bomblets from artillery strikes.
A soldier from Alpha Battery, Private Roger Valentine, lost his life when
he encountered an unexploded MLRS [multiple-launch rocket system]
DPICM bomblet. Moreover, there were still a lot of isolated Iraqi units out
there, some of which had either not been informed of the ceasefire, or did
not care. One night, for example, we were alerted to engage a renegade
Iraqi tank company.

I learned first-hand how dangerous it was a few days after the ceasefire.
I was out one day surveying an abandoned Iraqi cantonment area with my
driver, Specialist Malone. While checking out the area, I looked at my
watch, and realized that I was about to be late for Private Valentine's

memorial service, which was being held that day at Alpha Battery's position. Since I was running late, I decided to drive a straight line from my current location to Alpha Battery's position, rather than take the MSR (main supply route). That turned out to be a mistake, which came damn close to costing me my life.

As we were heading to Alpha Battery's position, I heard Malone ask in his Texas drawl, 'Sir, what are those rods sticking out of the ground?' I looked up and saw numerous mounds of dirt with small metal rods sticking out of the ground, spaced about one every 10 square metres [12 sq yards]. I got my binoculars out, and scanned the area. With the binoculars, I could tell that the metal rods were actually detonating rods sticking out about 15–31 cm [6–12 in] from the ground. Those were hastily buried anti-tank mines. We had wandered into a minefield, alone, miles away from the closest American unit. I immediately shouted, 'STOP THE VEHICLE, MALONE!' Malone came to a screeching halt, and gave me a quizzical look. I explained the situation to him, and then called the TOC [Tactical Operations Centre] to let them know that I would be late …

My first course of action was to get out of the vehicle and ground guide [it] around the anti-tank mines. This minefield had obviously been laid by the Iraqis in an extremely hasty manner. It was not very dense; only one mine every 10 m [11 yards] or so. I had one foot out the door of the vehicle when I remembered that soldiers generally do not lay just anti-tank mines; they usually lay anti-personnel mines as well, to kill the engineers or infantrymen who dismount from vehicles to clear the anti-tank mines. It occurred to me that the Iraqis might have forgotten to do that, but I was not about to risk that.

Malone and I ended up leaning out of our respective doors to look for mines as we drove out of the minefield at five miles per hour. The carriage of the HMMWV had enough clearance to roll over the anti-tank mines without touching the detonating rods and setting them off. What I was concerned about was one of the front wheels rolling over a mine and sending us sky high. Malone watched the left front wheel, and I watched the right front wheel. It took about 15–20 minutes to get out of the minefield, the longest 15–20 minutes of my life.[12]

Steven Dutch

Sergeant Dutch served with the 432nd Civil Affairs Company, US Army. The company assists in transition from military occupation to civilian government.

Monday, 25 March 1991

We went to Iraq today. We left about 09.30 hours on a nice sunny day. The road leads through the choke point, then turns north. Along the way we passed more burning oil wells in the Rawdatain [oil] field. At least 50 fires were visible, with another 20 or so in the distance to the east. The bus took us to Safwan, the first town in Iraq. Safwan is very poor and rundown, and not from the war. Many of the buildings are mud-brick, with wooden roof poles sticking out. It looks like an Indian pueblo or a town in Latin America. The contrast between what Kuwait did with its oil wealth, and what Iraq did with its, is starkly evident here.

Relations between the locals and the occupying troops seem remarkably amiable. The kids mobbed the bus for candy. Male dominance starts early here; even small boys push the girls aside. There's lots of unexploded ordnance around. EOD [explosive ordnance disposal] blew ammo about 15 times in the two hours we were there, and cleared our street three times to blow ordnance in a building across the street.[13]

Notes

1   Tracings in the Sand (www.gulfweb.org/tracings)

2   ibid

3   US Center of Military History interview, 10 March 1991

4   Permission of Donald Shawver

5   Permission of Bill Hobbs

6   Permission of John Pettit

7   Tracings in the Sand (www.gulfweb.org/tracings)

8   ibid

9   Courtesy of Britain's Small Wars website (www.britains-smallwars.com)

10 http://userpages.aug.com/captbarb/femvetsds.html

11 Permission of Lundy Hall

12 Permission of Andy Hoskinson

13 Permission of Steven Dutch

Prisoners of War

In the West, pilots, Special Forces personnel and other specialists who are likely to be shot down or ambushed deep behind enemy lines receive excellent training in escape and evasion procedures (E&E). This training prepares them for what they are likely to experience if captured by the military or police of totalitarian regimes where there is scant regard for the rules of war.

However, even for those who are prepared, being captured by an enemy is a severe psychological shock. It is a testament to the training given to those individuals whose stories feature in this chapter, combined with their mental fortitude, that though they were subjected to torture, they did not crack under interrogation. Sadly, their Iraqi torturers were never brought to justice.

Despite being a signatory to the Geneva Convention, Iraq consistently abused Coalition prisoners during the Gulf War. The 1949 convention lays down the following regarding the treatment of prisoners:

> *Prisoners of war must at all times be humanely treated. Any unlawful act or omission by the Detaining Power causing death or seriously endangering the health of a prisoner of war in its custody is prohibited, and will be regarded as a serious breach of the present Convention. In particular, no prisoner of war may be subjected to physical mutilation or to medical or scientific experiments of any kind which are not justified by the medical, dental or hospital treatment of the prisoner concerned and carried out in his interest. Likewise, prisoners of war must at all times be protected, particularly against acts of violence or intimidation and against insults and public curiosity.*
>
> *No physical or mental torture, nor any other form of coercion may be inflicted on prisoners of war to secure from them information of any kind whatever. Prisoners of war who refuse to answer may not be threatened, insulted, or exposed to unpleasant or disadvantageous treatment of any kind.*

These rules were not adhered to by the Iraqis when Coalition service personnel fell into their hands. The Iraqis had mistreated Iranian prisoners during the Iran–Iraq War, and the culture of prisoner abuse continued during the Gulf War. Mistreatment included physical abuse and torture, forced propaganda statements, food deprivation and denial of access to the Red Cross until the day of repatriation after hostilities had ended.

Bizarrely, the Iraqis paraded humiliated and abused Coalition personnel on world-wide television, thereby providing evidence of their crimes to the international community.

The treatment administered to those Iraqis captured by Coalition forces, on the other hand, was a radically different story. Coalition forces captured over 62,000 prisoners during Operation Desert Storm. During the ground war, 308 internees were treated by US military medical treatment facilities (MTFs). From the end of the ground war (28 February 1991) until the end of March 1991, some 8,979 internees were given medical treatment. Fragment wounds accounted for 44 per cent of the surgical admissions during the ground war; 23 per cent of surgical admissions required treatment for fractures. Surgical intervention was required in 28 per cent of Iraqi casualties admitted.

In total, American physicians treated more than 2,000 Iraqi prisoners of war after the war. Although most of the US military physicians returned to the US after the war, some physicians remained in the Gulf to care for the remaining US forces and also for wounded Iraqi prisoners.

The US Army had 1,500 physicians in the Gulf in total, including 831 from the reserves and Army National Guard. US Army physicians staffed 44 military hospitals with 13,000 beds. The US Navy had 843 physicians from various specialities, including general medicine, surgery, anaesthesia, internal medicine, family practice, psychiatry, paediatrics, radiology, ophthalmology, neurology, dermatology, pathology, and obstetrics and gynaecology.

Joseph Small

Major Small was a US Marine Corps pilot flying forward air control missions in an OV–10 Bronco.

For the first six weeks of the war [there] were mostly air strikes. It was 25 February (during the ground war) at about 13.00–13.30 hours in the afternoon. The Americans were moving through Kuwait and I was flying over them. The Army wanted to destroy all of the tanks. I tried to find the tanks, but it was hard because the weather was very bad; heavy fog and cloudy. It was also hard to see because oil wells were on fire, and there was a lot of smoke in the air that stretched for 160 km [100 miles]. While flying over an enemy trench base, my aircraft was hit with a heat-seeking missile. I was forced to eject from the plane.

An Iraqi unit of 12 men with rifles found me. They pointed their rifles at me, took away all of my survival equipment and weapons (pistol and knife), and put me in an SUV [sports utility vehicle].

They took me to a command bunker in central Kuwait. They reported that they had me, and other Iraqi men took me to Kuwait City.

I went through a very physical, painful interrogation while I was blindfolded and tied up. I gave them no information because I knew if I did other Americans would be killed, so they beat me. After a day and a half of interrogation, I was sent to Basra, the largest city in Iraq, for more questioning.

The next day, they drove me to Baghdad for more interrogations, which were even rougher. I was handcuffed for a whole day and a half; the handcuffs dug into my wrists far enough that I could see my bone. On the night of day two, I was taken to a prison cell, where I slept on the floor with one blanket during the cold winter.

My worst experience was hearing an Air Force captain in a cell close to mine scream in pain because of a very badly broken leg. Instead of giving him medical treatment, the Iraqi guards would enter his cell and kick his leg while he was on the ground. It was hard to listen to him in so much pain because I couldn't do anything about it. He couldn't do anything to protect himself, either.

The guards gave me one pitcher of water, a small loaf of bread, and they slopped some 'porridge' (which tasted like chalk) into a dish in the morning. In the evening, I got watery rice or greasy water/bone/gristle from boiled meat that the Iraqis ate. On the last day, I got half of an orange, a roll with marmalade, tea and rice. Compared to the other meals, this tasted very good. I was there from 25 February to 5 March 1991, when I was turned over to the Red Cross.

I stayed in Baghdad with the Red Cross on 5 March. I flew to Riyadh, Saudi Arabia, the next day with American and British escorts. All of the POWs were split up by their countries into groups. The Americans went to Bahrain and from there to a hospital ship, where we were checked up for four days. On 10 March, I arrived in Washington, DC, where I met up with my family.[1]

Rhonda Cornum

US Army flight surgeon Major Rhonda Cornum was on a search-and-rescue helicopter looking for a downed F-16 pilot on the last day of the war. Hit by gunfire, the Black Hawk smashed into the desert at 130 knots. With broken arms and other injuries, Rhonda Cornum was one of three crew members who survived the crash and was taken prisoner.

… I looked up and I saw five Iraqi guys with their, you know, rifles pointed at me. So then I knew I wasn't dead. And I knew I was captured. Then one of them reached down, grabbed me by the arm, and stood me up. And that's when he separated my already broken right arm. And then I knew I was pretty badly hurt and clearly, clearly not dead. I got taken down into a bunker and questioned a little about, you know. 'Who are you? What are you doing here?' That stuff.

… They … dragged me over to this group of Iraqi soldiers. And … this group of them, it was, like, a circle of them, and they opened up and they threw me down next to somebody else, and that was Sergeant Dunlap. And that's when I knew there was another survivor. The next thing was probably the scariest thing of our entire trip there. Because they just stood there and they put their handguns to the back of our heads, and we really thought they were gonna shoot us.

We thought, 'Well, you know, at the end of the war, they're gonna retreat. They don't want prisoners, and this will take care of that problem.' And, you know, who knows what they're thinking? But we both thought we heard them say 'Shoot 'em!'

And then nothing happened. They dragged us back to our feet and took us down to some other bunker to get interrogated some more.

They realized I was a woman when they stood me up. [Up to] that point, I had my flak jacket on and my survival vest and my weapon, all that stuff, and they started taking all this stuff off. And they took off my helmet. And when I fly, I don't wear pins and stuff in my hair, so that my hair stays up just because it's in the helmet. So they took off my flight helmet, and all this long, shoulder-length brown hair came out. [U]ntil then I'm sure they just thought I was a skinny guy. But, all of a sudden they realized, 'Oh my goodness, this is a girl!'

[W]e had maybe a 30-minute ride in the dark, to Basra. I'm not even sure I knew it was Basra, except that I … knew basically where we were going on the mission. I knew that was the only city that was around. And

... they took us to a prison there.... Well, I was just leaning back on the seat, and all of a sudden, I feel this guy sitting next to me, who puts his hands on my face and starts to kiss me. I thought, 'Well, how bizarre!' And ... I never, I don't know what I was thinking, but I really thought, 'Surely he can do better!' I mean, I've got ... a cut above my eye that's soaked with blood and ... I'm sure I don't smell very good. And I'm thinking, 'How can he possibly want to do this?'

[T]hen he ... unzipped my flight suit and started fondling me. And I thought, 'I can't believe it!' But there was no way to fight; I couldn't move anything anyway. I didn't really want to make him real mad, I didn't want to bite him. And so I did nothing. I just sat there. Except when he tried ... to take me by the back of the head and put my head down in his lap, and I couldn't because my arms didn't move then. And that was excruciating... I feel confident he knew he shouldn't be doing what he was doing. Because every time I'd scream, he'd quit. So I think the idea was that the guys in the front of the truck weren't supposed to know. I suspect that ... it was more he didn't want to get in trouble. I think if the other guys hadn't been there, he probably wouldn't have stopped either way. But I don't know that. I mean ... I don't know. I just was amazed that he would want to do that ... that was my first thought, really. Just amazed.

And that was really my biggest concern. I mean, a lot of people make a big deal about getting molested, and I'm sure it's a big deal. But in the hierarchy of things that were going wrong, that was pretty low on my list. Well next, he stopped, zipped my flight suit back up, 'cause we were obviously getting to wherever it was we were going. And I was grateful that it had been a shorter trip than it could've been.[2]

John Peters

British RAF Tornado pilot Lieutenant Peters was shot down on his very first low-flying mission to bomb an Iraqi airfield. He was captured and taken to a prison dubbed by Coalition POWs as the 'Baghdad Biltmore', where he was brutally beaten, tortured and displayed on Iraqi television.

Well ... you're taken into ... this room, and this time you've got a bag on your head, and ... they sit you on this stool ... and you've got these bright lights, you can feel these bright lights, you're sitting there, and you can feel people. They're very quiet, you can feel people, and then suddenly you get a voice in English, and that's the first time anybody's spoken to you.

'Name?'

[T]hen you're kind of thinking, am I right, this is the interrogation process? And to a degree, you know what's going to happen with the interrogation process. And you go, right, and that's when you start … trying to be evasive.

'Peters.'

'Rank?'

'Flight Lieutenant.'

And you get, 'Speak up! Speak up!' because you're always making sure you're very quiet so they can't hear you.

'Number?'

So you give them the number. And then they say, 'Are you pilot or navigator?'

And … we say … 'I cannot answer that question, sir!'

Because you're meant to give name, rank, number and date of birth. And I remember thinking, 'Ah, well, this is the interrogation process!' So I thought, 'Right, here it goes, I cannot answer that question, sir.' So I said … 'I ca … ' I didn't even get 'I cannot … ' and smash! And I remember just my head going; I was knocked off the chair!

And … suddenly I was back on the chair. And it was, 'Name?'

'Peters.'

Having worked their way round the body, they made me stand up and they threw my face against the wall, and then one guy just kicked my leg. And for all the hits, I'd damaged my leg quite, well, it felt, quite badly. I had difficulty walking; I was limping, and the guy kicked my leg. I just got this searing pain that went right down to my foot, right up the side of my body, from my knee. I yelped. And that was my mistake, the fact I yelped. Up to then you're grunting, but I let out a yelp. It's just a different sound, it was just a different sound of grunt and they recognized it, and I was on the floor.

They just yanked me up and … karate-chopped, from what it felt like, the heel of a boot, just into my knee. And I collapsed again, and they just pulled me up, smack! Pulled me up, smack! Pulled me up, smack! Pulled me up, smack! And somewhere in there while they were doing that they said, 'Are you pilot or navigator?'

'Pilot,' and it just came out. I couldn't, I couldn't stop it.

And that's when you realize you've broken to the violence.

'Rank?'

'Flight lieutenant.'

'Are you pilot?'

It's during the beatings … they're trying to speed you up and make you answer their questions. The moment they stop the beatings, they're putting you back on the chair. And they ask you a question, and you always delay and delay and delay, until you virtually can feel someone swing his arm. 'I cannot … ', then you anticipate the hit.

… [E]very so often they sort of take a break, and they leave you there, or they take you back to the corridor or another room and they put you there. That's when I really started to think, 'Don't let them get in your head. Whatever they do to you … if they get in your head they've won.' It is a mental fight. It's not physical … it's them trying to break you down. [E]ventually … I answered the question, 'Are you pilot or navigator?'

… And you know, in your own mind, that's when I suppose all the prisoners of war say they broke, as in, you succumb to the violence, because it's never going to stop.

And then they started sort of karate-chopping my knee again.[3]

Guy L. Hunter Jr.

US Marine Chief Warrant Officer Hunter and his commanding officer, Lieutenant-Colonel Clifford M. Acree, were the first US prisoners of war captured by the Iraqis when their aircraft, an OV–10 Bronco, was shot down on 18 January 1991. Hunter was incarcerated in the notorious Baghdad Biltmore during the Gulf War.

We were [captured] in the southern area of Kuwait. I thought, '*It's going to be a pretty long haul.*' Then we started driving, and I was really concerned about the Harriers (US jets) finding us moving on the ground and blowing us away. But nothing like that occurred. We got to Corps headquarters and they snatched us out of the truck and turned us over to these fellows.

From that point on, for an extremely long time I couldn't tell whether it was daylight or dark. It was just pitch black to me. We stayed there for some time – about a half-hour to an hour, I don't know. Then they loaded us into a vehicle and we proceeded heading north into Iraq, I assume. We received their 'welcome aboard' treatment several times all the way up. It was some good beatings.

That's when the rough treatment began. They marched us around to various places as though they were showing us off to all their various staff members. We were still blindfolded. They put another set of blindfolds over the ones we had and bound it extremely tight.

We could feel the blows, and it was getting worse. The beatings were all over. I wasn't thinking a whole lot, but I started praying for God to help me. My impression was they were hitting us with their fists, rifle butts and batons. You really don't let yourself feel anything … I thought for sure the colonel had lost consciousness a couple of times. I could feel [him] slump against me.

These guys were getting their kicks in because we were the first Americans they had captured after they had been bombed heav[ily] day and night. I guess they were happy to get their hands on somebody.

They put us in a holding cell where we sat and we shivered all night long. I heard one of the Italians, as I discovered later on. He kept begging them to loosen his handcuffs because he couldn't feel his fingers at all, or his hands.

They'd come by once in a while and feed us. We couldn't do it for ourselves. They would squat in front of us and I could hear the buckets moving down the line of prisoners. He'd say, 'Food, food,' and stick a spoon up to our mouth and we'd start eating away. Then he would say, 'Tea,' and hold some tea up to our mouth and we'd drink that or water. I'd nod my head when I'd had enough to drink.

I felt pure terror. I knew it was interrogation time because I could hear the other guys being interrogated, sometimes a word or two and then mostly just the sounds of it. It just sent spasms through my body, I'd just twitch. I was just drifting in and out of consciousness here.

The questions were posed in English: how many aircraft were at the airbases? How many observation aircraft and fighter jets? Where are you from? What should Iraq do to win the war? Why are you here?

'You think you will leave here?' an Iraqi general called … 'You will stay forever! Even when the war is over, you will never leave.'

I was scared I wouldn't get to see Mary and the children again. I had images of the kids in my mind, each saying, 'Hi, Dad.'[4]

Rogelio L. Carrera

Major Carrera was a Public Health Officer with the 489th Civil Affairs Company, US Army. He reveals that ordinary Kuwaitis were also subjected to brutality during the Iraqi occupation of their country. This account is from an interview given by Major Carrera to members of the US 116th Military History Detachment on 12 March 1991 at the 101st Airborne Division Command Post, Northern Province, Saudi Arabia.

Specifically, we dealt with Kuwaitis who had been captured by the Iraqis during their takeover of the kingdom of Kuwait and transferred back to Iraq. They had been incarcerated for, the majority of them, for six, seven months. At that time, they had received fairly brutal care and had been exposed … I was told by them, when I saw the evidence … [to] a fairly random, sporadic, but also at times well-formulated series of torture and general mistreatment. So that when we saw these people, what they had mainly suffered from is mental and physical exhaustion.

The severe skin problems, which were the result of improper hygiene. They all stated over and over again that they were not allowed to shower for the entire period (about six or seven months) they were prisoners. And so we saw the skin actually breaking down under the layers upon layers of dust, so the skin was unable to be exposed to oxygen. It started breaking down. We saw the victims of random mistreatment, whe[n] they were just sitting there: without any purpose.

[The Iraqis] were not even trying to get any information or were not even trying to punish the individual. But just because he was there and they were able to, the guard would take an iron truncheon and break an arm, and then not set it. So the individual is left there with a broken arm, in tremendous pain, and living in this filth[y] and hostile environment with a fractured arm, just because a man inflicted this pain.

Then there was more systematic torture where [the Iraqis] were in fact trying to get information. In this case, we saw individuals that were hung upside down by their ankles, and the soles of their feet were hit. And in one traumatic case, a gentleman had a bottle inserted through his rectum; shoved in his rectum as part of the punishment.

So we saw the remains of this. [Sometimes the injuries] were stable already. For example, we saw people who had fractured arms … four, five or six months ago, and therefore, when they came to us, they would need surgery. They needed orthopaedic repair with pinning or whatever, but for right now, when we saw them in the displaced civilian camp, they simply needed the stabilization of that.

They were all covered with lice, and, you know, in my experience, I think what we needed for these kind of facilities more than anything else was hygiene. To be able to give these people a shower and delousing, clean clothes, and a return to some degree of self-dignity. The medical problems, of course, are also the chronic medical problems you [can have]. A diabetic hadn't had medication for six or seven months. A hypertensive that didn't have his hypertensive medication for six or seven months. We saw a lot of that.[5]

Billie J. Maddox

Master Sergeant Maddox was Chief Ward Master with the 109th Evacuation Hospital, 44th Medical Brigade, 1st Support Command, US Army, in Saudi Arabia.

He's [an Iraqi] in his fifties. When I walk in the ward, the first thing he'll do when he sees me is throw up his hand and wave, 'Hey,' you know. That's the kind of people these are, you know. You'll walk around and see some of them give you the evil eye, or 'What am I doing?' They're scared. These folks are really scared to be in this hospital, and we try to assure [them] that, you know, they're in good hands; that we're not their enemy; and we just sort of pat them and just try to treat them like, you know, our own.

The American soldiers that are wounded at war here, they had a different war. We try to separate the EPWs [enemy prisoners of war] from the Americans. They hold no grudges against these boys. It's been a morale booster for some of our boys that go in there just to see them and try to talk to them, through the interpreter. It's been a morale booster for them, I believe, also.

They just know a few words like 'okay'. They know 'pain'. But you know, some of the nurses have drawn pictures, and they can relate to the pictures, you know, like 'time', and 'towels' or 'bath', and stuff like that. They've drawn pictures through the interpreter and that's how they communicate with the patients if the interpreter is not here.

We have shower units for patients and we have our EPW showers – we separate those. They have their latrines. The ones that are ambulatory, you know. We'll take them out and let them take showers or go to the bathroom and, you know, the ones that are in bed, they get a bed bath or whatever, you know. They're real sensitive about, you know, their customs. I know we had an incident where a man had to go to the bathroom and he wouldn't go unless we draped a sheet around him.[6]

Jim L. Manley

Sergeant First Class Manley worked in the Intensive Care Ward with the 109th Evacuation Hospital, US Army, in Saudi Arabia. He recounts a similar story to Sergeant Maddox that reveals the sensitivity shown by the Allies with respect to the cultural differences of their Iraqi POWs. This account is from an interview given by Sergeant Manley to members of the US Center of Military History in March 1991.

One of the EPWs in the ward needed to use a bedpan, so in a regular hospital, you just kind of bring the drapes around and drape it off, and give them a bedpan, and let them do their business. Well, this guy, he didn't want it draped around. He wanted the sheet thrown over his head, where he could kind of squat down on the bedpan beside his bed. That was the type of situation he wanted. But even just some of the corpsmen on the ward talk about when they took them out to the latrines, instead of sitting on the latrines, they'll jump up on the latrines and kind of squat down like a big bird. They won't sit down on the latrines. I guess it's different cultures. That's just their way of doing things.

To expound a little bit further on this war, it's almost like we're at war, but we're not at war with these people. The people that come in here, it's hard to think that they were actually out to try to kill us at one time, and now that we have wounded them and brought them in ... [W]e're actually picking up their casualties and bringing them in and treating them.

And they're getting the very best care that they could ever get in modern warfare. I mean, this is better care than they could get in Iraq, pre-war, the care they're getting here in this hospital and the other hospitals down the line. [I]t's been an eye-opening experience for myself, and I know it's got to be for the other people ... seeing these people come in.

I've yet to see any malice or hatred or ill will displayed by any of the EPWs. It's either, you know, they look at you and kind of ... you want to think, in suspicion. I guess they've been told that we're going to hurt them or we're going to do something to them. It's just not happening, you know. We're treating them. We're making them feel good. We're accommodating them. We're waiting on them almost hand and foot. This has been catching them really off guard.

How can these people go back to their country and have a person like Saddam tell them that we're the evil, 'the great Satan' and 'the infidels,' when they've been treated this way by us?[7]

Craig Berryman

The experience of being a prisoner of war can have long-term effects, both physical and psychological, long after the fighting is over, especially if the imprisoned is mistreated. Captain Berryman, US Marine Corps, was shot down near Kuwait City in January 1991. While he was held captive, Iraqi guards broke his left leg, beat him repeatedly and threatened him with shooting and mutilation. A lighted cigarette was twisted into an open wound on his neck. Berryman lost 11.3 kg (25 lb) in 37 days and contracted dysentery. When he returned to the US, a World War Two former prisoner of war warned the young Marine pilot that he would never forget the experience.

He said there would not be a day go by I didn't think about it. At first, I really didn't believe him. But in the 12 years since, he's been right. There have been days I'd like to go after some of them for what they did to me. Some days I'm happy to have survived and have my honour intact. There are a lot of emotions. I have some unfinished business over there.

I had so much hatred for those guys. I was thinking so much about how much I hated them for what they were doing to me, I wasn't concentrating on what we were trained to do, to plan escape and staying alive. I prayed I would have the physical strength and the mental ability to do that, and fortunately I did.[8]

Notes

1   https://www.weeklyreader.com/featurezone/eyewitness/ce_eyewitness01.asp

2   Permission of Rhonda Cornum

3   Copyright © 1995–2009 WGBH educational foundation

4   *Los Angeles Times*, 31 March 1991

5   US Center of Military History interview, 12 March 1991

6   ibid, 2 March 1991

7   ibid

8   Fox News 18 February 2003

Iraq: invasion and occupation

and

occupation

(2003–10)

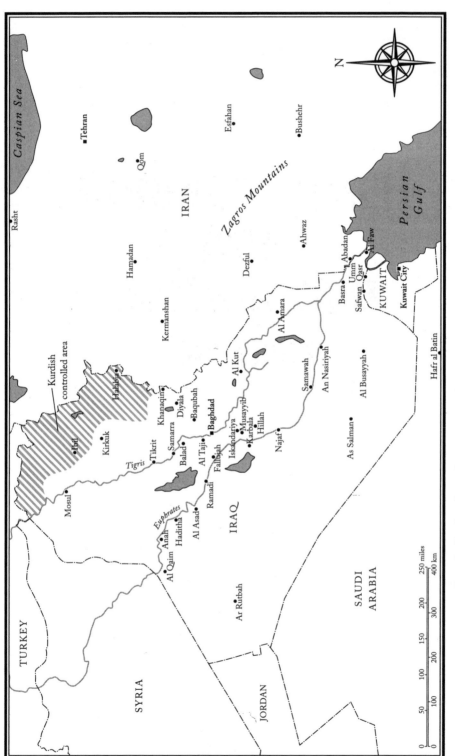

Iraq, indicating the major towns and cities where much of the fighting took place

Operation Iraqi Freedom

Having decided that 'regime change' was the only acceptable option, US President George W. Bush and British Prime Minister Tony Blair (b. 1953; prime minister of Britain 1997–2007) launched the invasion of Iraq in March 2003, codenamed Operation Iraqi Freedom. The ground campaign was led by US Army Lieutenant-General David McKiernan, the Commanding General of the Combined Forces Land Component Command (CFLCC), the ground component of CENTCOM. The strategy was a quick, two-pronged push from Kuwait up through southern Iraq to Baghdad.

Under the CFLCC, the ground 'main effort' was led by US Army V Corps under Lieutenant-General William Scott Wallace. V Corps was assigned the western route up to Baghdad west of the River Euphrates. Meanwhile, the 1st Marine Expeditionary Force (1MEF) led by Lieutenant-General James Conway was assigned the eastern route closer to the border with Iran. From a tactical perspective, for both the Army and the Marines, this was a very long projection of force – over 600 km (373 miles) from Kuwait to Baghdad, and more for those units that pushed further north to Tikrit or to Mosul.

The British 1st Armoured Division, which fell under 1MEF, was tasked with taking Basra, Iraq's second-largest city. The British faced resistance from members of the paramilitary force Fedayeen Saddam, and others still loyal to the Ba'ath Party. To limit casualties, rather than enter the city immediately in full force, the British opted for a more methodical elimination of opponents, combined with communicating with the population to explain their intentions. After several weeks of this, the British pushed into Basra on 6 April.

The main 1MEF force encountered some resistance as it pushed north, in particular at the town of An Nasiriyah, a geographical choke-point. Here, the Marines suffered casualties from a friendly fire incident with Apache helicopters. It was also here that the US Army's 507th Maintenance Company lost its way in the area and stumbled into an ambush in which some personnel were killed, and others, including Private Jessica Lynch, were taken hostage.

The area was blanketed by fierce desert sandstorms. In addition, the Fedayeen Saddam put up a stout fight. Moreover, additional Iraqi fighters inspired by the ambush carried out by the Fedayeen came from Baghdad to An Nasiriyah to join the fight. But Marine firepower proved overwhelming, and they pushed on to Baghdad along their eastern route.

In the west, the US Army faced a longer route through a less-populated landscape. V Corps began combat operations with two divisions under its command: the 3rd Infantry Division under Major-General Buford Blount and the 101st Airborne Division under Major-General David Petraeus.

The 3rd Infantry Division lunged for Baghdad, reaching Saddam International Airport on 4 April. The division launched its first so-called 'thunder run', a fast, armoured strike into the city on 5 April, and the second two days later. The purpose of the first, according to the Brigade Commander in charge, Colonel David Perkins, was 'to create as much confusion as I can inside the city'. The purpose of the second was 'to make sure, in no uncertain terms, that people knew the city had fallen and we were in charge of it'.

The 101st Airborne cleared resistance in southern Iraqi cities, fighting battles in Hillah, Najaf and Karbala. Just after mid-April, the division arrived in Mosul in northern Iraq, and set up its headquarters.

In northern Iraq, on 26 March, about 1,000 soldiers from the US Army's 173rd Airborne Brigade, part of the Army's Southern European Task Force based in Italy, made a parachute insertion. They secured an airfield so all cargo aircraft carrying tanks and Bradleys could land. Once on the ground, the 173rd expanded the northern front of Operation Iraqi Freedom by working closely with air and ground Special Forces and local Kurdish Peshmerga forces.

Initial Coalition plans had called for the US 4th Infantry Division to open the northern front by crossing into Iraq from Turkey to destroy Iraqi Army forces based north of Baghdad. This would also place limits on possible Kurdish ambitions to control more territory in northern Iraq, thus providing some reassurance to the Turkish government, discouraging it from sending its forces into Iraq to restrain the Kurds. In the event, this never took place.

On 9 April 2003, the statue of Saddam Hussein in Firdos Square in Baghdad was toppled. Two days after the 3rd Infantry Division's second 'thunder run', this event signalled for many, both inside and outside Iraq, that the old regime had ended. But US forces continued to flow into Iraq. The 4th Infantry Division, diverted from its original northern-front plans, was rerouted to Kuwait. Its forces began entering Iraq on 12 April 2003. The US 1st Armored Division also began arriving in the same month. As soon as it became apparent that the old regime was no longer exercising any control, widespread looting erupted throughout Iraq. Targets included government buildings and the former houses of regime leaders, but also private businesses and cultural institutions. Leaders of Iraq's National Museum in Baghdad, for example, reported that 'looters had taken or destroyed 170,000 items of antiquity dating back thousands of years'. Looters and vandals also targeted unguarded weapons stockpiles largely abandoned by former Iraqi security forces. The failure to stop these incidents indicated that although the allies had toppled Saddam Hussein, their quest to exert control throughout Iraq and establish a democratically elected government was only just beginning.

James P. L. Holzgrefe

Captain Holzgrefe was with the 17th Air Cavalry Regiment, 101st Airborne Division, US Army. The regiment led the division's aviation forces across the border during Operation Iraqi Freedom, and took part in fighting in Najaf, Karbala, Hillah, southern Baghdad, Mosul and terrorist training camps in central Iraq.

The invasion in March of 2003 was a really intense time. We spent about two weeks in Kuwait prior to the invasion, planning, training and getting acclimatized to the environment. I was a platoon leader at the time, in charge of four helicopters, ten pilots and six crew chiefs. Kuwait was pretty miserable. It was hot, sandy and windy. I'll never forget the night of the invasion. We were on the airfield readying our aircraft and trying to cram a couple of days' worth of water and food into every available spot. We had become accustomed to occasional missile attacks with the accompanying Patriot launch. You would hear an explosion, then an alarm would go off and everyone would put on their gas masks and move into protective bunkers. That night was the first time any of us had actually seen the Patriot launch and intercept something. It seemed to be overhead, but was probably several miles away. We went through the normal drill, but the sight of it added to the intensity of the moment.

That was the same night as the fratricide grenade attack by Sergeant Hasan Akbar at an adjacent camp [an American Muslim, Akbar killed two officers and injured 14 of his fellow soldiers of the 327 Infantry Regiment, 101st Airborne Division at Camp Pennsylvania, Kuwait, in a gun-and-grenade attack]. I think we were all ready to get out of Kuwait at that point, even if it meant going into Iraq.[1]

Tim Collins

Lieutenant-Colonel Collins made this speech to around 800 men of the battlegroup of the 1st Battalion of the Royal Irish Regiment, part of the 16 Air Assault Brigade, British Army, at their Fort Blair Mayne camp in the Kuwaiti desert about 32 km (20 miles) from the Iraqi border on Wednesday, 19 March 2003. The commander of the 1st Battalion, Royal Irish Regiment, Collins gave this eve-of-invasion speech, which has subsequently entered military legend.

We go to liberate, not to conquer. We will not fly our flags in their country. We are entering Iraq to free a people and the only flag which will be flown in that ancient land is their own. Show respect for them.

There are some who are alive at this moment who will not be alive shortly. Those who do not wish to go on that journey, we will not send. As for the others, I expect you to rock their world. Wipe them out if that is what they choose. But if you are ferocious in battle, remember to be magnanimous in victory. Iraq is steeped in history. It is the site of the Garden of Eden, of the Great Flood and the birthplace of Abraham. Tread lightly there.

You will see things that no man could pay to see and you will have to go a long way to find a more decent, generous and upright people than the Iraqis.

You will be embarrassed by their hospitality even though they have nothing. Don't treat them as refugees, for they are in their own country. Their children will be poor; in years to come they will know that the light of liberation in their lives was brought by you.

If there are casualties of war, then remember that when they woke up and got dressed in the morning, they did not plan to die this day. Allow them dignity in death. Bury them properly and mark their graves.

It is my foremost intention to bring every single one of you out alive, but there may be people among us who will not see the end of this campaign. We will put them in their sleeping bags and send them back. There will be no time for sorrow.

The enemy should be in no doubt that we are his nemesis and that we are bringing about his rightful destruction. There are many regional commanders who have stains on their souls and they are stoking the fires of hell for Saddam.

He and his forces will be destroyed by this coalition for what they have done. As they die, they will know their deeds have brought them to this place. Show them no pity. It is a big step to take another human life. It is not to be done lightly. I know of men who have taken life needlessly in other conflicts, I can assure you they live with the mark of Cain upon them.

If someone surrenders to you, then remember they have that right in international law and ensure that one day they go home to their family. The ones who wish to fight, well, we aim to please. If you harm the regiment or its history by overenthusiasm in killing or in cowardice, know it is your family who will suffer. You will be shunned unless your conduct is of the highest, for your deeds will follow you down through history. We will bring shame on neither our uniform nor our nation.

It is not a question of if [there will be a chemical or biological attack], it's a question of when. We know he [Saddam Hussein] has already devolved the decision to lower commanders, and that means he has already taken the decision himself. If we survive the first strike, we will survive the attack. As for ourselves, let's bring everyone home and leave Iraq a better place for us having been there. Our business now is north.[2]

Todd Brown

Major Brown commanded an infantry company in the 4th Infantry Division (Mechanized), US Army, during Operation Iraqi Freedom.

21 April

Just crossed into Iraq … what a shit hole! They are so poor here that the kids are running in front of the vehicles trying to get us to stop so they can hijack all our gear. It is a mugging, but they have nothing. I'm sitting in the back of the Bradley with the door open pulling security. It's hot. The people are cheerful and waving, but they are simply a suppressed nation. They are skinny with all smiles. Roads aren't too bad; the countryside is desolate, though. Houses are made out of mud, and it looks like they are desperately trying to farm.

This is my second convoy; the first time we broke down. These guys are slow as shit. Luckily I got decent sleep last night on the bench seats. There are all kinds of tank-fighting positions abandoned. Looked like they had plans to defend well south, but left the AO [area of operations]. They are dug in right off the highway on the desert floor. Saw 'el donkey' running from his herder. It was funny to watch.

The crazy aspect thus far is the unknown nature of this for the soldier. You don't know when the next hot meal is, the next shower, the next good night's rest … or the next rest for that matter.

The wind and dust here are absolutely horrible. They are everywhere. My Mohawk haircut was awesome, but now it has given way to the buzz cut. So much of this deployment has been lying around in the back of the track sweating it out with the master gunner 'Jonny Fogle'. Carlson 'the porn star', is just chilling up in the driver's hatch, not really all that fun. Your lips get so dried out, and your body just absorbs more and more dust. Eyepro [eye protection] is a necessity in this place. I really would like to write an eloquent description, but I don't know if I could capture the magnitude of vehicles, trash, crap, and the acrid smell of diesel. It is just a massive collection of the aforementioned products … mixed with omnipresent gritty dust. I so want to find a body of water and jump into it, wearing everything, for both the cooling effect and cleansing. Weapons maintenance is difficult here: my stuff is already filthy again.[3]

Jesse G. Odom

Corporal Odom was a member of the US Marine Corps and fought with the 1st Marine Expeditionary Force in Operation Iraqi Freedom.

I can still remember every detail; I can smell the burning oil and white phosphorous in the air. I can hear the thunderous explosions from the artillery and my heart beating uncontrollably. I remember the fear of the unknown and fear of the night sky dense with thick smoke. Alpha Company Marines were moving into Iraq in the effort to find weapons of mass destruction. After being the first company in the Coalition forces to enter Iraq, we were met with a heavy opposing force. We immediately destroyed the enemy tanks and continued fighting through the night towards our first objective, an oil pumping station. As we moved through the oil fields, I remember the feeling when I laid my eyes on a dead Iraqi for the first time. Chills ran down my spine as I gazed into the eyes of the mangled man. As the sun came up on 21 March, we arrived at the pumping station. After bombing around the compound we made our final approach to the fence that surrounded it. We scanned for enemy targets but only saw abandoned military equipment, including fully functional weapons of all sorts.

The Iraqis did not want to fight us. That thought ran through the minds of all of us and poisoned our brains. We were not alert, as before; some of us were too complacent. Just moments later, a fellow Marine stepped on a land mine, and shortly after my Platoon Commander was shot and killed a couple feet from where I stood. Seven if I remember correctly; seven Iraqi soldiers were packed in a pickup truck spraying bullets at us. They moved at least 115 kph [70 mph]. They headed right for us, but we did not just stand there. We returned an overwhelming amount of firepower. The truck still moved; the driver was still alive by some miracle. He came closer and closer. He had ducked down in the seat and amazingly stayed on the road that lay perpendicular to us. I moved behind a wall because I still heard bullets ping off scrap metal and our assault vehicle. I pulled the trigger a few more times as the bloody truck passed by.

Less than 100 metres [110 yds] after it passed me, the vehicle came to a stop. Marines still viciously shot at the stopped truck, but my mind was somewhere else. I yelled, 'Get the corpsman!' as I ran to him. 'He's shot, Lieutenant Childers has been shot.' I got to my knees and began to remove the chemical protective suit and his combat fighting gear. I then saw that he had stopped breathing. I tilted his head back and gave him a breath of air. He started to breathe again on my first try. 'Sir, you're going to be OK.'

As I noticed his wound, the corpsman arrived to assist me. He had been shot in the stomach. I applied pressure to the oozing wound as the corpsman prepared some gauze. It was at this time Childers would speak his last words on Earth. 'It hurts,' were the words that will haunt me forever. All of a sudden I heard a crack and then another. Machine guns were now going off as another hostile vehicle moved down the same road. We were going to get shot or hit by the vehicle if we did not move. I grabbed Childers by the shoulders and slung him over my back. I ran for cover. We were now safe from the car. I looked at Childers and knew he was about to go. His eyes glazed over as a single teardrop came from the corner of his eye. He died a painful death.

I was hurt not only because I saw a father-type figure go before me, but to see a grown man cry and urinate his pants hit me hard. Childers was the first American to get killed in the war. As we moved to Baghdad, I was always wondering who would be the next to get shot, or shot and killed. I knew that none of us were immune to death. At any given moment a pull of the trigger could change the life of any one of us. We all lived in suspense. It would take almost two weeks until the suspense would end.

Never in my life will I forget the day that death seemed inevitable.

Marines in Alpha Company will never forget 10 April 2003. We were in a firefight for nine hours that resulted in another death and 92 Marines getting shot or receiving shrapnel wounds. A man should never have to kill another, but I damn Saddam for putting us in that situation. Should I feel guilty? I was defending my life, wasn't I? Will I pay for my inhumane act for the rest of my life? I believe I will always feel guilty, but I could not have it any other way, otherwise I would have been the victim. As we moved through the streets shooting everything, I was put in the situation to kill or be killed. He jumped from around the corner and before I could get off a round, he had fired many. If my bullets were not accurate, he would have eventually shot me. I remember the panic when he jumped out; I froze for a split second. My heart rushed as I fired the first round and then he fell to the ground. I had a fear that he would get up and try to kill me again, so I put several more rounds in his body. When he finally stopped moving, I started to feel the feeling that still lies within me.

Bullets and rockets flew from every direction. Bodies were lying on the street sides. Blood was everywhere. Some of my close friends were shot and another one of my role models was killed before my eyes. Another scene that will haunt my dreams forever. I kept thinking to myself: when will this end? Will I get to see my fiancée again? Before I knew the time had come, we were finished fighting. We did not have to fear death from gunshot wounds any more. We can now take advantage of all the things we take for granted, like hot showers and talking to our loved ones on the telephone. We were back in America. We were fortunate because we only stayed in Iraq for four months and in Kuwait for one month.[4]

Justin D. LeHew

Gunnery Sergeant LeHew was platoon sergeant for Company A of the 3rd Platoon, 2nd Assault Amphibious Battalion (US). This unit was attached to Company A, 1st Battalion, 2nd Marine Regiment of Task Force Tarawa. On 23 March 2003, LeHew was taking part in the capture of three bridges in the city of An Nasiriyah.

We were over the bridge about five minutes when it seemed like the whole city came down on our heads. Fire was coming from almost every single building, and we could see swarms of Iraqis coming down the alleys. I remember thinking this is how Custer must have felt at the Battle of the

Little Bighorn. It would take more than four hours. I grabbed my corpsman, 19-year-old Hospitalman Alex Velasquez. When we reached the vehicle [an Amtrac], the first thing I saw when I went up the ramp was a leg, still in a MOPP (chemical gear) suit. [LeHew handed the leg to a wide-eyed Velasquez.] I said, 'Put this in my vehicle. We're going to find out who it belongs to.'[5]

Charles Blume

Captain Blume was the Wolfpack Fire Support Coordinator, 1st US Marine Division, which also fought at An Nasiriyah. This is his account of the action on 23 March 2003.

We had been ordered to begin to Recon [reconnaissance] up Highway 1 and the alternate routes called Lexus and Cobra. The CG [Commanding General] had told our CO to get up to Hantush and the Highway 27 Bridge over the Saddam Canal as rapidly as possible, and forget the alternate routes for now. As we pushed up, we definitely could feel we were getting well out in front of the division. We lost comms [communication] with the DASC-A [Direct Air Support Centre (Airborne)], and it was starting to get dark. We had some Cobras working in front of us earlier, and they had reported signs of enemy activity. Now, as we rolled up, we began to see abandoned weapons and equipment strewn all about along the highway. A suspicious vehicle was seen to our front that observed us and then sped away. ROE [rules of engagement] prevented engagement of the truck, even though it was acting suspiciously. As it started to get dark, we could all feel the hair standing up on the backs of our necks. You could tell something was about to happen.

Then, with Blackfoot [Bravo Company] in the lead, we began to see scattered tracers flying across the road in front of us from west to east. The scattered shots soon became a torrent of fire, and the entire battalion was engaged almost immediately. They opened up on us with mortars, heavy machine guns and RPGs [rocket-propelled grenades]. The tracers would seemingly explode when they hit the LAVs [light armoured vehicles]; it wasn't like the movies where they just bounce off. We later estimated the enemy at about an infantry battalion in size. There was fire coming from everywhere, and they were starting to mass and charge the column in groups. We were pouring 7.62mm and 25mm [rounds] on them, but they kept coming. There was no communications with the DASC, we were outside of artillery range, and there was no air [support] on station. Unable to reach the CO on the radio and even though we were not in immediate danger of being overrun, the Air Officer made the decision to call 'slingshot' over the guard channel. This brought in immediate CAS [close air-support]. ['Slingshot' was a radio brevity code that indicated an American unit was about to be overrun and all available fire support was to be vectored to its aid.] Before we knew it, there was air coming from everywhere. There were too many sorties coming to control individually, so we established an east/west buffer of 2,000 m [2,187 yards] off the road and in front of our column, and turned that fight over to Forward Air Controller (FAC) (A) with our ground FACs directing traffic closer. We estimate we got about 20 sections of fixed-wing [aircraft] in support of us that night.[6]

Doug Feiring

Communications Officer in the US Marine Corps. On 24–25 March 2003, Feiring was fighting for his life at An Nasiriyah with Regimental Combat Team 2 (RCT–2).

A short while later, we were setting up in what was definitely part of the city dump. The flies were horrible and there were stray dogs everywhere, but it was home. One of the dogs had a missing leg and we started calling him 'Lefty'. He became our mascot for the next two days. We kidded the Sergeant Major about 'his' dog for the rest of the war. Spirits were high and everyone worked with a professional sense of urgency and competence that I have never before witnessed.

We were having difficulty getting medevac helicopters into the city to pick up our wounded. It started with a few injuries, then dozens. Before long, we had nearly 50 casualties awaiting evacuation. The reality of the fierce fight was really setting in. It hit me hard when the Ops O [officer], who was working the Regimental Tactical radio net, yelled over to the Air Officer: '1/2 [1st Battalion/2nd Marines] has eight more medevacs; two urgent, four priority, and two routine! Two of them are routine because they're dead.' He threw the handset down. After several long seconds of stunned silence, the radio chatter picked up again, and everyone went back to his work.

During the attempt to find a bypass route around 'Ambush Alley', the amtracs and tanks of Bravo Company became mired in thick mud. Charlie Company pressed ahead straight up Route 7 through the alley. Their tracked vehicles became the targets of a withering hail of machine-gun fire and rocket-propelled grenades (RPGs). One RPG struck an amtrack with 23 Marines in it. Several were injured. A while later, an Air Force A-10 mistakenly attacked another Marine amtrac. Several Marines were killed north of the bridge.

It took several hours to organize and conduct the recovery of six stuck Bravo Company vehicles. It was a very tenuous situation as the Iraqis organized to exploit the Marines' predicament. Marines fanned out in a circle through the neighbourhood around the vehicles to provide security. Several wounded Iraqi civilians approached the Marines and requested medical treatment. Enemy fire increased and became more accurate as the Iraqis homed in on their position. 1/2's TAC CP [tactical command post] abandoned their stuck armoured vehicle, jumped in soft-skinned HMMWVs and moved back … where they could control the battle.

The Iraqis began a series of sharp counterattacks against Alpha Company on the southern bridge. We ordered 2/8 [2nd Battalion/8th Marines] into the battle to relieve Alpha Company, who was instructed to move north. I stood on the side of the road watching, waving and shouting encouragement to the Marines of 2/8 as they passed me heading north in their trucks towards the fight. I could only imagine what was on their mind as they rolled into close combat.

For the next several minutes, I listened on the radio to 2/8's Battalion Commander attempt to coordinate a link up between his lead forces and Alpha Company 1/2. The fighting in that area was heavy and there was a real danger that the two Marine units might mistakenly shoot at each other. It was too 'hot' at the bridge for the Alpha Company Marines to remain exposed attempting to affect the linkup. Finally, the two converging forces agreed that Company A would simply move out of the area and the 2/8 Marines would move in. Not the doctrinal method of conducting a relief in place, but effective nevertheless.

The north side of the bridge was in 'Ambush Alley'. 2/8 did not have sufficient forces to physically defend the northern side of the bridge. They set in their defences on the south side … and covered the north by fire.

Charlie Company 1/2 took the northern Saddam Canal Bridge next. To cross the bridge, they endured withering, effective fire from an Iraqi anti-aircraft gun. The 23mm machine gun was trained on the bridge from a prepared position 100 metres [328 ft] to the east.

At some point that afternoon, a two-star general flew in and came into our COC [Combat Operations Centre]. He was the Assistant MEF [Marine Expeditionary Forces] Commander. Word had gotten out that we were in quite a fight at An Nasiriyah and he came to ... assess the situation.

The commanding officer of RCT–1 was also present in our area. We were taking the bridges in order to facilitate his unit's movement north to the city of Al Kut. He wanted to know when he would be able to press his attack north. It wasn't going to be today.

As darkness and the enemy were closing in on Bravo Company, 1/2's CO prudently decided to abandon two of the amtracks that they had not been able to retrieve from the mud. Both Bravo and Alpha Company moved through Ambush Alley to reinforce the northern bridge.

1/2 was desperately low on ammunition. We called for a helicopter re-supply. We were told helicopters could not conduct the re-supply because there were no secure landing zones (LZs) in which the helicopters could land. Higher headquarters suggested conducting a ground re-supply in the morning. The Air Officer yelled in the radio that unless we got the helicopters in tonight, there would be no 1/2 to re-supply in the morning. That convinced them. We got our helicopters.

Sometime that evening the ALOC [Administrative and Logistical Operations Centre] arrived. They gave up on trying to pass the enemy prisoners to higher headquarters. They just loaded them in a truck and brought them to the fight with them.

Early morning of 25 March, RCT–1 began their forward passage. They went through Ambush Alley with 'guns a' blazing'. Not surprisingly, they shot one of our Marines as they passed through our lines. Fortunately, the Marine was wearing one of the new SAPI [small arms protective inserts] plates, the bulletproof inserts for our flak jackets. He survived the impact of several rounds into his chest.

By mid-morning, all of RCT–1's combat forces had proceeded through Ambush Alley and were working their way north. Eighty of RCT-1's logistics vehicles arrived at our position requesting to move through and join their unit north of the city. They had no combat vehicles with them to escort them through Ambush Alley. So we arranged for their security from our own resources.

The Iraqis were hitting us from buildings on both sides of the road. I heard two or three heavy machine guns and several rifles start to fire before we crested the top of the bridge. The LAVs in front of me immediately answered them with their 25mm chain guns. An instant later, my HMMWV reached the top of the arched bridge and my machine gunner opened up with his Mk 19. Looking out my window over the sights of my pistol, I saw two or three Iraqis firing rifles at me. I fired three shots. I knew I wasn't going to hit them. I was firing at targets over 100 metres [328 ft] away from a moving vehicle, but there was no way they were going to get a free shot at me or the vehicles behind me without experiencing a little danger themselves.

The firing continued on the other side of the vehicle for several more seconds. We anxiously awaited the next ambush as we raced through the enemy-controlled 4 km [2.5 miles] of Ambush Alley. The CO calmly came on the radio every 20 seconds, admonishing the lead vehicle to increase the speed. 'Pick it up, Light Horse.' 'Light Horse, pick it up.'

After what seemed like forever, we started up the rise of the second bridge. We clicked our weapons back on safe, and breathed a collective sigh of relief. We were re-entering friendly lines. We pulled over at 1/2's Combat Operations Centre, as the RCT–1 convoy sped nervously forward. 1/2 had established their Combat Operations Centre near the Iraqi 23rd Brigade Headquarters. After I completed my business with 1/2's communications officer, I took a walk around the enemy command post with COs of RCT–2 and 1/2. Remarkably, the Iraqis had their city defensive plan painted on one of the walls of the headquarters.

The 1/2 CO related how they captured the 23rd Brigade's commander the day earlier. Marines manning a vehicle checkpoint stopped and searched an ambulance attempting to cross into their zone. The ambulance driver stated that he was transporting a burns victim to one of the city's hospitals. A look in the back of the ambulance revealed that there was indeed an individual suffering from severe burns lying on the stretcher. However, a more thorough search disclosed that the medical personnel were wearing Iraqi Army uniforms under their rescue squad garb.

One of these officers turned out to be the local brigade commander. The burns victim was taken away for treatment while the enemy soldiers were held for interrogation.

The 1/2 CO told the Iraqi commander that we expected light resistance. He asked him why, if he knew we would hit them with overwhelming force, they decided to stand and fight. The Iraqi colonel stated that they were amazed and emboldened by their success against our lead elements. This confused the Marines for a short while and the 1/2 CO asked for clarification. The Iraqi stated that we had sent several trucks into the city to conduct a reconnaissance before our main attack. The Iraqis observed the US forces for awhile, then decided to attack. The Iraqi commander went on to relate that the US forces had fought so poorly, the Iraqis were convinced that they could successfully defend against the forthcoming American attack.

It was starting to get dark, and the wind and sand were starting to pick up, so we assembled our group to run through the gauntlet of Ambush Alley yet again. For the return trip, I commandeered a Squad Automatic Weapon (SAW) machine gun that wasn't being used and felt a little better about my chances in a firefight. We lined up our four vehicles – an LAV in the front, my vehicle, and the RCT–2 CO's vehicle, followed by another LAV. We had two tanks standing by to come to our assistance if we ran into any problems.

With only four vehicles in the convoy, we were able to travel at a tremendous speed. I sat sideways in the HMMWV's seat, facing outboard and ready to shoot anything that moved. Much to my relief, nothing did and soon we were across the southern bridge. We slowed to a safe speed as we re-entered friendly lines. It was getting dark fast and I was ready to be back in the relative safety of our command post.

Just as I was starting to breathe easy again, 2/8's battalion commander came on the radio and asked us to stop where we were. He related that a 0.8 km [0.5 mile] ahead of us, one of his HMMWVs had just been shot at by an Iraqi tank.

'Oh great', I thought, 'there's an Iraqi T–62 tank loose on the road in front of me!' Our two light armoured vehicles were ordered forward to help locate and destroy the tank that had now disappeared in the darkness. The wind started whipping ominously as I stood there, peering into the dark looking for the Iraqi tank I just knew was heading in my direction.

We arranged our defences the best we could. We had one AT–4 light anti-tank rocket launcher, two heavy machine guns, one light machine gun, rifles and a couple of grenades. We were very concerned about the possibility of shooting a Marine vehicle that might be travelling our way from the direction of the tank. The minutes ticked by.

After about a half an hour, several vehicles from 2/8's Combined Anti-Armour Team (CAAT) pulled alongside of us from our rear. We breathed a collective sigh of relief with the TOW [anti-tank] missiles pointed down the road. Their team leader stated they thought they knew where the tank was and were getting ready to call in artillery.

I was treated to the business end of the 'king of battle' up close. Round after round impacted no more than 915 metres [1,000 yards] in front of me. The artillery mission was repeated twice for good measure. As soon as the last round had impacted, the CAAT vehicles moved forward to ensure the tank had been destroyed.

An hour after we had stopped for the tank, we were given the go-ahead to move forward. After a seven-minute drive, we were back in camp. The wind had picked up and the sand was blowing hard. There was a storm front moving in.

That evening we moved 3/2 from their positions in the vicinity of the western bridge to a spot south of the River Euphrates Bridge near 2/8. We needed more combat power in the area to start clearing the city out. There were some minor engagements with the Iraqis occurring that evening, but the action was light enough for the night watch to handle without me.

It rained hard before I hit the rack that night. The farmer's field we were in was designed to trap and retain rainwater using irrigation techniques perfected over thousands of years. What it meant for us was thick mud everywhere. I was exhausted. A quick scan outside indicated that the skies were clearing. I decided it would be safe to sleep outside in my usual spot behind my truck. I took off my boots and socks and set them beside my helmet and flak jacket, where I could get them quickly in the middle of the night if required, and crawled into my sleeping bag.

By the time I realized it was raining, it was too late. It was pouring cats and dogs. I was still relatively dry and warm inside my sleeping bag, thanks to its Gortex outer shell, but my socks and boots were beyond hope. I tried to nudge them under the HMMWV and went back to sleep.[7]

Ernest 'Rock' Marcone

Lieutenant-Colonel Marcone was the battalion commander of the 1st Brigade, 69th Armor Regiment, 3rd Infantry Division, US Army. His unit has been described as the 'tip of the tip of the spear' in the advance towards Saddam International Airport on 3–4 April. His brigade also successfully fought off a counterattack at a key bridge on the night of 2 April.

The best piece of intelligence I got the entire war was that night [2 April]. We were told that an Iraqi commander brigade was coming from the airport area to try and retake the bridge. And that did happen. A commander brigade especially is, to me, more of a threat than armour, because its capabilities were so good.

But I was concerned to the north, because it was good infantry terrain, where the enemy could have infiltrated very easily into our positions. We determined that that was probably where that commander brigade would come. So we put infantry reinforced with armour, two companies, on that avenue. That's the way it happened, it turned out.

We got the first spot report, 'Tanks moving from east to west,' from Captain Gerald Robbins, my Charlie 369 commander, and then started to get the spot reports from Dave Benton and Chuck O'Brien who commanded Alpha 369, Bravo 37 Infantry. We started to get the spot reports of infantry moving in the north.

So now it looked like we had some sort of coordinated attack to try and retake the bridge. As the spot reports started to come in, and as we started to look at what we were facing at the time, we weren't sure what they were, because we were engaging at such long ranges … we didn't know if they were T-72 [tanks] or whether they were BMP [infantry fighting vehicles].

It was a very dark night – not much illumination at about [03.00 hours]. The moon had already gone down. We fought from [03.00 hours] until about [06.00 hours], almost steadily. What we ended up fighting were two brigades – the 10th Brigade of the Medina Division attacked from east to west, and then the commander brigade attacked from north to south. They tried very hard to coordinate this attack, but they just could not put it all together. They ended up piecemealing themselves. The 10th Brigade hits us hard first; we repulsed their attack. They came at us again; we repulsed the attack again.

Then the brigade, the infantry, started to show up in the north. They had the interior lines that were able to move assets around, and move artillery around and CAS (close air-support) to the critical points, and [we were] able to match fires against their concentrated attack avenues of approach. They did the best they could, and they came at us with everything they had: 15 tanks, 30 to 40 armoured personnel carriers reinforced with artillery mortars. The problem was that we could see them at long ranges, and we were able to engage and destroy them very effectively. The engagement didn't last very long.

We allowed them to come into the kill zone, in the engagement area. Once they got in, they couldn't get out, because behind them, artillery is falling, and behind the artillery, we had the close air-support coming in. The lead units were being engaged by main guns, machine guns and 25mm

[guns]. So they were under fire – suppressed immediately.

The units behind them all piled up on the road, and then our artillery and CAS came in, basically raking the column. It started at [03.00 hours]. The main attack [was] about [04.00 hours], and by [05.30 hours] they were completely destroyed. The 10th Brigade had ceased to exist.

The amazing part was that we didn't realize how big the force was we were fighting, and it was one tank company that fought that brigade.[8]

Kim Campbell

Captain Campbell was an A–10 pilot with the 75th Expeditionary Fighter Squadron, 332rd Expeditionary Operations Group, 332rd Air Expeditionary Wing, US Air Force. On 7 April 2003, she was flying an A–10 over the Tigris River, near the North Baghdad Bridge. In the squadron, Kim's call sign is 'Killer Chick', and on that April morning Campbell and her flight leader, Squadron Commander Lieutenant-Colonel Rick Turner, were waiting their turn in the 'close-air-support stack', the name US Air Force fighter pilots give for the circles they fly while waiting to be called to perform close-air-support missions.

When I felt and heard a large explosion in the back of the aircraft, there was no doubt in my mind. I knew exactly what it was. I knew I'd been hit [an anti-aircraft missile had sheared both hydraulic lines to her jet]. Our hydraulics are really what allow our flight control system to function normally. If the system is compromised, rudders, flaps and other critical flight and landing gear won't work. At this point there's really one option, and that's to switch to manual – the A–10's backup system of cables.

Ejecting in itself over friendly territory is one thing. Now, ejecting over enemy territory and going down over Baghdad, where we were just delivering ordnance on the Iraqi Republican Guard, is a totally different story. [So that left manual inversion, a technique that Campbell, like most A–10 pilots, had performed exactly once, during initial pilot training.] There's one sortie where you'll fly in manual inversion for a very limited time, to understand that it's just a little bit more difficult to fly. [She reached over with her right hand and hit the switch to put the A–10 into manual.] Instantly, the jet began to respond. It was a huge sense of relief. That's not a system you check in the preflight, so you put 100 per cent trust in the maintenance guys that it will work, and it did. It worked as advertised.

I had plenty of gas and the airplane was flying very well, so we decided to take it back to Kuwait. When it's your own Americans ... getting shot at, you want to do everything you can to help them out.[9]

Ken Brown

Lieutenant-Colonel Brown, a chaplain with the US Army's 101st Airborne Division, was at a camp in southern Iraq with young soldiers who had seen some of their comrades wounded or killed. His war diary entry on 9 April recorded what he said to soldiers when they came to him to talk about death.

You know, I think you see significant change in young people who face death – their priorities change. I had a young man come to me a couple of weeks ago that had seen a soldier killed and several wounded. He talked to me about, if he had been just a couple of seconds sooner at a certain location, he probably could have prevented that. I think what he was really getting at was something that I faced as a young man in Vietnam as an infantryman – that is, you're guilty [that] you're alive and your buddy is dead or hurt real bad.

You're not going to be able to explain the problem of evil or suffering or pain to someone when they're in the midst of it. Philosopher-theologian Anicius Boethius, who lived in the 4th century, once said about the problem of evil and suffering that it was much like a fairytale. That God was writing straight with crooked lines, that even when we cannot see the justification and the need for the things that go on, even though they may appear crooked to us, that God was writing with straight lines.

This young man in particular, all I did was just say, 'Well, you may come to the conclusion that God has spared you in this particular instance. Now what are you going to do with that life that you have now? Will you use it to do great things, to live a more moral and ethical life?'[10]

Ramzy Azar

Around 100 of the most critically injured Iraqi prisoners of war were treated on the USNS *Comfort* in the Persian Gulf. To communicate with their Iraqi charges, the ship's doctors relied on American translators like Lieutenant Azar, who spoke a Lebanese version of Arabic.

As a translator, we're dealing with people that are in pain; that are longing for their family and longing for something that is familiar. So it's very difficult not to get personal. I had to watch myself to make sure that I wasn't too comfortable around them, mainly because it has been a war setting. I've had some requests to exchange phone numbers and exchange addresses, but I've been a little bit hesitant to do that.

What has also ... stuck in my mind has been when I've been translating for this enemy prisoner of war. [T]his gentleman was quite tense. And he kept asking whether we were going to kill him. In this man's mind, he had this impression that we brought him onboard here to actually execute him. I reassured him that we were here to make sure that he was healthy. We wanted to heal him as best as we could. And you could just see a relaxed expression on his face, and all of a sudden this gentleman started to cry.[11]

Raad Al-Hamdani

Lieutenant-General Raad Al-Hamdani was the Commander-in-Chief of II Corps in the Iraqi Republican Army during Operation Iraqi Freedom. His summary of the invasion of his country provides a stark example of the overwhelming American military might pitted against Iraq.

On a field level, and with respect to my troops, I issued operational commands on 15 March [2003], which was the time of the arrival of the American 101st Airborne Division to Kuwait. This was an important criteria to me for the seriousness of the war. Accordingly, the first psychological orientation towards the war began on 15 March.

On the eve of 18 and 19 March, there was an air warning announcing the arrival of 20 enemy air targets, which entered the Iraqi territories from the western desert; passing over An Nasiriyah city, then over Iskandariya; after which they changed their directions.... The actual fierce time of the war began on the second night; which was known as Assadma Wal-Tarweea [Shock and Awe]. Baghdad was bombarded very heavily and savagely; over 1,500 guided missiles, and more than 550 laser-guided bombs launched by B-52 bombers on Baghdad. Part of these guided bombs weighs more than seven tonnes ...

On the strategic, tactical and psychological levels, as well as the will to fight ... we did not have any glimpse of hope to win the war. The Iraqi Army was exhausted, the war did not end with respect to the air conflicts;

it was continued outside the no-fly zones imposed by the United States and Britain, in violation of international law. Accordingly, the Republican Army and the leadership headquarters were subject to continuous attacks throughout the period between 1991 and 2003. Besides, we did not have the minimum air defence utilities. All these factors made us convinced that we could never win the war. However, our duty towards our country and our military honour forced us to fight to the end.

Nine months before the war began, I submitted this issue before the late president in a meeting. I clarified to him that if the high Iraqi strategy could not avoid the coming war, we should then change the mode of our strategic and tactical thought towards a kind of guerrilla fighting, which then I named as the Partial Use of Power, and dividing all Iraqi territories from the north to south and from the west to the east into sectors that are run by traditional forces which fight as guerrillas.

He [Saddam Hussein] listened to me for over 45 minutes, and when another commander wanted to intervene, he prevented him and told him that he was interested ... However, he did not agree to my proposition, nor did he agree to what other commanders said, especially with respect to the commandment of the army. He then took a decision which was, practically, correct. This decision provided for dividing Iraq into four territories of commandment and general control. What was wrong about that decision was that the commanders of these territories were political commanders, not military commanders. The Ministry of Defence and the Army staff commandment were not given a leading role in that war. Their mission was simply securing logistic and field requirements for the main four commandment sectors.

There were many reasons behind the fall of Baghdad. Certainly, three weeks can be reasonable with respect to differences in the power balance in that conflict.... the fall of Baghdad started on 2 August 1990, with the consequent sanctions, resulting in the exhaustion of the state, the Army and the Iraqi people, and the whole Arab nation as well, as a result. There was a huge amount of factors, the end of which represented the last stroke that broke the camel's back ...

However, the Americans used distant manoeuvring which kept their forces outside our reach. For instance, V American Corps, which was under the command of General Watts, moved through the desert approach near the River Euphrates. This approach was outside the effect of all our arms, except some cannon shots, which are called ... temporary positions; which is a style we use only for marking targets. We used it so that we would not give a chance for the enemy fighters or helicopters to destroy these cannons. Hence, the manoeuvre of the enemy was outside the effect of our arms; and our tanks which we relied on in the field had no air cover and were not protected by any other arm. Moreover, we had the American Abrams tank which was in the field against the Iraqi T-72 Soviet tank, and this was totally outside our technical measurements. Fighting depends on how modern your fighting system is.

Now, the latest tank which we owned was the T-72, of Soviet origin, which I received back in 1982 when I was the commander of a tank battalion in the Republican Army. On the other side, each American tank was protected by an Apache fighter which carried 16 anti-tank missiles named Hellfire, which worked by a system of Fire and Forget. The range of these missiles was 8 km [5 miles], while the maximum direct shooting range for a Soviet T-72 tank was 5 km [3.1 miles]. Over the Apache, there was an F-16 fighter, which could spot targets within 80 km [50 miles]. Over the two fighters, there was an F-15 fighter, which could spot targets within 120 km [75 miles]. Over these fighters were Blackbird espionage fighters, above which flew the AWACS [airborne warning and control system] fighters. Above all these flew the reconnaissance air systems; while the Iraqi tanks fought all alone; and we had only simple defence arms.

Besides, our air defence system was also incomplete. Therefore, we relied on the free ambush manner in which you assign an expected mission; we did not work through a mutual shared-intelligence system. The battle was unbalanced, and the enemy, with his huge equipment and modern technology, was capable of movement and managed to separate our troops from each other. Consequently, our Army felt greatly disappointed, and despite their courage, our soldiers were not capable of manoeuvring and fighting in the way the enemy did.

In addition, there was the foreign propaganda and media, and the opposition parties, as well as the Iranian media, which played a very vital role in discouraging our army. Added to this is the absence of political awareness. The enemy managed to push for the end of the troubles in Iraq by removing Saddam Hussein. These propaganda strategies were not very well comprehended by the Iraqi people in general and the Iraqi Army personnel in particular. We believed that President Saddam relied heavily on his good luck; and he believed that he had a mission to perform under the protection of Almighty Allah.

In his answer to one question, he said, 'Do you know why we will humiliate America and make it kneel at the gates of Baghdad? This is because Allah did not prepare any army for them except the army of Iraq. If America fought with the ex-Soviet Army; people would have said that a great power is fighting a great power; but when it comes to the Iraqi Army, which was exhausted, tired and poorly armed and manages to humiliate and defeat the American Army, this is all done under the Divine protection and care.'

There was a feeling that the very last moment of the war would be decisive and triumph would be to Iraq through the protection and care of Almighty Allah. It was noticed that the late President Saddam Hussein, after any crisis throughout these 15 years, he went to cross the River Tigris from the same place that he crossed in 1959 when he was saved by his good luck. Hence, he was optimistic, and he was thinking in the same manner of Frederick the Great … in the decisive moment … after the death of … the Czaress, the European alliance against the Germans collapsed. Such was [Saddam's] feeling, and such is the feeling of all leaders who believe themselves to be very important. He also believed that Russia would be the final solution.

Strangely … [at] that meeting on the morning of 7 April, while the American forces were moving to Baghdad from the north, west, east and south of Iraq, he raised his hands triumphantly, saying that victory was in his hands. He was very steadfast, and quiet. On 6 April, while he was sitting in a bus stop near Umul-Tubul Mosque in Baghdad, American tanks passed through the highway leading to the airport. He was astonished and asked, 'What are these tanks?' A brigadier named Hameed answered him that they were American tanks. Very quietly, he pushed his aides to fight, and two of these tanks were destroyed. He was extremely quiet, and dealt with things as if luck was on his side and Allah would not forget him.

Three months before the war … we all stood on a big bridge known as al-Qaed Bridge ('The Leader' bridge), in Jurful-Sakhar region over the River Euphrates. I told them that the enemy would cross this bridge. This bridge is similar to the one over the Rhine which the US 6th Division crossed in 1944 and settled the Rhine battle … I assigned a force to destroy the bridge, and I assigned a commander for this force. I also authorized the commander-in-chief of the Al-Madina Al-Munawara Division to destroy the bridge the moment he felt the enemy would cross it. Ten days before the beginning of the war, I consulted the supervisor of the Republican Army, Qusay Saddam Hussein (1966–2003), God bless his soul, about this bridge. I said to him that this bridge would be an important part of Baghdad's defence system. I preferred to destroy the bridge right then. He asked to wait until he got the permission of the president. The answer was no. The same thing was true for many other bridges, like the Al-Kifil Bridge, over which a fierce battle took place on 26 March 2003, which was lost by Iraqi troops. The problem continued.

On 2 April 2003, I was summoned to Baghdad to meet with the president. However, I met with the defence minister and with Qusay Saddam, God bless his soul. At that moment I had my own information; I knew the location of the enemy; I had my own deep reconnaissance forces which supplied me with information about the movements of the enemy, especially near the Euphrates ... I insisted on destroying the bridge and the meeting lasted for three hours. We also discussed other issues.

... I was in need of more troops; they demanded that I withdraw other troops. They believed that was not the real effort of the enemy, and the actual forces would approach us from the west, from the Jordanian border. Their measures were not punctual, and more American troops were arriving. They occupied Al-Majar; and the 82nd Airborne Division landed over Haditha and occupied the Haditha Dam.

As discussions were going on the phone rang, and it was I who picked it up. The speaker told me that the enemy was crossing the bridge and that the news was very painful. I returned very quickly, and a battle began. Many of our forces were involved: the engineering units, the 10th Brigade, and other forces, but we lost the battle due to the fierce air strikes. We tried to recapture the bridge back before the dawn of 3 April, but we failed.

The stupidity of the American strategy, and the domination of the new conservatives, who are now being called the new idiots, in imposing certain criteria as regards supporting the strategic position in regards to Iraq. Sure the United States is a superpower, and has its own decision-making institutions, a respectful military institution, as well as a political institution. However, it appeared that the domination of the new conservatives [Neo-Cons] had led to imposing strategic criteria on which the war was built, [the] top of which was destroying the Iraqi Army, toppling the regime and occupying Iraq.

The second factor which helped the Americans in this war was a strategic misappreciation on the part of the Iraqi command. There was a merging between Saddam Hussein, being a strategic and political leader of Iraq, and Iraq as a state. Those who know the personality of Saddam Hussein know that there was no clear separation between Saddam and the state ... Saddam Hussein was our destiny ... No one was able to change this destiny.

Any way you look at what happened, we figure out that there was a change in the international strategy which Iraq and the Iraqis paid for. The second point is the Iran–Iraq struggle ... after the success of the Islamic Revolution in 1979. Throughout this war, and the previous struggle during the Shah's regime, Iran could not achieve its goals. However, in this war the Iranian leadership managed to bring down a very big foe, Iraq and Saddam, for a very small price, through the American and European alliance. The current problem in Iraq is a political one, in addition to the security issue. They also put sacred schedules for democratic changes to ... Iraq. Democracy, as we know, is history and heritage.

The British in 1921 came with a project of building Iraq, so they brought a skilled elite, who were also Sunnis, Shi'as, Christians, Kurds, Mandeans and Yazidis. Unfortunately, the Americans came with the project of destroying the state; and who adopts such a project does not need skills. A powerful bulldozer would be enough to destroy it.

The current political map is simply a map for conflicting political powers, in which no powerful one dominates. Iran is the big winner from the situation in Iraq. Unfortunately, there is no regional power that can balance the power of Iran in order to protect the interest of the country and the Iraqi people. All Iraqis will regret, those who participated in the political process, and those who stood against it, because the outcome ... [for the] coming five to ten years will be painful and Iraq will not be ... as it was, with its huge strategic weight within the Arab world. Such is Iraq.[12]

Notes

1 *University of Virginia Magazine* feature, summer 2008
2 BBC News, 20 March 2003
3 Battleground Iraq, Department of the Army, Washington, DC, 2007
4 Iraq War Veterans Organization, Inc
5 Used with permission from *Stars and Stripes*. © 2005–2009 *Stars and Stripes*
6 US Marine Corps 2003, With the 1st Marine Division in Iraq
7 © 2004 Iraqi-Freedom-Diary.com
8 Copyright ©1995–2009 WGBH Educational Foundation
9 Used with permission from *Stars and Stripes*. © 2005–2009 *Stars and Stripes*
10 National Public Radio, Inc
11 ibid
12 *Russia Today* interview, 10 April 2008

Fighting the insurgency

The relatively easy conquest of Iraq in 2003 resulted in the Coalition shifting from regime-removal to assisting a new Iraqi leadership to improve security, establish a legitimate government and rebuild the economy. However, in the immediate political vacuum, Iraq was soon awash with tens of thousands of former armed forces and police personnel from disbanded units, and flooded with weapons. Violence exploded in Sunni-dominated central Iraq, where Ba'ath Party and Former Regime Elements (FRE) launched attacks on Coalition forces. Shi'a Arabs, long oppressed by Saddam Hussein, also assaulted Coalition forces. To compound the problem, foreign fighters from Syria, Saudi Arabia, Egypt, Jordan and Iran flooded into the country to fight the Western invaders. Some estimates put the number of insurgents in Iraq in 2004 at 200,000.

In Sadr City (a district of Baghdad), the radical Shi'a leader Muqtada al-Sadr led an uprising between April and June 2004. Controlling the Jaish al-Mahdi (JAM), or 'Mahdi Army', a loose grouping of religious militias and criminal gangs, al-Sadr's revolt was eventually crushed by American firepower, with an estimated 800 Shi'as killed.

Although the Coalition forces also retook the city of Samarra from insurgents in October, by the end of 2004 the number of insurgent attacks per day in Iraq had increased from 25 early in the year to 60 by the year's end. In addition, though the majority of insurgent attacks (around 80 per cent) were targeted against Coalition forces, the Iraqi population suffered approximately 80 per cent of all casualties. Insurgent tactics grew more sophisticated, with a dramatic increase in casualties and in the numbers of car bombs, suicide bombings and roadside bombs.

For those Coalition soldiers on the ground in Iraq, 2004 was a year when an alien land appeared to be infested with enemy fighters, and where death seemed to be around every corner. Misery, boredom and terror were the most common emotions experienced by Coalition troops in 2004.

Don Nitti

Lieutenant-Colonel Nitti, Commander of Alpha Company, 404th Aviation Support Battalion, was stationed in Tikrit, Iraq, with the 4th Brigade Combat Team, 4th Infantry Division, US Army. Alpha Company is an Aviation Intermediate Maintenance Company with the primary mission of conducting aircraft repairs. For ten months, the 4th Brigade combat team flew more than 33,000 helicopter hours.

December 2003

… My unit deployed to Operation Iraqi Freedom in March 2003, and after a brief stay in Kuwait, we convoyed 960 km [600 miles] into Iraq. Since April 2003, the units of the 4th Brigade Combat Team have been stationed at Forward Operation Base Speicher in Tikrit, Iraq.

The environment in Iraq has been harsh, on both personnel and equipment. The … temperature has ranged from 1.7°C to 49°C [35°F to 120°F] … The summer was extremely dry, with seven months of no precipitation and regular periods of high winds and sandstorms. The fine sand covers everything, and it is impossible to keep things clean. The fall and winter months have brought a substantial amount of rain, which has created a lot of mud and some flooding.

While living conditions vary widely between units … our conditions [are] austere, but adequate. For the first few months, the only rations available were MREs (meals, ready-to-eat) and limited water supplies. There was restricted bathing, and the only structures were tents. We now have a civilian-contracted dining facility that is one of the best in Iraq. We have built makeshift showers, constructed some offices and work areas, and although we are still living in tents, we have air conditioning and heat, which helps to regulate the temperature to some extent.[1]

John B. Nails

Captain John Nails was a US Army company commander in a tank regiment in Iraq, February 2004.

Not all of Iraq is a big desert. The river valleys are loaded with date palm groves, vineyards and sunflower fields. The ground is covered in waist- to chest-high grass. Vegetation is very thick. The roads are elevated from the fields, and are usually bordered by walls, fences or canals, which cross the landscape in all directions of the compass. Most groves are separated into 2–4 hectare [5–10-acre] plots surrounded by walls or fences. The walls and fences provide good cover and make great obstacles, as do the canals. Most canal bridges will not support a tank's weight.

The towns and villages have narrow streets; more narrow than Europe. Electrical wires hang about 2.4–3 metres [8–10 ft] off the ground and cross each other in no particular pattern. Running an M1 tank through these areas is possible, but due to the amount of collateral damage, it would be unwise. Remember, we are restoring the Iraqi infrastructure, not destroying it … Key leaders (platoon sergeants and up) need to carry a couple of body bags and sets of rubber gloves. Initially, my battalion chain of command felt [this] was counterproductive to morale. What was actually counter-productive to morale [were] the pieces of human remains my soldiers had to pick up and place on a litter and cover with a blanket because nothing else was available. Remember, not all casualties will be Americans. We are a civilized nation, and we recover the remains of our enemies and civilians as well.

Expect combat stress and have your chaplain and medics locate and tie into your servicing combat stress teams. Have the combat stress teams pay periodic visits to your soldiers. It will pay off in the long run. Let your soldiers know that the effect of combat stress makes you no less a man.

Think before you announce, 'On the way' with a high-explosive anti-tank round. The [insurgents] will fire at you from or near occupied homes. Once the sun comes up, you will see several small children emerge from these homes. Imagine if you would have let go with your big gun. How many deaf children on the block did you create? How will this impact community relations? Use appropriate force. Yes, there are times to let loose the big bullets, and I am more willing to let one fly than most, but make sure it is an informed decision, and a price you are willing to pay.[2]

Ismail Hussein Ali

Ismail Hussein Ali was an Iraqi colonel of police based at the busy Karrada police station in Baghdad in early 2004. Like all police stations in Iraq, the Karrada station was a fort of concrete walls and razor wire to try to keep out suicide bombers who had been targeting Iraqi policemen. Throughout that year many policemen were kidnapped, tortured and killed by the insurgents.

These suicide bombers come by car. If you shoot and kill them, they will still reach the target, so we had to put up these barriers, which are a painful sight. We have no choice. Lots of police have been killed and injured through these suicide bombings.

There have been difficulties. If we take Baghdad as an example, there was incredible chaos after the war. Bandits everywhere. So when the police were back on the streets, the people welcomed us in a very unusual way. People told us they did not like us before, but that they liked our new role.

In Saddam's time, connections were important. Now we try to convince our employees to let the people know that they are equal in front of the law, and that the former connections aren't there anymore. There have definitely been problems with some of our policemen misbehaving. But we now have clear rules supplied to everyone. I go out to other offices [to talk to people about this]. I personally see the misbehaving policeman and see if it is possible to change him. Now we feel that we are working with freedom without any pressures.

In the time before, I was an investigating officer, so you conducted an investigation and you found who the criminals were, and when you had the evidence against them, you had it ready for the court, and for sentencing.

We, the Iraqis, will be the deciding factor in our future. Things are acceptable for the time being, and we hope for better things in the future. Terrorism is a big issue. It targets the people as well as the police, and it targets the infrastructure as well. These people are foreigners and not Iraqis. But some of the people who attack the Americans are Iraqis. I would like to see the Americans stay to supervise a new government.

There are lots of competing parties, and there is the risk of a civil war, and ethnic war, and there are those foreign parties that would like to push a war forward. Even under the old regime, even though things were extremely harsh, we never had suicide bombings like [the ones at Karbala and Kadhimiya]. We had a hunch that something like this might happen. The aim of these terrorists is to create a civil war. If the Coalition forces leave Iraq, there would be a bloodbath very shortly.[3]

Murray Rice

Staff Sergeant Rice was a combat medic with the 3rd Armored Cavalry Regiment, US Army, who, on 20 July 2003, was caught in a roadside ambush against American troops in Iraq. That day he was part of a convoy delivering $750,000 earmarked for police salaries, water and sewer services.

I don't know why, but everything looks like slow motion coming at you. We didn't have the kind of secure communication that units with more money and equipment had. Whatever we encountered, we ha[d] to deal with it on our own. All I know is I had three magazines changed and rotated through my weapon before I even knew I was doing it. I didn't think of anything except shooting back, because that's how they trained me. Anybody that says they weren't scared, something's wrong with them. Yeah, I was scared. You don't think about it then, but when you're sitting in your safe, secure zone, you just think about how lucky you are.[4]

Chris Bain

Staff Sergeant Bain was a reconnaissance and chemical weapons specialist with the US Army Reserve. On 8 April 2004, just as the convoy he commanded was rolling out on a mission, a group of insurgents attacked the Al Taji base camp. He describes what happened to him and the long-term consequences in the account that follows.

There were four to six of them. They hit us with small arms, around 17.30 or 18.00 hours. The sun was going down. I'm sitting in the back of a truck, sitting there relaxing. I was hearing mortar fire, and I asked if it was all out-going. It took about 50 seconds for the first round to hit, about 50 metres [165 ft] in front of us. We jumped out, throwing people under cover for protection. I just stayed out there too long, making sure my guys were protected.

[A mortar round exploded 1 metre (3 ft) in front of Bain's face, ripping off his whole left forearm. Then he was shot in the right elbow.] I can tell you second-by-second. It comes back to me every day. All I saw was all the blood. I was under a truck and just gushing. I lost 1.5–1.6 litres [3–3½ pints]. I'm lucky I didn't bleed out. With all the adrenalin and all, I didn't feel my arm. I was crying over my [nearly severed] finger.

Everything was like slow motion. I saw a medic. He was going, 'What hurts?' I couldn't hear him, but I read his lips, saying, 'What hurts?' I said, 'My finger, it's killing me.' He said, 'Your finger? Have you seen your arm?' I said, 'What's wrong with my arm?'

I have a hard time going to sleep, and [react] every time I hear something loud, like the 4th of July, which is the worst holiday for me now.[5]

Joe Day

Warrant Officer Day was an Australian fighting with US Marines in Iraq. In April 2004, he took part in an operation in Fallujah, which was to act as a prelude to the major battle that took place in the city seven months later. Australia sent 2,000 troops to Iraq as part of the US-led Coalition but by April 2004 only 850 remained.

On the evening of 12 April, we received fresh orders to move south, link up with Regimental Combat Team 7 and redeploy to near Fallujah. We were to assist other 1st Division troops to secure some of the troubled areas and main roads around the town in an operation called Ripper Sweep.

We moved to Al Asad, about 150 km [94 miles] to the north of Fallujah. We used it as a staging area in preparation for the operation. We moved to clear all roads to the west of Fallujah. Artillery fired over our heads; fixed-wing and rotary-wing aircraft were attacking (insurgent) positions. It was almost like the war all over again. We were prepared for a big fight as we moved through. Our force was so large and must have appeared so daunting for the enemy that they fled in front of us, abandoning their positions.

We met little resistance on the opening day. There was one close call, when a roadside bomb exploded near a Humvee. Luckily, nobody was seriously injured … we searched every house and questioned every male of military age. Some were detained for further questioning.

We found and cleared many roadside bombs along all the roads we covered. We moved further south to cordon the town of Ash Amerya. The town had a population of about 25,000 people. I thought that it was an insurgent stronghold, feeding fighters to Fallujah. We searched the town without incident and re-established law and order. It was assessed that, once again, the enemy had fled the town before we arrived. This was of some concern because it meant that they were able to gain early warning of our movements.

I went with the CO [commanding officer] to a bridge at the western entrance of Fallujah. It was like a scene out of World War II. Marines in heavily fortified sandbag bunkers guarded the bridge. The sounds of battle were all around. It reminded me of when we were preparing to move into Baghdad nearly a year before. I realized that this bridge was the one that (US) civilian contractors' bodies had been hung off after being dragged through the streets by a mob of barbaric young men.

My blood boiled as I realized this was what started the whole thing in the first place. Now, people were dying in there. All because of some evil desire to kill Americans and for some hollow cause (if any at all). Marine losses were the highest they had been since our return. That thought angered me as I pondered where all this was going.

Soon we received orders to redeploy to the eastern side of the city. We were to cordon the small town of Al Karmah, about 10 km [6 miles] to the northeast of Fallujah proper. This town was a known stronghold of mujahedeen insurgent fighters. They estimated there were up to 500 and they wanted to fight. This rang true when our movement was stopped by the discovery of several roadside bombs.

As we surrounded the town in the classic cordon, the discovery of more and more bombs was getting to be some kind of record. In the end, we had found 61 IEDs (improvised explosive devices) … all successfully destroyed.

We attacked the town on or around 20 April. With the exception of one firefight in which eight enemy were killed (and no losses on our side), there was no enemy to be found. Rumours were rife that some members of the media had deliberately let the word slip out so as to avoid a bloodbath. I don't know if that is true or not. If it is, that is a very dangerous course of action for us, as it will certainly cost lives in the future.

We remained in the town for the next few days, continuing our searches and detaining suspects as we went. It was decided that we would get some rest in a forward operations base, which was just outside Fallujah itself. The base was known as Camp Fallujah and was well protected by walls, wire and fortified positions. There was fresh food there and phones, an internet cafe and a PX [post exchange/retail store]. We were in heaven after weeks in the field …

The next day we returned to the field to tighten our cordon on Fallujah and its surrounding towns. We still had a sizeable force in Al Karmah. Rocket attacks were becoming more prevalent, and our artillery was coming into play now with counter-battery fire.

A few days later, a ceasefire was declared, and the battalion was ordered to return to Al Asad, and then its own area of operations further to the north, at Al Qaim.

After nearly a month-long operation, we are now at our base camp and preparing for the next operation. We don't know where we are going or what the mission will be. Our base camp is a lot smaller than the ones to our south. There is no fresh food and water is scarce. We sleep in an abandoned building with no air-conditioning, nor any other luxuries.[6]

James Ross

Sergeant Major James Ross was a member of the 4th Battalion, 5th Air Defense Artillery Regiment, 1st Cavalry Division, US Army. During Easter 2004, he and his unit were involved in the fighting in Iraq.

We depart Camp Blackjack, Baghdad International Airport, at 05.30 hours. The patrol consists of 28 soldiers ... mounted in eight M114 'up-armour' Humvees. Each Humvee has three- or four-man crews and a crew-served weapon mounted in its rotating turret ... I am riding in the lead Humvee with a squad leader, driver and gunner.

At 05.45 hours, we pick up 'J', our translator, at the Titan Company Headquarters. Everyone calls him J because his Arabic name is too tough to pronounce. We drive about a mile and turn north on an expressway that serves as a military supply route (MSR) ... The route runs south all the way to Kuwait and northeast through Fallujah, about 30 km [19 miles] from Baghdad, which makes it a popular road for insurgents.

The countryside along the MSR is primarily rural. Farmers live in the villages to our left and right. We head north on the MSR about 8 km [5 miles], and we come across a large crater that has been blown in the road ... Someone has blown an improvised explosive device. A civilian car is broken down in the crater. Obviously, the car's driver didn't see the crater and drove right into it. The patrol positions its vehicles around the area and investigates the scene.

... A sergeant, a specialist and I follow the firing wire back to its point of origin. The three of us jump over a 1.5 metres [5 ft] wide concrete culvert that holds about 1 metre [3 ft] of water. About 30 metres [35 ft] further, the wire ends at the corner of a yard, about 200 metres [220 yds] northeast of the crater.

We contact the patrol leader, 1st Lieutenant Tracy W. Doubler, on our handheld radio and tell him what we found. He directs the Humvees off the MSR and moves them east onto a road that flanks a small dirt road. Then the patrol leader, a platoon leader and a platoon sergeant move to the culvert to develop a plan of action. The platoon stays on the far side of the culvert. Since the sergeant, specialist and I don't want to jump back over the culvert, we stay on our side of the culvert. An Iraqi farmer who lives in a nearby village comes up to us and tells our interpreter that for the last few weeks men have been showing up in the area and threatening the residents if anyone speaks of their activities. He says the men are very intimidating and basically have all of the locals scared. He says all the insurgents have guns and threaten to kill anyone who talks.

We thank the man for the information, and Lieutenant Doubler decides to search the house. He tells … us to stand fast because the platoon is going to move its vehicles into position to conduct the cordon and search … The patrol leader and platoon leaders head back towards the Humvees, while the three of us wait on the far side of the culvert.

Before they reach the Humvees, we are ambushed by insurgents firing small arms from about 400 metres [440 yds] away on the west side of the MSR. The platoon members rush to their Humvees and begin returning fire. For the three of us trapped behind the culvert between the insurgents and the platoon, there are few options. As bullets fly all around us, we move backwards about 6 metres [20 ft] and take up prone fighting positions. The specialist tries to jump back over the culvert, but doesn't make it across and ends up waist-deep in water. The patrol leader yells for him to start shooting with his M203 grenade launcher. Because the water is waist-deep and the culvert walls are angled, the specialist can't get out of the culvert. He gives up trying, locks and loads his grenade launcher, and starts firing controlled bursts about every 30 seconds …

The specialist directs the grenade rounds into a ridgeline about 400 metres [440 yds] to the west, where we believe the ambush is coming from. After about two minutes, the sergeant and I grow tired of dodging bullets, which are zinging by so close that you can hear them snap. I look at the sergeant and tell him that we need to get the fuck out of here. We get on our feet and jump over the culvert. I help pull the specialist out … Rounds are flying all around us, and we have no choice but to run for it. I yell to them, 'Run for the vehicles.' We are completely exposed and in the open, so we run as fast as we can towards the vehicles.

Weighted down by our gear, we aren't able to run as fast as we'd like. It's a 150 metre [165 yd] sprint to the Humvees with no cover. I really don't like our chances. As we dash for the vehicles, bullets whiz by our heads and kick up dirt around us. It's a miracle none of us are hit. We somehow make it to the vehicles safely. The specialist tells me later that, when I got to our Humvee, my eyes were so big with fright that they were filling up my Eye Safety System goggles. It's surreal. I can't believe I am standing there without a scratch.

Using the vehicles for cover, we fire back at the ambushers with all of our small arms and crew-served weapons. The platoon sergeant notifies the battalion command post that we were almost 'black' on ammo and to have a re-supply waiting at ECP 7. Once the attackers stop firing, and we are convinced that the area is reasonably clear, the patrol leader has a team search the house and question the residents. The platoon forms a 360° perimeter to ensure we are safe.

During the search, we start to receive mortar fire. The first round explodes about 300 metres [330 yds] to our east. The second round falls about 200 metres [220 yards] away and causes a very large explosion, probably by hitting a house or a car. The mortar fire is starting to get too close for comfort, and the lieutenant gives the order to line up on the MSR and return to ECP 7 for ammunition re-supply. Simultaneously, the mortar crew adjusts fire and mortar rounds start landing all around us. It's obvious we need to get out of the area because we are sitting ducks. The patrol leader gets on the radio and tells everyone that we are moving back to ECP 7. As we are pulling into ECP 7, we notice a convoy leaving Baghdad International. It consists of 20 fuel tankers and a couple of five-ton gun trucks. A sergeant in the lead vehicle tells us the convoy is headed away from the ambush site.

First Sergeant Paul Peterson of Foxtrot Battery meets us with the ammo at ECP 7, and re-supply takes only about 10 minutes. We head back out towards the MSR and, almost immediately, we see black smoke coming from the northwest ... As we travel one kilometre [0.6 miles] further, it becomes obvious that the convoy we saw leaving ECP 7 is under attack ... An ugly scenario unfolds in front of our eyes. The convoy had been attacked within the previous 10 minutes. Two fuel trucks had been completely destroyed and are blocking the three lanes of the northbound MSR. The convoy personnel, about 50 of them, are up ahead about 400 metres [440 yds] and are being attacked from both sides of the street. They are in big trouble. The only way we can get to them is by taking a dirt trail on the right side of the MSR.

It's a textbook ambush waiting to happen and everyone knows it. We also know that we either run the gauntlet or the personnel in the convoy gets hammered. I grab the radio hand-mike and notify the platoon to expect to get hit as soon as we pull off the MSR onto the dirt road. The dirt road branches northeast about 200 metres [220 yards] and then turns back towards the highway. Running parallel to the dirt road is 2.4 metre [8 ft] high patch of grass and reeds that mask the enemy location. I don't know how I know they are in there, but by looking at the burning fuel trucks, I can just envision insurgents waiting to spring an ambush.

With our Humvee in the lead, we pull onto the dirt trail and, just as expected, we get ambushed. A rocket-propelled grenade streaks out of the weeds and misses by less than 30 cm [1 ft]. Rounds are flying everywhere. They are firing at us, and we are firing back. If one of the rocket-propelled grenades hits our Humvee, it will be a disaster. The entire platoon will be trapped on the dirt trail in the middle of the kill box. We make it around the turn and, with the platoon in full throttle, we move back onto the MSR and position ourselves around the disabled fuel trucks.

The convoy has taken many casualties, and one soldier with a head wound is in a critical condition. Most of the other wounded are suffering from gunshot wounds to their extremities. Our medic immediately starts to consolidate the wounded and sets up a triage. Doubler gets on the radio and calls in a dust-off [medical evacuation] request. He's told that a medevac helicopter is on its way.

The platoon immediately takes charge of the scene and lets loose with all its weapons systems. On the radio, I call battalion and ask for air and armour support. The battalion commander, Lieutenant-Colonel Todd Morrow, tells me he's sending everything he has our way. Small-arms fire is flying at us from both sides of the highway and, periodically, mortar rounds are landing within 200 metres [220 yards] to our front. Two Apache helicopters arrive and provide air cover for an inbound medevac Black Hawk. A soldier tosses a red smoke grenade so the medevac knows where to land. The medevac picks up the wounded and is gone in three minutes max.

The Apaches roll in and use their main guns to strafe the ridgeline. Everyone is cheering. Suddenly ground fire hits the tail of one of the Apaches, and it plummets to the ground and explodes. The whole incident lasts about three seconds, and it's a horrible and helpless moment as we witness the deaths of two pilots who bravely gave their lives to protect us. The soldiers from the convoy are not very organized, and most of them are not even shooting back. Peterson and I move down the line of fuel trucks, yelling … at the drivers … to get the fuel trucks turned around so that we can get them out of the kill zone. Many of the fuel trucks have blown-out tires, so we direct the drivers to start changing tires as we provide cover.

The Bradleys dispatched by battalion arrive and lay down covering fire. Some Bradleys cover the Apache crash site. MPs arrive and go to the crash site. It takes about 30 minutes for the convoy personnel to change tires and get their vehicles turned around. Again, my Humvee takes the lead and escorts them back to ECP 7.

Foxtrot Battery's 3rd Platoon rolls out from Camp Blackjack to meet us and assist in the movement back to ECP 7. Once we arrive at ECP 7, we get the convoy personnel staged on the west side of the Hesco barriers. Suddenly, we come under attack again. Small-arms fire zips towards us from a house about 500 metres [550 yds] north of ECP 7. The platoon lines up all its crew-served weapons along the barriers and, with the tower guards along the western wall joining in, light up the house. The 4–5 ADA Bradley Linebackers [short-range air defence vehicles] at ECP 7 let loose with their 25mms.

Once the house and the insurgents inside are destroyed, the convoy personnel get back in their vehicles and head home towards Camp Victory. It is now about 14.00 hours, and Doubler tells me that I don't need to go back out with the platoon. He says that I have seen enough action for one day. The platoon still has six more hours to go on their patrol. Although it's one of the hardest things I've ever done, I get back in the Humvee and complete the patrol with 2nd Platoon. It was one of the longest 12 hours of my life.[7]

Brian Wood

Sergeant Wood of A Company, 1st Battalion of the Princess of Wales's Royal Regiment, British Army, won the Military Cross at the 'Battle of Danny Boy', named after the vehicle checkpoint nearby, some 24 km (15 miles) south of the city of Al Amara, on 14 May 2004.

We were conducting a vehicle checkpoint, but we were told to mount up sharpish. We heard that there'd been an incident with the Argyll and Sutherland Highlanders, and someone had been hit by a grenade and another had been shot in the arm. Our role was to extract them. [On the way, their Warrior vehicles were ambushed by insurgents from the Mahdi Army. Then came the order to dismount and fix bayonets onto their SA80 rifles.] The adrenalin going through my body was like nothing I'd ever felt before. I just led my boys in and hoped for the best. We've got a lot of firepower with the Warrior, so I'd never dreamt we would be told to dismount and engage in close-quarter battles. It hadn't happened since the Falklands War [1982], and fighting in the trench with the enemy down at your feet was an experience I'll never forget. The thing I remember is the blast. It just sucked all your breath away. And the fire. The smoke was just unbelievable – it was full of toxic black smoke and there was no noise from the vehicle, nothing.

The gunner, Private Samuels, was shouting, 'The boss is dead!' I looked and the boss [platoon commander] was lying at the bottom of the vehicle. We had two injured, and I was injured myself with a blast to my face. One of the boys in the back had pierced an artery in the leg and one had shrapnel to his nose, which was dangling down. I had to patch them up and then give first aid to the platoon commander. The diesel tank in the back had split, so we were up to our shins in diesel, and there was a fire in the left-hand side.

I put the fire out with the fire extinguisher, but totally forgot that you were supposed to use it and get out of the vehicle – so it took all our oxygen away. But it did put the fire out. I must have done something right, because we were still alive.[8]

David Bradley

In August 2004, Major Bradley was commanding B Company, the Princess of Wales's Royal Regiment (PWRR), a group of 120 men attached to the Cheshire Regiment, British Army. He and his men were operating from the Shatt al-Arab Hotel, Basra, a large British military base. Basra is located along the Shatt al-Arab waterway, where the Rivers Tigris and Euphrates flow together into the Persian Gulf. In the increasingly lawless Iraq of 2003–04, a radical Shi'a militia group known as the Mahdi Army (numbering around 6,000 combatants) began to flex its muscles. In April 2004, the Mahdists, led by Muqtada al-Sadr, had launched attacks in Baghdad and had taken control of Kut and partial control of Najaf. By the first week of August, the Mahdi Army was involved in fierce clashes across central and southern Iraq with US, British and Italian forces.

9 August 2004

It wasn't a normal day. It was at a period in our tour when the Mahdi Army uprising was gathering pace and was clearly reaching some sort of culminating point. We had experienced some sporadic yet heavy fighting before then. Our camps had been attacked a lot and we faced ambushes and IEDs [improvised explosive devices] out on the ground, but certainly no worse than others were experiencing. There had been periods of weeks where very little had happened, and other times where a lot had happened. It wasn't consistent one way or another. But as we entered the beginning of

August, a number of events had taken place nationally that meant that the activity in Basra was increasing at a rapid rate. The Americans were closing in on Muqtada al-Sadr, the leader of the Mahdi Army, in Najaf, so that was causing the tensions between the Mahdi Army and the multinational forces to increase. There was also a lot of posturing going on between Iraqi groups, who were trying to gain influence with the new Iraqi government.

At the beginning of August, therefore, there really was increasing tension, an increase in camp attacks and [an] increase in IEDs. A couple of days before, the Mahdi Army had taken over the centre of Basra, but instead of sending the British Army in to clear them, the view of local Coalition commanders was that it was an Iraqi problem. We needed to find a political solution, so they were allowed to remain there. Around the edges of Basra the generals were engaging with the Iraqi governor and the police chief to try and work out a solution with the Mahdi Army. At the same time, though, we were hearing from our intelligence that more fighters were pouring into the city.

Losing the Najaf battle, they were coming south to Basra because they thought there was a chance they might win that. And around the margins we were fighting battles to keep our supply routes open. They were attacking the camp more and more. As a soldier I felt we were probably giving them too much freedom. I was talking to my platoon commanders, and we all felt we would rather go in and clear them now rather than give them a week to dig in. We felt that it was a job that had to be done, but we wanted to do it on our terms rather than on theirs.

There was a base in the centre of Basra, in the old state buildings, where a satellite company of my battle group was being attacked more and more intensively, and they were struggling to be re-supplied. Our camp was being attacked, too. We could not sleep in tents at night because the rocketing and mortaring were too intense, so we moved into the Shatt al-Arab Hotel, which is next to an old airfield in the north of Basra, which was Battle Group Headquarters for the Cheshire Regiment: three Cheshire companies; D Squadron, Household Cavalry Regiment; and ourselves, B Company, 1PWRR. We were battle-grouped as the only Warrior company in Basra with the Cheshire Battle Group.

B Company of the Cheshires was based in the old state buildings and was having a tough time of it. On 9 August, as the only Warrior company in the battle group, we were the operations company/quick reaction force with armed vehicles which could get into the city relatively safely and quickly. That morning we were on standby, waiting for something to happen, because the tension was clearly building.

We heard rumours that the Mahdi Army was attacking an isolated police station, which in fact they were. Fairly early, one of the bases south of us, an old Iraqi naval base, had reported seeing a large group of armed militia in front of the base. So I went down with a couple of platoons … to that base, but we didn't find anything. I left a 'call sign' [usually a multiple of two vehicles and 10–12 people – in this case, two Warriors] outside to act as protection for the base, and we went back to the hotel.

Back at base, I was enjoying a late lunch of pie and chips when we started hearing firing down in the south of the city. Someone came in and said, 'Sir, can you go to the Operations (Ops) room? They want to talk to you.' I went to the Ops room where I met the Ops officer and the second-in-command, who was the acting commanding officer of the battle group (the commanding officer was on leave at that time). He said that the Royal Artillery thought they had lost a call sign. 'We are not quite sure; we are still waiting for confirmation.' As stated above, in order for some sort of political solution to be achieved, the city centre had been put out of bounds. It was a lesson we had learned in Northern Ireland. No one could go in, which stops unnecessary contacts happening. So we looked at this big out-of-bounds box on the map, and we thought: where are they going to be in this particular area? Eventually word came through that the call sign was somewhere near the old Ba'ath Party headquarters, which was right in the middle of the out-of-bounds area, opposite the headquarters of the office of Muqtada al-Sadr himself – enemy headquarters, essentially. Right in the middle of bandit country!

They had been ambushed, and rather than turning back to base, they had kept going and got themselves trapped. They were cut off in the centre of town. I was looking at the Ops officer and thinking, that is a bad place to be lost. I asked for confirmation that they were still there, because if we went in there it was going to be bad. I didn't want to be chasing a load of gunners who were actually safe and sound and having their scoff [food] at another base. Luckily the call sign commander had a mobile phone, and he reported that he had actually abandoned his Land Rover vehicles. They left their vehicles because they had been fired on and they felt they couldn't drive on any further. They abandoned their vehicles, left their radios, ran through the streets and broke into a house. We didn't know where they were or where they abandoned their vehicles. Worryingly, they didn't know where they were, but thought that they were near the old Ba'ath Party headquarters. My orders were, 'You need to go and get them.'

I had to rush back to my company Ops room and give a quick warning to the lads, 'Call sign lost in town, we need to go and get them out. Follow me.' We jumped into the Warriors, headed south into the area and picked up the other call sign that was still waiting outside the gunner's base. We had five Warriors to start with. Two call signs plus my Warrior. Another two followed fairly quickly afterwards, so that made seven.

We set off and got to a point where there was a Cheshire patrol that had stopped because there was a massive amount of firing going and they couldn't go any further. We used our Warriors to fire and manoeuvre down the main highway into Basra, which was a wide thoroughfare. It was a dual carriageway all the way to the centre of town, so we could advance two groups abreast. There was a central concrete reservation that channelled us to a certain extent, but we had a bit of room for manoeuvre because we could get past each other. So I started manoeuvring the call signs down the highway.

In a Warrior, you can batten down so everyone is under cover; i.e. close all the hatches so that shrapnel and small-arms rounds can't get in. Unfortunately, the Warrior has a very poor sighting system when battened down, so you can't see very well to defend yourself, spot the enemy or find a lost patrol. So we actually patrolled in what we call 'head up', where the commander, armed with a rifle, is slightly exposed from the shoulders upwards in the turret, looking for the enemy. He can then spot the enemy and … talk to the gunner, and the gunner with the armament (30mm cannon or 7.62mm chain gun) can engage the target. And at the back, two people are usually also 'head up' to protect your rear and provide extra firepower. You therefore are exposed, but equally no one can creep up on you from behind. If you batten down, you have many blind spots in such close country: you could motor down an alley and get an RPG [rocket-propelled grenade] round up your arse without seeing it coming – that was a big concern.

Sometimes I was in the lead, sometimes I wasn't. We were soon being fired on from both sides. We engaged one ambush point and pushed straight through it. We continued firing and manoeuvring down this highway. I remember hearing firing, looking up and being conscious of the rooftops. The insurgents would often fire from the rooftops. I thought, I just want to cover those rooftops to see if anybody was up there. As I was looking to the left, there was this sudden bang, and then I felt this pressure. I remember being flung to the side of my cupola. We had been hit by one or more RPG rounds.

I looked down and saw this dark grey explosion near my right-hand side, on the edge of the turret. It looked nasty, just thick, dark grey, and I felt this pressure spreading over me. I held my right hand up and saw what looked like a cloven hoof – my hand was split and was a mass of blood, bone and flesh. At the same time I felt a pressure in my chest. At first I thought the rounds from the RPG hadn't detonated for various reasons, but had bounced off my Warrior.

However, in the fog of the battle I then thought that an RPG round had hit me and was slipping into the turret. I tried to get onto the internal intercom and shout, 'Get out, get out, RPG in the turret, RPG in the turret!' Then I realized that my body was on fire. My right side was on fire and being in a vehicle on fire is a scary prospect. You don't want to be on fire in a vehicle, so I used my one good hand and patted it out and luckily it didn't do much damage to the hand. I then thought about the RPG round and tried to warn the lads to get out, and then hoisted myself up with my good hand and climbed up on top of the turret. I remember looking down into the hatch at my gunner, who looked up at me and said, 'Sir, get back inside! Get back inside!' As he was shouting at me, I was really conscious of the sound of bullets just pinging off the vehicle and all around me. I could hear high-velocity rounds whizzing past me very close, and I thought, this isn't a good place to be. So I got myself back into the turret and dropped down under cover.

I started to take stock of the situation. I looked at my hand and knew I needed medical attention. Unbeknown to me, the vehicle had been hit by seven or eight RPG rounds, and nearly all the blokes in the back had been wounded (all of them were knocked out for awhile). I was badly wounded. The only people that weren't wounded were the driver and the gunner, but they couldn't talk to each other because all the radios were out of action. So there I was, telling everyone that I was injured and needed to get back, calling my other call signs to join the fight, warning them that we needed a medevac [medical evacuation], that I was going to get myself back to base and that I needed someone to meet me there. No one heard it because the radio was broken, so I was talking to myself!

I thought, I need to take stock. What have I got? Right hand – it looks bad. I could move my thumb and thought that was a good thing (I knew the importance of keeping a thumb). I thought, I want to keep my thumb. I remember thinking about an officer in the regiment who had made the rank of captain and who had lost two fingers on one of his hands in Northern Ireland. He still managed to work through the ranks and become a captain. If he can do it, I can do it. It's not too bad. You know, in 4–6 weeks I will get myself sorted and I will be back with the lads.

I could not see out of my right eye, but I could see light. There was blood in it, and I thought, well, I can see light; it's not black, a bit blurred. My hand and my eye – they were the two injuries that I was aware of. I was also very aware of the pain. We kept morphine injections under our body armour, so with one hand I whipped out a syringe and banged it into my leg. At the same time I was conscious of my gunner, Private Carl Yee-Lim, on the chain gun [7.62mm gun coaxial with the 30mm cannon] firing and the enemy clearly still attacking us. He kept firing, the vehicle started to move and I tried to tell the driver (Sergeant Pike) where to go, but no one could hear me. He wasn't my normal driver, but as an experienced NCO [non-commissioned officer], he knew how to handle the situation. He did brilliantly.

I knew the right way to go, which was to do a 180° turn to get back to where we came from; he wasn't quite so sure, though. So we drove further south, deeper into the battle area. Fortunately, Basra is laid out like a US city, so if you keep turning right, you actually get back to where you started from, which is what he did. He got us back to base. As we were moving along, I thought, it shouldn't take this long. I was drifting into unconsciousness, and my gunner, in between firing the chain gun, was leaning across the ammunition bins that were separating the two of us, shaking me and saying, 'Wake up, wake up,' (you are always taught in first aid that if someone is seriously wounded, you need to keep them with you). I was thinking, why is he waking me up? Perhaps I am badly wounded; no, I can't be.

There's a strange train of thought going through your mind. There is the moment when you are hit. It's like, I don't fucking believe it. I've been hit. It's just a surprise. You expect to go down in a blaze of glory. Bang, shot dead. Or receive a flesh wound. You don't expect to be maimed and seriously wounded. It isn't something that goes through your mind. You expect to have a bullet clip your shoulder and be able to carry on. You don't expect a very nasty maiming: that nasty blast wound that knocks you over and prevents you from carrying on.

So we are going along, and I am sitting with my knees up and trying to wrap up my hand to stop the bleeding. I then see my rifle mangled in the corner of the vehicle, and realize that actually what I felt being pushed against me was not an RPG, but the force of my rifle going into my chest, and then it slipping down into the vehicle. After what seemed like an age, we eventually got back to the nearest base, which was the Royal Artillery base. As we pulled in, I remember feeling faint, but not too bad. I was determined to get out using my good hand to hold onto the top of the turret, walk down the front of the Warrior and then jump down. I did this, but as I jumped down, some lads appeared with a stretcher and I just flopped back onto the stretcher – at that moment I felt incredibly weak. I thought, I can't walk any further. I didn't think I was going to die, though.

They took me to a room where they were setting up a mass casualties reception area, because a lot of the lads in the back of the Warrior were injured as well. They put my stretcher on a table and the doctor comes up and starts asking me what's wrong. In the vehicle I remember my gunner saying, 'Sir, Sir, is your jaw okay?' And I am thinking, I don't want facial reconstruction, and I don't want to drink through a straw for six months, please. I remember using my tongue to feel all my teeth, going around the inside of my mouth from left to right, top and bottom, expecting it at any moment to stick out through a bloodied hole in my jaw. It never did, thank heavens.

The doctor, who was checking me over, cutting off my blooded clothes, kept asking how my jaw was. But after checking my jaw and my teeth, he saw that there was no problem, and I thought, thank heavens for that. He asked me if I had taken morphine, which I had, and I could tell him where it was hurting. You don't remember the pain particularly, it's an odd thing. Although I remember taking the morphine, I don't remember being in pain (back in the UK a doctor said people don't remember the pain as the body cuts that particular memory out).

I was conscious all the time. I remember my driver, Sergeant Pike, running up as they were cutting my clothes off me and saying, 'Sir, Sir, I've had a quick look and your family jewels [genitals] are all right.' I knew I was all right! I remember asking about the company and the vehicle. I remember thinking, fucking hell, if the company commander has been hit in the first 20 minutes, there must be fucking carnage down there. Fucking hell, they need help. They haven't got their company commander, they need someone to take control. How is the company? How's the wagon? (You get very attached to your vehicle.) Zero Bravo. How is Zero Bravo [my Warrior's call sign]? I talked to the guys afterwards, and they asked why was I so worried about the vehicle? I suppose in my twisted sense it was important to me to know that Zero Bravo was all right. The vehicle looks after you, so you want to make sure it is okay. My Warrior was a brilliant vehicle. A few dents on it, a few bits knocked out of it, but very reliable. They took a lot of punishment and gave it back, which is all you can ask for. They always got you home.

After being checked over and patched up, I was put into a wheeled ambulance on a stretcher, which was bloody dangerous, but which was the quickest way to get up to my own base, the Shatt al-Arab Hotel, where there was a medical squadron. When I arrived, I remember being put on a treatment table and another doctor examined me. It was the doctor that I used to meet at daily battle-group orders, or 'prayers', as it is called. The last time I [had seen] him was across this table, and the next thing I am lying on it, and he is looking pretty shocked, staring down at me, doing his job, fixing me up. Again I was asked about my jaw and I'm thinking, please don't let it be broken. I remember being really tired and saying, 'Doctor, just patch me up, because I want to go back and kill those fucking bastards.' I remember at that point starting to be really angry. I wanted to get back out there, but I also remember saying, 'I am tired of this, just knock me out.' That was one of my last thoughts.

They flew me by helicopter down to the field hospital in Shaibah where they took me into theatre. The Czech surgeon who was attached to the field hospital gave me a five per cent chance of surviving, apparently. At first he couldn't work out what was wrong with me. They were losing me on the operating table. What had happened was that a piece of shrapnel had entered my right shoulder and had gone into my chest, where it had severed a vein. I was bleeding to death. Luckily, he was a chest surgeon by trade and had a feeling that there was a problem with my chest, so he made an incision at the top of my chest and blood spurted out. So they had to open my chest. Unfortunately, they didn't have the correct opening tools, so they had to use a pair of plaster shears to cut. They cut me open, found the piece of shrapnel and got it out before I bled to death. Then they didn't have the correct equipment to seal my chest. He did the best he could, though.

I came round in a strange, morphine-induced state. I remember being told that I was being moved, and that I needed my helmet. I remember thinking, I don't know where my helmet is! Then I thought, I am in fucking hospital, you are the nurse, you find me a fucking helmet. How am I supposed to find my helmet? I am lying here practically unconscious, and you are asking me where my helmet is? I thought, just my luck to have survived an RPG round and I will die in a helicopter crash on the way to Basra air station because I didn't have a helmet on.

The next day they flew me back to Britain. Because my chest wasn't sealed, they couldn't pressurize the aircraft cabin (I was in an intensive care ward in the back of a C-17 transport aircraft). They couldn't fly above 3,000 metres [10,000 ft] and had to keep low throughout the flight, which is very hard work for the pilots. I was hit on a Monday, they kept me overnight in a field hospital, and I flew out on a Tuesday. I arrived in Selly Oak Hospital, Birmingham, UK, on the Wednesday. [9]

[*But David Bradley's personal battles were only just beginning ... see page 232 in 'Casualties of war'.*]

Drew David Larson

In October 2004, Captain Larson was serving with the 82nd Medical Company (Air Ambulance), US Army. He served two tours of duty in Iraq and co-piloted a Black Hawk military helicipter air ambulance during those tours.

One of the missions that stands out in my mind was a Point of Injury (POI), because a lot of times we fly to the actual battle positions that are prepared for us, but we went to what we call POI. We went to right where they were injured. They weren't evacuated out because a vehicle was hit by an improvised explosive device, or IED as we call them nowadays. That IED just demolished his vehicle. I remember flying in and there was a fire, and I'm thinking to myself, 'Is that a Humvee?' I couldn't tell what it was. There was a tire on top of it. The tire had been blown off and went so high it came back down on top of the vehicle. A lot of soldiers in that particular one were killed, but there was one that was still alive, burned [on] maybe 70 per cent of his body, and that soldier got to Fort Sam Houston in Texas, which is one of the premier burn centers in the world, inside 48 hours. He was taken back ... there was no waiting. We took him to our resuscitative surgical suite, that was right there where we were located, and they didn't do anything but intubate him so he could breathe, give him painkillers and put him back on our helicopter. We didn't even stop flying and took him all the way to the echelon that was going to fly him out of Iraq, which is more than we usually fly. We flew farther. We usually go to our main body company, and then they take the soldier from there to the next echelon, but that stop takes 10 minutes, 20 minutes sometimes, and we determined this guy doesn't have that much time. We took him. We bypassed it, worked out the fuel, because we flew with a covert escort, a covert gunship escort, and one covert came up and took over for the other covert, because we had more fuel than they did. He got back to the States inside of 48 hours. I listened to the Vietnam Veterans ... talking about 12, 24, sometimes 48 hours before they could get a medevac altogether, and this guy's back in the States. That's one of those things that sticks out in my mind, because I have pictures ... some of the other soldiers that didn't make it in the back of my helicopter ... I also realize how much we did for that soldier, and how much we're able to do just by our speed and our projection of force, because we spread ourselves out to cover as much ground as possible. That's why I wanted to fly for the Medical Service Corps and not for the Aviation Branch, because I wanted to fly Medical Evacuation.

We are actually fairly protected. I'm armoured below myself, behind me, on my side, and then I'll wear a protected vest. We're pretty well protected. The aircraft itself, the Black Hawk, is just an amazing machine. They've gotten shot up and shot up and shot up and they'll just keep flying. Last year, we took a round in our rotor cuff, and I didn't even know the round had hit the aircraft until the next morning when our Crew Chief was doing an inspection of the aircraft. He came back in and he's like, 'Hey, you know we got a round pulled out of the rotor cuff?'
We didn't even know it hit us.[10]

Ladda 'Tammy' Duckworth

Helicopters are not invulnerable, though. Major Ladda 'Tammy' Duckworth of the Illinois Army National Guard was flying one over Iraq on 12 November 2004. She remembers seeing a ball of flame after an RPG hit her helicopter, and wondering why her legs couldn't work the control pedals.

I found out later the pedals were gone, and so were my legs. I didn't know I was hurt. We had started taking some small-arms fire, and I turned to my co-pilot and said we could be in for some trouble. As the words left my mouth, there was a big fireball at my knees. [Her pilot-in-command, Chief Warrant Officer Dan Milberg, managed to land the helicopter safely.]

That was the last bit of stress that caused me to blackout. This didn't change who I am. I'm an air assault pilot. I'm not about to let some guy who got lucky with an RPG decide how to live my life. For me to sit around and feel sorry for myself, that's going to dishonour my crewmates' efforts to save my life. I'm not about to pass up the second chance [climbing back into a Black Hawk cockpit] I've been given.[11]

Jason Whiteley

Captain Whiteley led Dog Company's 100 men and women who formed
the headquarters support unit for the US Army's 1st Battalion, 8th Cavalry
Regiment. At the end of November 2004, he was with his unit in the south of
Baghdad City. At the time there was an American television crew embedded
with the soldiers of Dog Company, recording the day-to-day reality of life for
US soldiers in Iraq.

What surprises me is how much support [the insurgents] have among the
people. Just right now, for example, we are trying to recruit people to guard
the highway, the main highway that people use to go to work. We have had
a lot of bombs on that road, assassinations (one this morning) and no fewer
than 100 IEDs [improvised explosive devices] in the past month. There
will be 100 men guarding that road. Yesterday someone distributed a flyer
saying, 'If you try and defend this road, you will be killed; your families will
be killed.' Today we were supposed to have 100 people here at 10.00 hours,
but there is no one. One letter was that effective in turning off the entire
security apparatus. Speaks volumes, I think.

Just down the road, they shot the [man who was fixing the road]. We
were fixing that road so that farmers could take their stuff to market, but
they killed him and set his vehicle on fire. Now we can't find anyone else
to go down there and finish the job. I can't find anyone else to finish
the highway. You're not working for the US Army; you're working for your
own government.

There's too much violence. Too much learning needs to be done on
behalf of the populace about how one interacts with the government,
which allows your participation. There is a lot of infrastructure repair that
needs to be done in order for this government to effectively rule. I mean,
the highways have to be rebuilt; [the] power grid needs to work; the fuel
situation is terrible. We have gas lines that are 3.2 km [2 miles] long. These
very simple problems that promote civil unrest have to be solved somehow,
and then people will turn their attention to institutions and how
institutions distribute power, and then they will be successful. But I think
you are talking 10 or 20 years from now, if I were going to bet.

And the Iraqi people do not want democracy. They don't care that the
Americans are here. They just want security. They want to be able to go to
school and come home without getting shot in the face. Kids want to play
in the street without an RPG coming down the road.[12]

Benjamin Morgan

Private First Class Morgan was also a member of Dog Company while it was stationed in south Baghdad in November 2004. The company's role was to protect senior officers from attack as they moved around dangerous areas of Baghdad. The company also helped to rebuild a power station, kept the only oil refinery functioning and the main north–south highway open.

I'm the gunner. They gave me a .50-calibre [machine gun] that can destroy everything the enemy uses – house, vehicles. When I signed up to be a tanker, I never expected to be on an HV [Humvee]. I knew I would be in a combat MOS [military occupational specialty], figured someday war would come. Here I am, doing what I can do.

We try to take as many captive as possible. We have a lot of informants. The population helps us. They call in tips about bombs or weapons; we go out and arrest them. Nine times out of ten we get the guy we are after.

The .50-calibre Browning machine gun fires three rounds every two seconds, big recoil, shakes the vehicle, tears through anything and goes through any armour apart from our tanks, sets it on fire. Nothing like rocking a .50 when going down the road. Thought ceases when you are firing at the enemy. It's all training; it's all instinct. All you are doing is trying to take them before they take you or your friends out. It's your job.

There is a very big risk of VBIEDs [vehicle-borne improvised explosive devices, or car bombs]. One single one is capable of taking out all three HVs, so we don't let anyone near us. We keep them back behind what we call the trigger line. They pass that mark, we fire a warning shot. If they don't back off, engage if you have to; aim for the engine block. A kill radius on a VBIED is sometimes 100 metres [330 ft]. A deadly weapon.[13]

Josue Reyes

Private Reyes was another member of Dog Company stationed in south Baghdad in November 2004.

You don't really think about people actually trying to kill you. You just do it. You see a guy running away, and he has an RPG. It sounds kind of savage, but if you don't kill him, he will kill you. You lose everything; you get numb. Out there, I don't remember feeling tired, hot, cold. I just remember shooting my rifle. I don't remember sounds, moving the truck into place. Afterwards my uniform was soaked in sweat. Then you start feeling really tired, feeling the bruises. You just do it, I guess.

I don't really feel fear. I try not to think about it. More when I go out the gate, I feel anxious, nervous, but not fear ... I feel more a sense of anger sometimes. You see an Iraqi just looking at you, and you wonder why is he looking at you? ... Or a car that won't get out of the way – sometimes you just get angry and want to ram it off the road. Or when you're in traffic and cars don't want to move, so you get out and tell them to move. They don't understand, and sometimes you just want to wring their neck....

People tell me to speak up back home. Here you have to be tough with people; you have to be aggressive. Give an inch, they take a mile. I used to be nice to these people. Some people here think if you are nice to them, it's a weakness. You just have to learn to be tough with people – iron fist, velvet glove. They tell you 'hearts and minds'. Then you got to be mean, then nice. You don't know what to be. On the roads you have to run people off the road. There could be a VBIED or a guy taking his kids to school. So you have to be all things at once. That is the hardest part. You're always thinking, which one are you going to be, a nice guy or a mean guy.[14]

Notes

1   Madison Online, 'A Black Hawk Pilot's View of Operation Iraqi Freedom', 5 November 2008

2   *Armor Magazine*, February 2004

3   *Observer*, 7 March 2004

4   *Washington Post*, 19 March 2006

5   Used with permission from *Stars and Stripes*. © 2005-2009 *Stars and Stripes*

6   Courtesy of Digger History: an unofficial history of the Australian & New Zealand Armed Forces (www.diggerhistory.info)

7   'Ambush at Holy Week' by Sgt. Maj. James Ross (*Air Defense Artillery Magazine*, January-March 2005)

8   BBC News, 29 April 2009

9   Permission of David Bradley

10 Drew Larson Collection (AFC/2001/001/53032), Veterans History Project, American Folklife Center, Library of Congress

11 Used with permission from *Stars and Stripes*. © 2005-2009 *Stars and Stripes*

12 Copyright © 1995-2009 WGBH educational foundation

13 ibid

14 ibid

The Battle of Fallujah

On 8 November 2004, around 15,000 American and Iraqi troops launched Operation Phantom Fury in Fallujah, following weeks of aerial bombardment by US aircraft. The assault was an attempt to regain control of the city from insurgents in preparation for national elections in Iraq scheduled for January 2005. Fallujah had a population of 300,000 civilians, though up to 70 per cent had fled by the time of the ground attack. The resulting battle was among the fiercest combat experienced by the US Marines since the Battle of Hue in 1968 during the Vietnam War.

US officials estimated that up to 3,000 hardcore insurgents, under the command of Abu Musab al-Zarqawi (the head of al-Qaeda in Iraq, killed in a US air strike on 7 June 2006), were in the city when the assault began. Prior to the assault, Prime Minister Ayad Allawi declared a state of emergency across Iraq, except for the Kurdish area of the country, as violence flared in anticipation of the assault on Fallujah. A round-the-clock curfew was imposed on Fallujah, and residents were warned not to carry weapons.

On 9 November 2004, US air strikes destroyed an apartment complex and train station prior to troops pushing into southern Fallujah. By 17.00 hours, American troops in the northeastern part of Fallujah had advanced about 732 metres (800 yds) into the city. Other units in the west of Fallujah faced heavier fire, which slowed their advance.

By 10 November, US military officials announced they controlled 70 per cent of the city. Targeted air strikes continued with laser-guided bombs being used to destroy buildings that contained insurgent forces. American commanders said US troops and Iraqi Security Forces had secured the neighbourhood of Jolan in the northwestern part of the city with less resistance than expected. US forces also saw a lack of resistance by insurgents as they captured and crossed Fallujah's main east–west highway. However, American units in the southwestern neighbourhoods of Resala and Nazal ran into heavy resistance. General George W. Casey, the top American commander in Iraq, had predicted that resistance would be stronger as US troops pushed into the heart of the city – he was right. Some soldiers reported being fired on from mosques and that some women and children were seen firing on soldiers.

By 12 November 2004, Coalition officials asserted that they had achieved control over approximately 80 per cent of the city. Three days later, though, the Americans were still battling isolated pockets of insurgents, mostly on the southern side of Fallujah. By 15 November, 38 US troops, 6 Iraqi soldiers and an estimated 1,200 insurgents had been killed; around 275 US troops were wounded as well.

On 16 November, US military officials announced that American troops had secured Fallujah, but that there were still sporadic instances of insurgent activity. By the end of November, Fallujah had been secured, and the grim battle was finally over.

Sergeant Earl J. Catagnus, Corporal Brad Z. Edison, Lance-Corporal James D. Keeling, Lance-Corporal David A. Moon

This is an extract from 'Infantry Squad Tactics in Military Operations in Urban Terrain During Operation Phantom Fury in Fallujah, Iraq', a paper written by the above-named individuals who were members of a scout-sniper platoon from the 3rd Battalion, 5th US Marine Regiment, following their combat experience in Fallujah in November 2004. Catagnus returned to active duty with the Marine Corp in 2003 to take part in Operation Iraqi Freedom and kept a journal of his experiences. Edison was his right-hand man, helping to shape ideas, while Moon provided input about combat mind-set and tactics, and Keeling offered the expertise of an assaultsman on subjects such as demolitions and door breaching.

The streets are narrow and are generally lined by walls. The walls channelize the squad and do not allow for standard immediate action drills when contact is made. This has not been an issue because the majority of contact is not made in the streets, but in the houses.

The houses are densely packed in blocks. The houses touch or almost touch the adjacent houses to the sides and rear. This enables the insurgents to escape the view of Marine over-watch positions. The houses also are all made of brick with a thick covering of mortar overtop. In almost every house a fragmentation grenade can be used without fragments coming through the walls. Each room can be fragged individually.

The two types of insurgents that the squads are engaging will be labelled the Guerrillas and the Martyrs in this evaluation. The Guerrillas are classified by the following principles:

1. Their purpose is to kill many Marines quickly and then evade. They DO NOT want to die. Dying is an acceptable risk to the Guerrillas, but their intention is to live and fight another day.
2. The tactics used are classic Guerrilla warfare. The Guerrillas will engage Marines only on terrain of their choosing when they have tactical advantage. After contact is made the Guerrillas will disengage and evade.
3. Their evasion route normally is out of sight of Marine over-watch positions.

The Martyrs are classified by the following principles:

1. The Martyrs' purpose is to kill as many Marines as possible before they are killed. Time does not have any significance. The Martyrs want to die by the hands of Marines. The final outcome of their actions results in dead Marines as well as their death.
2. Their tactics directly reflect their purpose. The Martyrs will make fortified fighting positions in houses and wait. Marines will come, they will fight, and they will die in place.

Both the Guerrillas and Martyrs employ the same weapons. The weapons used are mostly small arms, grenades and rocket-propelled grenades (RPGs). The Martyrs have used heavy machine guns and anti-air machine guns, unfortunately, with good effects.

Fixed-wing CAS [close air-support] is an enormous weapon that has great effects on the ground. The major problem with it is the amount of time it takes to get bombs on target. It took entirely too long for bombs to be dropped when Marines were in contact. The minimum safe distance of the ordnance was too great in order for even the block to be isolated and that allowed the enemy to escape countless times. Fixed-wing CAS should be used for deep targets. It should not be used when Marines have isolated the structure and trapped the enemy inside. A tank or CAAT [combined anti-armour team] section can be more effective. Marines do not have to be withdrawn from the cordon.

In contrast to fixed-wing CAS, rotary wing CAS was extremely timely, but the effects on target were not extraordinary. The Hellfire missiles used did not bring down entire structures, but they did do some damage.

By far the best two supporting arms used were tanks and CAAT. Tanks and CAAT were the infantryman's best friend. The battle would have been incredibly bloodier if it hadn't have been for tanks and CAAT. The tanks were able to provide a 120mm direct fire weapon on the spot of any contact within a matter of minutes. The thermal sights were able to pinpoint the exact position of snipers and then effectively neutralize them within seconds. CAAT was able to use its M2 .50-calibre machine guns and Mk 19 grenade launchers to breach as well as destroy buildings where fire was received from. CAAT also helped the squads by clearing the buildings that lined the street in their lane. The infantry should never attack in MOUT [military operations in urban terrain] without tanks or CAAT.

Mortars and artillery proved effective by forcing the enemy to stay in the houses and not allowing the enemy to fight the Marines in the streets.[1]

John F. Sattler

Lieutenant-General John F. Sattler (US) assumed command of the 1 Marine Expeditionary Force on 12 September 2004 and took up the command of the joint and Coalition forces at the second Battle of Fallujah in November 2004.

The battle was fought by a force of about 15,000, including US Marine, Army, Air Force and Navy units, plus British and Iraqi units. The main force swept through the city from north to south, down corridors.

All the streets into the town were sealed by known thugs and murderers. The Iraqi Prime Minister Ayad Allawi determined that Fallujah had to be cleared to keep from exporting terrorism. Thugs could come to Fallujah, get their missions, ammunition and training, and move out to other parts of the country to execute their missions. The only way to stop these thugs was to clean them out.

The task organization was two Marine regimental combat teams [RCT-1 and RCT-7], each with two Marine battalions and an Army battalion. One of the Army battalions led the fight coming down from north to south. We also had six Iraqi battalions that fought very well. In all, we had about 10,000 service members who actually went into Fallujah. We also had about 5,000 other soldiers, airmen and sailors in support.

We did a number of feints from the south and east – made the enemy think he knew from which directions we were going to attack. It worked. Our intelligence showed the large number of road blocks, berms and indirect fire, sniper and fighting positions the enemy established in the south and along the east to defend the city. When the sun rose on the day of the battle, we had all of our forces north of the town, but it was too late for the enemy to shift his positions.

We cleared somewhere between 15,000 and 20,000 buildings, most about three times. After the initial sweep, the thugs got in behind us, so we doubled back to attack south to north and cleared the same buildings again. Then, after we secured Fallujah, we went through every building a final time to make sure we cleaned out all the caches.

In all, we killed about 2,000 enemy thugs and took about 1,200 people into custody in Fallujah II, including a number of non-Iraqis. Every male of military age captured in Fallujah was at least vetted; many went to detention facilities. We were careful how we handled the captured Iraqis – our goal was not to create more enemies in this process.

There were probably between 3,000 and 4,000 enemy in Fallujah II. Before the fight, some of the thug leaders inspired the masses, and then ran as the citizens evacuated.

We didn't bring people back into Fallujah until 23 December. We began opening up the city by little districts, a total of 18, one at a time. This allowed us to get the rubble out and open services in the districts before the people returned.

We fired more than 6,000 artillery rounds during the battle. Every round was in response to enemy action – there were no prep fires before the attack, no harassing and interdicting fires. Every round fired was controlled by a forward observer [FO] or, in some cases, an unmanned aerial vehicle [UAV].

This is how good the artillery was: the ground warriors were willing to call in artillery rounds within 150 metres [164 yds] of themselves. One advantage of urban combat is friendlies can move back one row of buildings or get down below a wall to afford more protection from incoming rounds than in open terrain. We cleared danger close fires at 100 metres [109 yds] for the 81mm mortars, down to 50 metres [55 yds] for the 60mm mortars.

Fallujah II was fought in a city 8 km sq [5 miles sq] with 15,000 to 20,000 buildings that had about 10,000 soldiers, Marines and Iraqis attacking north to south, some swinging east to west and some attacking back from south to north. Aviation, artillery, mortars plus UAVs [unmanned aerial vehicles] had to be deconflicted, with their effects orchestrated, to prevent fratricide, be most effective and limit collateral damage or injuries to non-combatants. All that had to happen in a fog of intense house-to-house combat for ten-plus days in a constrained urban environment.[2]

Michael Erwin

Lieutenant Erwin fought with the 2nd Battalion, 7th Cavalry Regiment, 1st Cavalry Division, US Army, in Fallujah.

After 12 hours of air strikes, our US Army Cavalry Task Force was the first unit to enter the city. Our M1 tanks and Bradley fighting vehicles engaged every enemy strongpoint we came across. Moving deliberately and violently, it took until 10.00 hours the next day to get 3.2 km [2 miles] into the city. Our three companies of armour killed many insurgents that first day, and weakened numerous defensive points in preparation for the Marines' attack.

Our intelligence shop was flying a UAV to determine where the enemy was. Our Raven is a very small plane with cameras, launched by being thrown into the air, then controlled remotely. We flew it for several hours and reported locations of insurgents on roofs and in the streets.

The Marines' mission was to follow the tanks and fight the mujahedeen building to building. In the first day of fighting, the Marines took tough casualties, sometimes battling the enemy hand to hand. Along the way, they found huge caches of weapons, suicide vests, bomb-making factories, torture chambers and slaughterhouses – evidence of the presence of foreign fighters – and more than 650 roadside bombs.

Marines came across several houses rigged to explode. 'Refrigerator bombs' were used as a last-ditch effort against our units after they forced their way into houses. We were very disturbed to find one house with five foreigners with bullets in their head, killed execution-style. Marines also came upon a house where a soldier in the Iraqi National Guard had been shackled to the wall for 11 days and left to die. Some of the torture chambers were extremely gruesome. These insurgents are sick people.

Several houses contained high-tech equipment where the enemy conducted meetings. In Fallujah, they had a military-type planning system. Some of the fighters were wearing body armour and helmets just like ours, and were armed with expensive ... armour-piercing bullets, machine guns and RPGs. Soldiers came across bodies of fighters from Chechnya, Syria, Libya, Saudi Arabia, Jordan and Afghanistan. This was a city full of trained fighters from all over the Middle East, whose mission in life was to kill Americans. It was the wrong city for them in November 2004.[3]

Willard Buhl

Lieutenant-Colonel Buhl was the commanding officer, 3rd Battalion, 1st Marine Regiment (US Marines) in Fallujah.

The fighting experienced in Fallujah was some of the most violent I have observed over my career in the US Marine Corps. We were up against determined adversaries who were well armed, and had prepared defensive fighting positions in complex urban terrain. The 1st Marine Regiment (RCT-1) advanced into the western half of Fallujah with the Thundering Third (3rd Battalion, 5th Marines) and the 2nd Battalion, 7th Cavalry, armed with M1A2 tanks and Bradley infantry fighting vehicles. Marines, sailors and soldiers aggressively attacked the enemy and maintained relentless pressure on him until he was reduced to operating in small isolated groups, hiding in homes.

As I mentioned above, the fighting was extremely fierce. During our advance, we uncovered enemy insurgents from many different neighbouring Arab countries, large quantities of weapons and ordnance of every type, sensitive items such as passports of murdered hostages, torture rooms, propaganda studios, military-skills training centres, etc. As we had long suspected, Fallujah proved to be a massive sanctuary and cache site for the enemies of peace. Indeed, the extent of the ordnance located in this city is such that the city continues to experience daily explosions, as our Explosive Ordnance Disposal teams destroy newly discovered explosives and munitions.[4]

Ryan 'Doc' Scholl

Commander Scholl led Strike Fighter Squadron 81 (VFA-81), US Navy, at Fallujah, and reported that his fliers and their Super Hornet fighters got close enough to the enemy to see the firefights in the streets.

It's a very difficult yet satisfying relationship between a pilot, with a God's-eye view of the city and the fight, and a joint tactical air controller on the ground, who is in the middle of this firefight, and the cross-talk that goes on between you to be able to successfully put a weapon in the right spot and eliminate the fire that he's taking. It takes time, it takes a lot of imagination, it takes patience. But again, I'll fall back on the training and the joint procedures. Those two things combined enable us to be successful.

That (GBU-38 [joint direct attack munition]) reduces our probability of damaging surrounding areas. [It allows fliers to preserve] the walls of the houses that are right next door to it. One of the rules of engagement is positive target ID [identification]. We have to have that. We have to see what we're going after.[5]

Mike Regner

Colonel Regner was the operations officer for the 1st Marine Expeditionary Force (US Marines) in Fallujah.

There would be certain pockets of resistance, as the roads and the alleyways would not allow armoured or mechanized vehicles. And in those city blocks [that] might have had alleys of 1 metre [3 ft] wide, it was an individual fight, man to man: spider holes where guys would pop out of; after a Marine would go by it or a soldier would go by it, they'd pop out and attempt to shoot the Marine in the legs or in the back. So it became a very tenuous fight, that if you weren't streetwise – and you got streetwise about an hour into this operation – you'd find yourself a casualty.[6]

Michael Burgoyne

Captain Burgoyne was the commander of Battery A, 3rd Battalion, 82nd Field Artillery, 2nd Brigade Combat Team, 1st Cavalry Division, nicknamed Gator Battery. The battery's hardware comprised Paladin 155mm howitzers.

The troops on the ground give us exact coordinates and requested support, and we will fire at those coordinates and hopefully destroy the enemy they are engaging. We destroyed an enemy command-and-control headquarters; we've killed enemy snipers, bunkers, mortar teams, enemy squads: just about anything we were called upon. There was a Marine platoon that was ambushed by about 70 insurgents. The enemy was dug in at a trench line, and the Marines were engaged pretty heavily. They called in support and we disengaged the enemy. Later on, Marines came up to our firing line and thanked my guys for saving the lives of the platoon.[7]

Brian Drinkwine

Lieutenant-Colonel Drinkwine was a battalion commander with the 82nd Airborne Division, US Army. He served in Iraq in 2003–4 and was also deployed to Afghanistan in support of the 2004 national elections as part of Operation Enduring Freedom. At the beginning of 2010, Colonel Drinkwine was a commander of the 4th Brigade Combat Team, 82nd Airborne Division. He and the men and women of Task Force Fury were responsible for the training and mentoring of Afghan security forces in the southern and western parts of Afghanistan.

Fallujah is the centre point of the war. You got to be steely-eyed out there. There are good people down there and in the midst of them are a handful of evildoers. We have told the local leaders we know that there are evildoers. But we are not here to spray up the town. We say, 'You shoot an RPG, you can expect some steely-eyed killers who will kill or capture you.'[8]

Aubrey McDade, Jr

Sergeant McDade of the 1st Platoon, Company B, 1st Battalion, 8th Marine Regiment (US Marines) earned the Navy Cross for his bravery in Fallujah on 11 November 2004. He is the 15th US Marine to date to receive the Navy Cross for actions in the 'War on Terror'. Aubrey is currently a drill instructor with Charlie Company, 1st Recruit Training Battalion.

[The insurgents] had night-vision goggles or something, because they had a bead on me. They started firing into the bushes. It was so dry, the bushes caught on fire on top. [McDade made it unharmed to Lance-Corporal Andrew Russell, whose leg had nearly been severed by machine-gun fire.] I kept on the flak jacket and the Kevlar (helmet) and my weapon. I had heavier stuff, and a pack, and a magazine of extra ammo. The gear will protect you, to a point, but it wasn't going to be able to stop all the stuff they were sending down-range. So, I just took it off and hoped that if I moved fast enough, they wouldn't be able to hit me. [Once he had Russell slung across his body, he fell back; the insurgents followed.] The rounds were getting real close to me, so I just tossed Russell as far as I could and just [lay] down in the road. When it lightened up, I dragged him the rest of the way to the CCP [casualty collection point].[9]

Major Zarnik

Air Force KC-135R Tanker Aircraft Commander Zarnik, United States Air Force Reserve, recorded his thoughts about retrieving and repatriating the first 22 American military troops to die in the Battle of Fallujah in November 2004.

I thought that I was prepared for the acceptance of these men until we landed at Kuwait International. I taxied the jet over to a staging area where the honour guard was waiting to load our soldiers. I stopped the jet and the entire crew was required to stay onboard. We opened the cargo door and, according to procedure, I had the crew line up in the back of the aircraft in formation and stand at attention. As the cargo loader brought up the first pallet of caskets, I ordered the crew to 'Present Arms'. Normally, we would snap a salute at this command. However, when you are dealing with a fallen soldier, the salute is a slow, three-second pace to position. As I stood there and finally saw the first four of 22 caskets draped with the American flags, the reality had hit me. As the Marine Corps honour guard delivered the first pallet on board, I then ordered the crew to 'Order Arms', where they rendered an equally slow three-second return to the attention position. I then commanded the crew to assume an at-ease position and directed them to properly place the pallet. The protocol requires that the caskets are to be loaded so when it comes time to exit the aircraft, they will go head first. We did this same procedure for each and every pallet until we could not fit any more.

I felt a deep pit in my stomach when there were more caskets to be brought home and that they would have to wait for the next jet to come through. I tried to do everything in my power to bring more home, but I had no more space on board. When we were finally loaded … and fuelled for the trip back to England, a Marine Corps colonel from 1st Battalion came on board our jet in order to talk to us. I gathered the crew to listen to him and his words of wisdom. He introduced himself and said that it is the motto of the Marines to leave no man behind and it makes their job easier knowing that there were men like us to help them complete this task. He was very grateful for our help and the strings that we were pulling in order to get this mission done in the most expeditious manner possible. He then said, 'Major Zarnik, these are my Marines and I am giving them to you. Please take great care of them, as I know you will.'

I responded with telling him that they are my highest priority, and that although this was one of the saddest days of my life, we are all up for the challenge and will go above and beyond to take care of your Marines. '*Semper Fi*, Sir.' [*Semper Fi* – 'Always faithful' has been the Marine Corps motto since 1883. Likewise the response that follows.] A smile came on his face and he responded with a loud and thunderous, '*Ooo Rah.*'

He then asked me to please pass along to the families that these men were extremely brave and had made the ultimate sacrifice for their country and that we appreciate and empathize with what they are going through at this time of their grievance. With that, he departed the jet and we were on our way to England.

I had a lot of time to think about the men that I had the privilege to carry. I had a chance to read the manifest on each and every one of them. I read about their religious preferences, their marital status, the injuries that were their cause of death. All of them were under the age of 27, with most in the 18–24 range. Most of them had wives and children. They had all been killed by an IED … Mostly fatal head injuries and injuries to the chest area. I could not even imagine the bravery that they must have displayed and the agony suffered in this God-forsaken war. My respect and admiration for these men and what they are doing to help others in a foreign land is beyond calculation …

The stop in Mildenhall was uneventful, and then we pressed on to Dover where we would meet the receiving Marine Corps honour guard. When we arrived, we applied the same procedures in reverse. The head of each casket was to come out first. This was a sign of respect rather than defeat. As the honour guard carried each and every American flag-covered casket off the jet, they delivered them to waiting families with military hearses. I was extremely impressed with how diligent the honour guard had performed the seemingly endless task of delivering each of the caskets to the families without fail and with precision. There was not a dry eye on our crew or in the crowd. The Chaplain then said a prayer, followed by a speech from Lieutenant-Colonel Klaus of the 2nd Battalion. In his speech, he also reiterated similar condolences to the families as the colonel from the 1st Battalion back in Kuwait.

I then went out to speak with the families as I felt it was my duty to help console them in this difficult time. I wanted to make sure that they did not feel abandoned, and more than that, appreciated for their ultimate sacrifice. It was the most difficult thing that I have ever done in my life. I listened to the stories of each and every one that I had come in contact with, and they all displayed a sense of pride during an obviously difficult time. The Marine Corps had obviously prepared their families well for this potential outcome.

So, why do I write this story to you all? I just wanted to put a little personal attention to the numbers that you hear about and see in the media. It is almost like we are desensitized by the 'numbers' of our fallen comrades coming out of Iraq. I heard one commentator say that 'it is just a number'. Are you kidding me? These are our American soldiers, not numbers![10]

Notes

1   Courtesy of Edward S. Marek, Lt. Col., USAF (Ret.) and his excellent website www.talkingproud.us
2   *Second Battle of Fallujah – urban operations in a new kind of war* by General John F Sattler © 2006 US Field Artillery Association
3   Courtesy of Free Republic (www.freerepublic.com)
4   Courtesy of Edward S. Marek
5   ibid
6   ibid
7   ibid
8   ibid
9   Used with permission from *Stars and Stripes.* © 2005–2009 *Stars and Stripes*
10   Courtesy of Edward S. Marek

A long, hard slog

As 2005 began, the number of attacks against Coalition forces and Iraqi civilians increased. Insurgent attacks also became more sophisticated and deadly, as car bombs and suicide bombers began to take their toll. The major bombing attacks of 2005 included: 114 killed in a suicide car bombing against jobseekers in Hillah (28 February); 90 dead when a suicide bomber detonated a fuel tanker in Musayyib (16 August); 182 fatalities as a result of a suicide car bomber targeting labourers in Baghdad (14 September); and 80 dead in multiple bombings in Baghdad and two Khanaqin mosques (18 November).

The situation worsened in 2006 as sectarian violence threatened to tear the country apart. Attacks against Coalition forces and Iraqi units were already high, especially in the Sunni triangle (the area west of Baghdad, around the town of Fallujah), but the bombing of a Shi'a mosque in Samarra in February 2006 triggered fierce round of sectarian violence. Civilian casualties rocketed as Islamic radicals sought to create a 'chain of retaliation' that would engulf the country.

In response, US President George W. Bush, following consultation with the Iraqi government, announced a new strategy in January 2007. Additional troops would be sent to Iraq and another carrier strike group would be deployed to the Middle East. The Iraq troop surge was announced by President Bush on 10 January 2007.

The troop surge was designed to regain control of some regions that were de facto controlled by insurgents. It was concentrated in Baghdad and the western province of Anbar – the most violent parts of the country. By June 2007, there were 160,000 American troops in Iraq, and many were 'embedded' within Iraqi units in order to assist them in suppressing insurgent activity in the two regions. Side by side with the military effort were construction efforts to rebuild the country's infrastructure, and initiatives to encourage political progress between rival groups. Most important was the need to protect the Iraqi civilian population.

There is no doubt that the surge was successful. Under the direction of General David H. Petraeus, the rate of violence in Iraq had been reduced by 80 per cent by the end of 2008. Part of the reason for this reduction was the increase in the size of the Iraqi security forces, which grew by 200,000 between 2005 and 2007. By the middle of 2008, the Iraqi Army numbered 180,000 troops. In mid-2009, there were still 134,000 American troops in Iraq.

Joe Haman

Corporal Joe Haman, 3rd Platoon, Kilo Company, 3rd Battalion, 1st Marine Regiment, fought at Haditha in November 2005. On 4 October 2005, the US 2nd Marine Division launched Operation Bawwabatu Annaher (River Gate) in the cities of Haditha, Haqlaniyah and Barwana. Some 2,500 Marines, soldiers and sailors from Regimental Combat Team 2, plus Iraqi security force soldiers, participated in the operation. The aim was to deny al-Qaeda in Iraq the ability to operate in the three Euphrates River Valley cities and to free the local citizens from the insurgents' campaign of murder and intimidation.

As soon as it [IED] went off, Sergeant (later Staff Sergeant) Raphael – our squad leader – told us to gear up and stand by. Our squad was on React because we already had another squad on patrol from the COP [command observation post].

Air – helos – saw insurgents that split into groups. One of the groups ran into another house in a palm grove. Air picked them up going in. Then one of the helos shot two missiles into the house. It blew out the roof, put a big hole in the roof; smoke was coming out. We were told to go into a house by a blue car. The car was parked between two houses. We didn't know which house was the right one.

The point man kicked in the door. Lance-Corporal Blankenship was on point. Corporal Bautista, my fire-team leader, told us to stack up [a tightly grouped combat formation] and go in. I was the second man to the door. I wanted to throw a frag [fragmentation grenade]. I had never thrown a frag into a house before.

Our squad leader, Sergeant Raphael, told us to wait for the smoke to clear, but our adrenalin was pumped up so we just rushed in. We couldn't see anything, so we turned our flashlights on. Nobody was in the house, the house was clear. We were at the wrong house. Somebody said it was the house to the southwest – catty-corner. Lieutenant Zall said to clear the other house, but don't frag it this time. Blankenship tried to kick the door down. It knocked him down, he couldn't do it. So Lance-Corporal Ghent bashed into it a couple of times. He couldn't do it either.

Everybody was laughing. The third time he [Ghent] knocked it in and fell down. I jumped over him. I saw a room to the right and one way out in the back corner. The door was almost closed. Then a grenade came out the door. It bounced off my foot and went off. I don't remember anything after that for a while. I was hit but I didn't know it. Somehow I was inside the room to my right. I don't know how I got there. Bautista called my name. I guess I woke up. I got up and started shooting at the door. We backed out of the house. It was one of the lessons we learned at Fallujah. When there is somebody inside, just back out and call in air strikes.

Lance-Corporal Garcia and Lance-Corporal Vetor went to the side of the house. I saw them so I went with them. I was still real groggy. It was an American grenade and it really rang my bell. I thought I was okay. Then Vetor looked back and yelled, 'Grenade!' One blew up behind me. I got hit in my right back triceps and in the back shoulder. I knew it had hit and it burned a little. It didn't hurt until hours later. Then the hole in my underarm swelled up as big as a golf ball and I was bleeding out of it. Lieutenant Zall got hit real bad. Zall got hit in the legs. He was evacuated and 'Doc', our [US Navy Medical] Corpsmen, was wounded. Lance-Corporal Garcia got hit as well.

Vetor checked Garcia and me and said we were both good. Then an AK burst came in and sprayed in front of us in an arc. We thought it came out of the window, so we started lighting up this window. Then we heard an explosion go off, maybe on top of the roof.

We kept yelling for Lance-Corporal Ghent, Corporal Bautista and Sergeant Raphael. We couldn't get a response from them. We could see the helos flying around. We didn't want to get a rocket. We didn't know where anyone was. Vetor said to pop the white flare to let them know where we were. Somebody started lighting up the house with the two-forty [M-240G machine gun]. We popped a red star cluster (pop-up flare). Then Bautista popped a green flare.

He [Vetor] took off running first. I went second, and then Garcia came. We wanted to run across the road to where there was some cover. Then a seven-tonner (cargo truck) or two pulled up and Marines started popping out. As soon as they saw us, Sergeant Raphael [on the roof of the house next door to the insurgents] started yelling for cover fire.

We regrouped and found out where everybody was. We saw the docs putting Lieutenant Zall and our Doc into either a seven-tonner or Humvee to medevac out. Then we ran back to a house across the street from the one the insurgents were throwing grenades from.

Marines went to the top of the roof on the house and started shooting M-203 grenades at the insurgents. I stayed inside the house with Lance-Corporal Stefinitis, watching over the civilians who lived there. There were eight people. We got them all in one room while everybody else went on the roof to engage. I smoked a cigarette. I still didn't know [how bad] I was hit. Stefinitis was bleeding from grenade hits to his nose and face.

Grenades were flying all over the place. I think everyone on the roof got wounded. I know we had nine guys wounded in my squad. From then everything went to shit. We called for air. I stayed downstairs....

Then we all took off, jumped about a four-foot wall, ran down to the palm grove, climbed the hill and went back to the house we used for the COP and waited for the air to hit. We waited 15 to 20 minutes for air to get there. I think they dropped two 500-pounders [227 kg], but it could have been 1,000-pounders [454 kg]. They blew the house all to hell.[1]

Charity Trueblood

On 5 December 2005, Airman 1st Class Trueblood, 732nd Expeditionary Logistics Squadron, was driving an up-armoured Humvee near the middle of a 30-vehicle convoy. Just outside Balad, the lead vehicle spotted what looked like a roadside bomb. As the vehicles slowed to examine the bomb, the convoy was ambushed. Trueblood's actions in the battle won her the US Army Bronze Star.

You just go. As soon as the attack starts, you return fire and get out of their range. I moved the [Humvee] towards the side of fire to block the unarmoured ones, but we all started moving. We wanted to get out of there so no one would get hurt in the fire, but you can't drive too fast or stop too fast when someone is holding onto the hood. You have to be pretty careful.

[Once out of the flames' reach, Trueblood jumped out of the car with the first-aid kit to treat the contractor.] He had a through-and-through gunshot wound. It entered in his right arm, completely missed bone and came out between his shoulder blade and his spine. When we got back, the guys asked what I did to the Humvee, because there was blood all over it.

You react. When something happens, at least in my case, you react, and you deal with it later.[2]

David Swan

In 2005, some 400 Vermont National Guardsmen and women were deployed to Iraq as part of Task Force Saber. Most went to Ramadi, the capital of Anbar Province, at the time one of the most dangerous parts of the country. David Swan commanded 27 men as part of Task Force Saber, and his unit patrolled in the Tamim area of Iraq. Task Force Saber set up observation posts and checkpoints along the roads near the base in Ramadi and was responsible for keeping the roads clear of roadside bombs. These checkpoints sometimes came under fire from insurgents. The task force was also responsible for combat operations, counter-insurgency operations and training the Iraqi Army and police.

The gun trucks were roving through the town. They came into an ambush: probably seven insurgents that ambushed them with heavy machine-gun fire. [T]he squad leader started manoeuvring his men. We returned fire and ended up killing two insurgents at that point. And then we started doing house searches after that to see if we could get any more insurgents.

The houses were your typical Third World kind of houses. Some people had nice furniture. Some people would have just a mattress on the floor. A lot of people were driving around in Mercedes, but they wouldn't have anything in the house.

I feared more for my men's sake than I did for my own sake. That was the hardest part for me, because I was in command of the 27 guys there and it was pretty hard – you just never knew what was going to happen next, five minutes from now or a day from now.

I had one soldier that was severely wounded. He lost an eye and the pinkie on one hand. And he had a leg injury. We had a lot of injuries due to the IEDs. When the IEDs would impact, a lot of guys would suffer concussions.

I think that there's some things that unless you were there, you're not going to understand. And you won't be able to discuss, you know, things that happen over there or people that didn't actually come home with us – people from my company that didn't come home. You know, that's a very difficult situation to deal with.

I personally don't think I have too many mental issues. But I know that you just can't do a year in combat and expect to come home after seeing so many traumatic events, life-altering events that aren't normal to everyday life, and to not be scarred in some way.[3]

Damon Rooney

Twenty-year-old Damon Rooney was a also member of Task Force Saber, trained to load ammunition into the guns mounted on tanks.

At first, it was definitely overwhelming, not so much that I didn't know what to do in the seat, but just knowing that this is the real thing. You know, the last time I'd sat in the gunner's seat before coming to Shelby [Camp Shelby, Mississippi] was during my basic training. I sat there. I touched off a main gun round, okay, you get out of the seat, next guy gets in. And now, you know, I was in the thick of it.

We had to go out one night – we were escorting the Iraqi security forces, training them up, and Catamount Company called us up, saying we need to run a snap raid. They had a high-value target come up through intelligence, and you know he's in this house right now, we need to get him. And this was at night, so I had the thermal-imaging system on the tank on, which picks up heat signatures. I noticed a pack of dogs running across the road, and obviously it was hard to tell they were dogs because at that distance, they just look like little specks. But I noticed one of the dogs was climbing up the side of a building. And I told my tank commander, 'You want to have a look at this? There's a guy up on the roof.' He was like, 'Well, how do you know it's a guy?' and I was like, 'Well, I never saw a dog climb a roof.'

He was overlooking right where they were conducting the snap raid in a known IED location. Judging by the fact that the Iraqi people had a curfew, they had to be [insurgents]. They could be in and around their houses, but you weren't supposed to be on the roof past 22.00 hours at night, and this was at 02.00 hours in the morning.

And so we got the clear to engage him, we deemed him as a threat. We had this 50-calibre machine gun with a special mount ... there's a lot of work you have to go through, properly lining it up with the sights and inputting ballistic solutions into the tank's computer to use it correctly. And as I got the clear, you know, 'Storm 2 (that was my call sign), you have the clearance to shoot.' I was like, this is it; this is the real thing. This is my proving point to say, could I actually kill a man? And I ranged and engaged the target, effectively neutralizing the threat, and that was a big moment for me. It was the first time I was put in that situation.

More would come later, but I knew that I could do the job that I had to do over there. I don't look upon it in a bad way, I think it's sad, you know, that people had to die, but at the same time, I didn't do it just to kill them. I was doing it to protect the lives of other soldiers, you know, my friends, guys that I trained with, guys that I knew. And, I do think about it often.[4]

Jordan Paquette

As a member of Task Force Saber, Jordan Paquette spent a year patrolling the streets of Ramadi, Iraq. At this time the insurgents tended to employ hit-and-run tactics. Firefights could last from 10 seconds to 10 minutes, day and night. It was difficult to know what each day woulde bring, resulting in constant strain for Coalition troops on the ground.

Ramadi is, I haven't really seen much of other parts of Iraq, but from what I've seen, it's pretty well developed for what they have. It's a small village, a lot of sheep herding. I was surprised at how civilized it was, as far as how they have their towns set up … actually I was kind of impressed. I thought it would be more mud huts and stuff like that, but some of the buildings were actually, inside (we did raids and stuff like that), very impressive, multiple-story houses and very elegant work done inside the building. So it was surprisingly very nice.

At the beginning, they [the locals] were kind of shy, and didn't really know how to accept us as military soldiers, but after a while they would come outside. You [could] kind of tell that they would accept us, because they'd come outside, and they'd have their children play outside. That's a good sign that they respect you, because if their children are outside, they feel safe enough to let their children play. So that made us feel good. We have pictures with some of the kids, you know, holding their thumbs up, which is really good, letting us know that they support what's going on.

[A]s far as the military is concerned, it's one of the most dangerous places to be. At one time, I was on one of the OPs [observation posts] and a sniper shot ended up hitting the ground about 1.5 metres [5 feet] from me. At that point, I was like, okay, it's real now. We're not playing anymore, it's real.

[B]efore I left [for Iraq], I know a lot of things I took for granted. My parents are always going to be there; my sisters are always going to be there. And … you come over here and they're not there. It's that one [thing] you really miss and you really want to have, but just remember that it's the small things that matter. The small things: telling your family that you do care and you love them, because there may be one day where that round that hits 1.5 metres [5 feet] from you ends up tagging you and you won't be able to come home.[5]

J. J. Bixby

Bixby, an infantryman with Task Force Saber, patrolled the streets of a town in Anbar Province. In 2006 Anbar had more attacks per day than any other province in Iraq. A US Marine intelligence report at the time declared the prvince to be lost to al-Qaeda. In September 2008, however, the US military turned over control of Anbar Province to the Iraqi government

We had our body armour, which had ceramic plates in the front and back. We carried side protectors, which were two more ceramic plates on the side, Kevlar helmet, and seven magazines for your M16. I carried four smoke grenades, stun grenade; you had a medical kit that you carried with you, extra ammo and pistol ammo. Then you carried your rifle itself, your side arm (your pistol), and by that time, you're well loaded-up and it's kind of hard to move. Actually, I think I was able to find a scale over there, and when I stepped onto the scale, with my full combat load and kit, I was pushing about 160 kg [350 lb].

We were in the Tamim area, which is just outside of Ramadi. Most of Tamim itself was really dense, urban-type structures. Short alleyways, short roads and cross-streets, until you got out to where there was more open roads and stuff.

It was pretty active. It was actually pretty heavily active. It was right in Anbar Province, which is right by the last sector out there in the west that's seen the most activity right now. I don't think there was a single day that went by that something didn't happen. We'd usually take small-arms fire, maybe sniper fire, IEDs.

We would typically try to get out and interact with the people that lived right in that area. Tried to figure out what was going on; if they had seen the insurgency operating in the area when we weren't there. It got to the point where you got to know people in certain areas, you could tell when things were normal, when things weren't normal, and there were definitely areas where you just didn't dismount at all, because it was such a hot area.

You'd get used to the amount of people that would be outside, outside by their shops or their stores, or the people walking on the street or sitting outside on the doorstep. And then a few hours later, you may come back by through there, and it's deserted. There's nobody near anywhere, the streets are quiet. Nobody's outside; that was usually a sign. The hairs would go up on the back of your neck that something's not right here.[6]

Lara Yacus Chapman

Captain Lara Chapman, US Army, served in Iraq between January and December 2006. When she wrote this account she was a First Lieutenant.

One particularly rewarding job I had was being the officer in charge at the main gate to Camp Taji [located about 19 km (12 miles) northwest of Baghdad]. My unit was responsible for screening all of the traffic entering the base – pedestrians and vehicles, US and Iraqi.

Being at times the only female US soldier at the gate, it often fell to me to search Iraqi females for contraband and suicide-bomb vests. It was a little scary the first few times because their clothes are loose and flowing, and hiding explosives on women is a known terrorist tactic. The first woman I had to search was crying profusely because her husband had been detained for suspected insurgent activity. She was coming to the base to find out what happened to him. She had two young children with her: a dirty but adorable little girl about three years old, and a boy of about six.

They were sweet, innocent children, and a little shy to be around an American soldier – and a female one at that. I smiled and waved to them, and the little girl soon decided she could stop hiding behind her mother. The next time they came through the gate, the children remembered me and were full of smiles. I always made sure to bring out bubbles or little toys for the kids. She was just an average Iraqi woman who was concerned about her family. Without her husband at home working, she and her children were at risk and didn't have the income they needed. I really felt for her, but at the same time, it was sobering. I had no idea what her husband had done. Had he been involved in the deaths of soldiers that I knew?[7]

Andrew A. 'Drew' Fuller

Captain Fuller, US Army Special Forces, was in Iraq from September 2006 until November 2007. His account appeared in the *University of Virginia Magazine*.

I spent 15 months on a military transition team, living and working with an Iraqi Army battalion to help train them: a mission that I believe is the best exit strategy for the US. It was definitely an eye-opening experience. Although most of the soldiers we worked with had good intentions, we knew that some of them were actually insurgents who were working for both sides. For them, it's just economics. They'll work for whoever is paying more that day, be it the government or the insurgency. Pretty soon we learned to use that to our advantage: when the Iraqis were scared to be in a particular area, we knew that there was a good chance an attack was coming.

I learned that lesson my second night in Iraq. I was riding in a Humvee on a mission in northern Iraq, and there was an Iraqi Army Humvee in front of us. All of a sudden, it stopped and the driver refused to go any further, saying that the area was too dangerous. We had to keep moving, so my Humvee took the lead. A few minutes later we were hit by a roadside bomb and attacked from an adjacent building with rocket-propelled grenades and AK-47 fire.

We did what we were trained to do: we fired back, cleared the building that the ambush came from and captured our attackers. They ended up being al-Qaeda-linked foreign fighters – not even Iraqi. Luckily, none of us was injured, but I thought to myself, 'Man, this is going to be a long deployment.'[8]

Alex Horton

Specialist Horton served for 15 months in Iraq as an infantryman with the US Army's 3rd Stryker Brigade, 2nd Infantry Division, in the cities of Mosul, Baghdad and Baqubah.

6 May [2007] began for us like so many days before it, in the pre-dawn shadows of Baqubah. I had just returned from leave and was not too anxious to start patrolling again, with ten months of combat behind me and five left to push through. We searched houses, courtyards, roofs, trash piles and warm bodies throughout the morning. Our squad was designated to take a roof to overwatch other squads manoeuvring. On the way to the trucks to grab cases of water, we heard the first reports of Alpha Company having hit an IED way down on Trash Alley, the road so dangerous we were usually barred from driving on it at all. We heard at least one man was

dead, and they were trying to get to any survivors.

I was left behind on the Stryker [eight-wheeled armoured personnel carrier] to watch the rear as my squad moved to their building. Throughout the day we kept hearing reports about Alpha Company's loss. The number kept climbing. During the midday heat, the final tally came in. Six men were killed, along with a Russian reporter. Only the driver survived …

When I read about the six soldiers killed in the house explosion in Diyala a few days ago, I knew immediately it was the Stryker unit from Germany that had replaced us. It was at the beginning of a new offensive to clear out the remaining insurgents after last summer's Operation Arrowhead Ripper [involving 10,000 US and Iraqi troops – June to August 2007]. This attack underscored a vital truth: despite a countrywide decline in attacks, Diyala remains one of the most dangerous areas for American soldiers in which to operate.

For an area that contains 40 per cent of the violence of Iraq, it's been quietly pushed aside by the media in favour of Baghdad and Anbar provinces. One look, however, shows a dynamic history of a region that became an insurgent safe haven two years ago and remains one today. Once a popular retreat for Ba'ath Party officials, Diyala is at the epicentre of a flow of Sunni Iraqis who moved out of Baghdad, some 56 km [35 miles] to the southwest. It houses a mix of both Shi'a and Sunni sects, but the provincial government is predominately Shi'a. It shares its borders with Iran to the east and Kurdistan to the north, creating a microcosm referred to as 'little Iraq'. What sets it apart from the deserts and towns on the outskirts of the province is the valley that contains dense palm groves that flourish on either side of the Diyala River.

The treetops provide natural concealment from unmanned drones and attack helicopters. The roads are narrow and unpaved, creating logistical problems for giant American vehicles. The insurgents quickly found the environment suitable for their operations and began pouring into Diyala in 2006, overwhelming the small task force from 1st Cavalry. Al-Qaeda in Mesopotamia declared Baqubah their capital in Iraq. During the surge's first few months in 2007, even more Sunni insurgents were drawn to Diyala, going where we weren't. In March, my Stryker battalion was sent to put out the fire that had been raging since the year before, as all eyes were on Baghdad. For months we fought daily to retake the neighbourhoods of Baqubah, one by one, until reinforcements from our brigade arrived to take part in the first major offensive of the surge.

Operation Arrowhead Ripper commenced in late June with the US Air

Force pounding wired houses with 227 kg [500 lb] bombs. We had seen these houses before and took heed of the enemy's adaptability. They hit us with IEDs, so we got out and walked. In response, they placed IEDs in houses, where vehicles couldn't protect us. Three men in our brigade were killed when a house they were searching came down on top of them following an explosion. It's a deadly tactic that isn't new, but remains very dangerous when Coalition forces conduct searches in hundreds of homes in a renewed effort to clamp down on insurgents and weapons coming into the area. Diyala was the forgotten fight of 2007.

He was walking down the street in the middle of the night, AK-47 in tow, without a care about curfews or carrying an automatic assault rifle in the open, strolling along like it was the most natural thing in the world. He didn't likely hear the Americans infiltrating into the city, walking from a mile [1.6 km] away as to not alert anyone with the hum of Strykers [armoured vehicles] growing louder and more ominous. He certainly didn't hear the sizzling crack that ended his life a split second before he hit the ground in a tangled mess of limbs; the only thing uttered posthumously about him said over static radio waves: 'One enemy KIA.'

It had only been 20 minutes into Operation Arrowhead Ripper, the first large-scale ground offensive in Iraq after the surge, and already one insurgent was leaking his fluids into the street. We expected a final stand, a decisive battle, a moment of reckoning where hopefully our dead wouldn't stack as high as the enemy['s]. Our battalion had been holding Baqubah for three months, sustaining high casualties in a town that al-Qaeda declared their central hub in Iraq. Holding it with us was 3rd Brigade of 1st Cavalry, a unit that was taking a considerable amount of casualties since they had arrived several months prior. We would fall under their command, but would soon take control of the area, giving them a rest by giving them the job of securing main roads in and out of town. A company of Cavalry Strykers was with us for the same purpose, and our snipers and scouts were inflicting their fair share of enemy deaths with their long scopes and small teams, pairing with a mortar platoon at times. For regular infantry, there were two companies, Alpha and Bravo. In just a couple months, our numbers dwindled so drastically that we could combine both companies to form a proper textbook infantry company.

Daily firefights and ordnance falling from the sky kept the routine and mundane at bay. We held several of the neighbourhoods on the east side, creating combat outposts continually manned by rotating platoons within the company. Two smaller, dangerous neighbourhoods stood on the west side, Mufrek and Khatoon. Mufrek was the neighbourhood Chevy died in on our first day, and ten days later (and a few blocks away) was the scene of a vicious IED that took several limbs from the Stryker occupants and left a burning hull. West of the Diyala River was the bad side of a bad town that we cleared and re-cleared, but never held permanently. There simply weren't enough men to control the entire city with the shrinking manpower we had.

Operation Arrowhead Ripper was the overdue answer of desperate calls for reinforcement. In mid-June our sister battalion, 1/23, along with a company of 82nd Airborne and another out of Hawaii, arrived at FOB [forward operating base] Warhorse. We were grateful about their arrival, but not the growing lines at the internet and chow hall. The offensive was going to be huge, with air assaults and ground infiltration happening in the middle of the night. It would last for weeks, with the full support of helicopter gunships and aircraft dropping bunker busters. There was a new rocket system called a Glimmer that we had never heard of being used, where recent digging and bombs were identified in the road by helicopters or satellites, or some damn thing. Rockets would then fire straight down, creating a huge crater and destroying any IED in its wake.

With Baqubah's bloody past, it was expected that this offensive was going to rival Fallujah in terms of destruction and casualties. The insurgents knew it was coming and had ample time to prepare their deep-buried IEDs that had been lying in wait for months for just one American convoy to pass, justifying countless hours of waiting. Gates leading to courtyards were locked and chained shut so that no one could take cover behind a wall as machine guns lay in ambush, firing volleys down the avenue. As the insurgents prepared, we prepared. Rifle magazines and belts of machine-gun ammo were changed out with armour-piercing rounds to penetrate ceramic plates and make sure anyone shot would be down for the count. We had found countless vests in caches and on the bodies of insurgents killed, making us aware of how well they protected themselves. Nearly everyone was filling backpacks with extra ammo, extra grenades, shotgun rounds, crowbars, bolt-cutters, smoke grenades, batteries, knives and stickers used to identify cleared houses. We were cleaning our weapons, checking sights for accuracy and putting fresh batteries in night-vision goggles. We were calling and emailing family and friends, letting them know we'd be gone for a while, and that we loved them.

Weighed down with armour and extra equipment, we set out in the early hours of 19 June. The task force was starting in the south and clearing up in unison as one unit. We had the privilege of clearing Khatoon, the toughest nut to crack and our most unfamiliar area. Though 1/23 had their whole battalion, we were given the neighbourhood because of experience. They'd take Mufrek, the smallest section of the west side. We pulled up along a main road and filtered out of the Strykers and into the black abyss of a huge field. There was a road running parallel to us that we didn't take out of concern for small IEDs targeting dismounts. Instead we had chosen the less-beaten path, a garbage- and sewage-strewn open area dotted with wild chickens pecking the trash at their feet. We would find, clear and hold a tall building until daybreak and begin clearing in the morning sun.

Before getting there, our first platoon spotted a man walking down the street with an AK-47 slung over his shoulder. Muffled shots filled the air, no louder than the tin cans sent flying with awkward kicks from fumbling soldiers in the darkness, tink-tinking against rusted scrap metal. Over the company radio, the report came in. One enemy KIA. Well, shit. Now they know we've arrived.

We found a house high enough to see the landscape surrounding us and decided it would be home for the next couple hours. It was abandoned, like countless houses in the ghost town of Baqubah. On the floor in the living room was a pile of bootleg DVDs, the kind sold at the bazaar on our base. On top was a box-set of 28 Clint Eastwood movies over four discs. Once the building was cleared and security was on the roof, I trotted down the stairs to rummage through the neglected treasures of entertainment. My backpack was tightly packed with chemical-detection spray and 40mm grenades, but I found some room and crammed in the DVD set. So far, this mission wasn't so bad.

I joined the rest of the squad on the roof, replacing a guy that took my spot as I was pillaging on the floor below. It was still dark and oddly quiet, muted whispers and a gentle wind the only sounds to be heard. Dozer was behind me facing the other direction, watching the road for any movement as I looked over a swath of houses and fields. In a low voice, he suddenly calls out that he sees something. Four men run across the road to a small shack, one of them holding a bag that is quickly tossed in the weeds. He's not the only one to see them; infrared lasers dance on the figures from another area, quite possibly our third platoon or the scout platoon. Dozer makes the call and opens fire, cutting down a couple of the men with a burst of his armour-piercing rounds as Dodo fires alongside him. The other guns burp in perfect harmony, sending sparks on the road as God knows how many rounds are being fired at these four guys. One of them tries to climb a wall to safety and is shot in the back, making him drop like an anvil to the cracked pavement as blood streaks and splatters on the wall. I watch the whole thing unfold from over my shoulder, wanting to get into the fight, but holding my position on the opposite wall. All four men lay in varying degrees of death and dying. We'd wait [for] the sun to rise before going down to survey the damage. We didn't want to take the chance of walking into an ambush set by any unseen figures.

Dawn came, and with it, glimmer rockets and bunker-busting bombs. There was intel [intelligence] on several explosive-rigged houses and IEDs before the operation started, and they were being destroyed en masse as birds sang their morning tunes.

It was daylight, and another squad was sent down to check out Dozer's handiwork. They walked up to the guy who should have been the first one dead and saw he was still holding onto life by a thread, literally. His bottom half was almost completely sawed off from his torso, and he was throwing up his legs and twisting them like a freakish sideshow. He kept demanding water, but no one had any, other than their backpack reservoirs with a personal hose. When his demand of water wasn't met, he threw rocks at the soldiers surveying the area. A pistol was found on one of the bodies, and a grenade not far from the half-man. When they came back to check on him, he was dead.[9]

Patrick Sanders

The main base for the British Army in Iraq was Basra Palace, built by Saddam Hussein, but hardly used by the Iraqi dictator. A sprawling collection of buildings, it was the target of insurgent rockets and mortar rounds, and for the British soldiers it was invariably hot. Basra Airport was outside the city and was a relatively safer base for the British Army, but the route between the two locations became known as 'Ambush Alley'. In 2007, Lieutenant-Colonel Sanders was the commanding officer of 4 Rifles Battle Group, in charge of Basra Palace.

We had known for awhile that we had to leave Basra Palace, but it was a hugely difficult matter with a lot of political complexities. We decided on a night move, and it was broadly successful. We had one IED [improvised explosive device], and three soldiers received minor injuries.

We … faced a lot of action while we were at Basra Palace, and our guys

Soldiers from the US Army 24th Infantry Division serving with the US-led allies in Operation Desert Shield check an M-21 anti-tank mine in January 1990.

US paratroopers from the 82nd Airborne Division on desert patrol during Operation Desert Shield.

US troops arrive in Saudi Arabia to take part in Operation Desert Shield during the Gulf War, January 1990.

US soldiers guard captured Iraqi POWs somewhere in the Iraqi desert in February 1991. Iraq's invasion of Kuwait in August 1990 led to the First Gulf War, which began 16 January 1991.

British Engineers from the 7th Armoured Brigade blow up a mine field in the Saudi Arabian desert in January 1991.

Several members of the US Special Forces celebrate their victory over the Iraqi Army in Kuwait City. Allied forces rolled into the city on 27 February 1991.

Members of the US Air Force 491st Expeditionary Air Evacuation Squadron and the US Navy Fleet Hospital Eight team up to unload wounded service personnel at the US Naval Station in Rota, Spain on 2 April, 2003 during Operation Iraqi Freedom.

An F/A-18 Super Hornet takes off from the flight deck of USS Nimitz which entered the Persian Gulf on 7 April 2003 to support Operation Iraqi Freedom.

An Iraqi man and his donkey make their way out of Basra while Irish Guards, 7th Armoured Brigade, British Army, man a vehicle checkpoint.

Commander of the 1st Battalion, Royal Irish Regiment, Lieutenant-Colonel Tim Collins gave an eve-of-invasion speech to around 800 men of the 1st Battalion on 19 March 2003, just before Operation Iraqi Freedom. The speech has now entered military legend.

US Army 3rd Division soldiers provide covering fire during a gun battle outside the VIP terminal of Baghdad International Airport during the dawn advance towards the Iraqi capital on 4 April 2003.

US Army 3rd Division 3–7 infantry soldiers patrolling the outside perimeter of Baghdad International Airport on 8 April 2003, supported by a Bradley infantry fighting vehicle.

Iraqi citizens topple a statue of Saddam Hussein in one of Baghdad's squares on 9 April 2003.

Major David Bradley commanded B Company, the Princess of Wales's Royal Regiment, British Army, in Basra in August 2004, and was seriously wounded during fierce clashes wih insurgents of the Mahdi Army.

US Marines of the 1st Battalion, 3rd Marine Regiment keep watch during house-to-house searches in the city of Fallujah during November 2004.

have acted with immense courage. I could have stayed on there for another six months; we would have been able to defend ourselves, and killed a lot of people in the process, but what would that have achieved?

Some of the militias fighting us are nationalists and they do not like foreign troops in their country, and that is probably a healthy thing. Ninety per cent of the violence in Basra City was directed at foreign forces, and by us leaving, that violence should go down, so it was probably time for us to leave.

But there are also a lot of thugs among the militias, and I am glad that British forces played a part in showing the local population that one can stand up to them. Was the war in Iraq justified? It is too early to tell. If Iraq manages to be at peace with itself and its neighbours then it would have been worthwhile. If that doesn't happen, questions will be asked.[10]

Qais Mizher

Captain Mizher, formerly of the Iraqi Army, was in Basra in March 2008. The Battle of Basra took place between 25 and 31 March 2008, and involved 30,000 Iraqi Army troops and police and 16,000 members of Muqtada al-Sadr's Mahdi Army. The battle ended indecisively, although the Mahdi fighters did withdraw from Basra's streets. In the aftermath of the conflict, the Iraqi government was forced to dismiss some 1,300 soldiers and policemen who had deserted during the Battle of Basra.

I walked, ran and crawled into central Basra on Thursday, constantly dropping to the ground because of gun battles between Mahdi Army militiamen and the Iraqi Army and the police.

The rest of my stay in the city went like this: on Friday evening, the hotel I had somehow found open was showered with bullets, smashing glass on several floors and knocking pieces out of the stone façade. The next morning, Iraqi Interior Ministry forces in a part of the city they supposedly controlled were ambushed with heavy weapons at a hotel 45 metres [50 yds] from mine. On Sunday morning, after I had hired someone to drive me out of the city, an Iraqi soldier fired at our tyres, but missed. We did not stop.

Iraqi forces started their assault on the Shi'a militias in Basra on Tuesday. Whatever the initial goal of the operation, by the time I arrived in Basra it was a patchwork of neighbourhoods that were either deserted or overrun by Mahdi fighters. There were scattered Iraqi Army and police checkpoints, but no place seemed to be truly under government control.

Travelling anywhere was difficult, because of the violence that the Basra fighting had caused all over the Shi'a south and the curfews that the government had imposed. Somehow I made it to An Nasiriyah, about 160 km [100 miles] northwest of Basra, and persuaded a taxi driver with a GMC truck to take me to Basra.

The driver knew the road well. He took the old highway south; he knew that a checkpoint at a small town along the way would not let anyone through. So he turned off the road and drove several miles through the open desert to another road, and continued south.

That is when we started to see terrible signs of the conflict in Basra. I counted about 20 civilian cars coming north with coffins strapped to their roofs, heading to bury their dead in the Shi'a cemetery in the holy city of Najaf. My driver and I were unsure about the road ahead, so we flagged down a family driving in the opposite direction. As we did so, a woman in the passenger seat began frantically waving a piece of white cloth – a white flag – out her window.

It turned out that she was terrified that we might be members of the Mahdi Army, who she said had put bombs and snipers all along the road where the family had just passed. Once we calmed her down, she suggested another way.

Before we drove off, my driver had an important thought, asking the woman, 'Could you give us your flag? You left the city, and you don't need it anymore.' She kept her flag, but gave us another piece of white sheet. We used it often. At one point, we passed a huge plume of smoke at a place where a major oil pipeline had been bombed. We drove slowly into what looked like a deserted city, and at a certain point, my driver refused to go any further. I said fine and got out, but before I left he had one request: could he have the white flag? I tore it down the middle and gave him half.

Somehow I found another driver to take me within a couple miles of the city centre, which I had been told government forces controlled. When that driver would go no further, I had to walk, but by then I saw trucks filled with Mahdi Army members speeding through the streets, wearing black masks and carrying AK-47s and rocket-propelled grenades.

Gun battles broke out unpredictably, so I ran or walked when it was quiet, then dropped down and sought cover when I could hear shooting. After 45 minutes or so, I came upon the Rumaila Hotel in a central neighbourhood called Ashar. Amazingly, it was open, with six or seven guests inside and a couple of employees. I was so exhausted I didn't think twice, just checked in.

The next day I moved around as much as I could. The common observation was this: there was nowhere the Mahdi either did not control or could not strike at will. I am not sure what gunfight poured bullets onto the hotel on Friday. I just heard the gunfire and the windows shattering; as far as I know, no one in the hotel was hurt.

On Saturday I was talking with a colleague on my cellphone when a gun battle started right outside the hotel. It was so loud I couldn't hear the voice on the other end of the line anymore. I dived into a corner of my room and waited for it to end.

A while after the shooting stopped, some other residents of the hotel and I went outside. The street was littered with the shells of heavy machine guns where the Mahdi Army had fired towards another hotel, the Meerbad, where Ministry of Interior officials were staying, perhaps 45 metres [50 yards] away. We could see their pickup trucks, now full of bullet holes, in the parking lot of the hotel.

I decided to leave Basra. I took the white flag with me.[11]

Graham Cushway

After serving in the British Army, Graham became a private security contractor in Iraq. He worked alongside Coalition forces and made some interesting observations on the strengths and weaknesses of Coalition members.

After asking to deploy to Iraq and Afghanistan three times with the British Army, and either having had paperwork lost or being turned down for administrative reasons, I gave up and went to Iraq in late 2006 as a private security contractor to do what I thought would be much the same job, but for six times the money. In fact, everything worked out much better than I expected, and my tour was far more rewarding than a military tour would probably have been able to offer. The company I worked for was the biggest British-owned private security company (PSC) in Iraq. My personal role was working in intelligence. While the company I worked for had the largest number of intelligence staff in theatre of any British company (up to 36 staff at any one time), we were spread thinly throughout the country, with at most three or more in each of the regional command centres.

Intelligence operators for PSCs are asked to do a lot more than their military counterparts. The most immediate task was briefing the company's own bodyguard teams, but PSCs have numerous other customers as well. Other PSCs' personnel would wander into the intelligence cell looking for information. Iraqis would bring us important information, because they didn't trust the military. These individuals required proper debriefing. The intelligence that we collected was for the client, which in our case meant US military personnel (who could be anyone up to the rank of general). These also needed to be briefed.

The teams were interested in operational details in extreme detail. For example, one of my daily briefs on Route Irish [the road that links the International Zone – IZ, also called Green Zone – with Baghdad International Airport] stated: 'Be aware that a fence post has fallen and is pointing into the road, approximately 100 metres [328 ft] past the southern end of the Force bridge.' This kind of information was vitally important.... At the other end of the spectrum, we would be asked to provide strategic national and regional level briefs for senior US officers. Our daily brief was also used by the rest of the PSCs, as well as a variety of NGOs [non-governmental organizations] and other companies operating in Iraq. In most cases it was their sole source of intelligence. Because it was written in plain English rather than military jargon, it also found favour with senior US military officers, some of whom admitted to reading it ahead of official military sources due to the high quality of information and sheer readability.

... In contrast to the British, American forces tended to be both generous with their information and friendlier, although that didn't stop them putting a few bullet holes in our Union Jack at Camp Fallujah [home to 8,000 US service personnel]. Well, their firing range was over the back of our camp, and a few of the National Guard soldiers who trained there might well have been shooting in the wrong direction by mistake. The US Marine Corps (USMC), the best unit I worked with in Iraq, gave us everything they had intelligence-wise – often far more than we needed. The nicest of all the nationalities were the Australians, who had a small intelligence contingent based near An Nasiriyah. It was a pleasure to walk into their well-ordered intelligence cell, although it was a far cry from the vast facilities run by the USMC and the US 1st Cavalry Division in Fallujah and Baghdad, mostly because the Australians were always smiling and were remarkably quick and generous with the tea and cake.

There were a lot of differences between the various nationalities in theatre. The PSC dealt with French, Italians, Danes, Poles, Czechs and Romanians, as well as one lost-looking soul who used to rock up to briefings in Baghdad wearing the little-known uniform of the Fijian Army. However, aside from in the south, it was obvious that Iraq was a US operation....

A few Puma helicopters used to ferry the SAS [Special Air Service] around Baghdad, but Black Hawks were everywhere. Even the main American PSC, Blackwater, had its own small helicopters, which were MH-6 Little Birds, carrying sniper teams. These were occasionally a menace. Stories abounded that one sniper had fallen onto the DFAC [dining facility] (the US-managed catering facility) roof. Another had reportedly fallen in the Tigris. The fact that Blackwater didn't always clear their operations with the military also led to at least one collision with a UAV [unmanned aerial vehicle]. Still, some of the boys also told me that when they were out on the road, the Blackwater helicopters would sometimes fly escort. This help was greatly appreciated, particularly as there was never any guarantee that military aircraft would stop for a PSC call sign. Helicopters are vital for modern military operations. Reading reports about a lack of helicopters in Helmand Province, Afghanistan, in the papers, I can't help comparing British policy with the Americans. The disparity in jets was also noticeable. US jets were very common, particularly F-18s. I remember watching pairs of F-18s delivering air strikes in Fallujah. Aside from large numbers of C-130 Hercules transports, I never saw an aircraft from another air force, although I will never forget the vast roar and accompanying ground tremor as a British Nimrod warmed up at Basra Airfield.

For a Brit, working with the Americans was interesting. I was in Anbar when the USMC went into Fallujah and Ramadi for the final time, as part of General Petraeus's 'Surge' strategy. For us, it manifested in a sudden drop in workload. From having to make sense of and interpret over 100 separate attacks every day, we were suddenly down to 30. A week later it was 30, and then, memorably, not one single attack across the entire province. Of course we concluded at first that it was just a blip. However, as the weeks turned into months it became increasingly clear that in fact the Americans had finally won. They had succeeded in doing something that was not achieved in other areas: they had successfully engaged with the Iraqis and convinced them to stop fighting. However, to do this took overwhelming force. I was also in Baghdad when the same strategy was attempted there, with exactly the same result. Make no mistake, we won –

I was there – but to clear out Baghdad, the Americans deployed 80,000 additional troops in the city.

It pains me to say it, but the comparison with the Brits in Basra was not inspiring. Constant inappropriate pledges to cut troops, and attempts to 'do deals' involving handing key facilities to local militias, in return for quickly broken promises not to attack British troops, just made the situation more dangerous, eventually leading to a loss of control there and a serious loss of British prestige with the Americans. The Brits always thought they were better at engaging with locals than other nationalities, but their unwillingness to accept civilian casualties also meant that they lost face with the locals. By contrast, the Americans always backed up their charm offensives with an alternative 'very big stick' option. In addition, there were never enough Brits to get the job done and they simply didn't have enough kit, so it is difficult to say if their strategy would have worked. What they did prove, though, is that you can't fight a war on a shoestring.

PSC operations are luxurious by military standards. Although some PSC call signs are involved in activities similar to war fighting, most PSC tasks are routine, i.e. moving civilian contractors about, escorting convoys, or static security. Because they are primarily armoured taxis, PSC vehicles are luxuriously appointed, being armoured SUVs with air conditioning and padded seats. The contractors themselves were well equipped with Nomex jumpsuits, and the best body armour and helmets, as well as weapons and seemingly endless quantities of ammunition. I travelled with a smaller PSC on occasion, as well as with my own, and found there were few differences in terms of procedure, although the other company had slightly lower-quality equipment and vehicles. While on the road, the teams, which were then moving in three-vehicle convoys (although this later changed to four), are constantly on the alert and talking to each other via their earpieces and radios, pointing out potential obstacles or threats, such as oncoming vehicles or debris in the road which could conceal an IED. How they behaved towards civilians depended entirely on the location. Travelling with teams in the south seemed to involve a lot of smiling at children and waving at the local police. The atmosphere was relaxed and secure, although my first impression was one of surprise at the fact that in Iraq which side of the road you use is strictly one of choice. Locals hurtling down the wrong side of the road ('going kamikaze') was completely normal and was something PSCs also did whenever they felt it was necessary. The terrain was nasty, scrubby desert with the occasional sludgy brown river, broken up only by shanty towns, and the surprisingly numerous wreckage of Iraqi tanks and other military vehicles destroyed during the two Gulf Wars. The team members loved pointing these out to me, surmising with some justice that, like most intelligence personnel, I am an armour geek.

Moving around Fallujah was entirely different. The vehicle which picked me up from Camp Stryker was not what I was expecting after the smiley, wavy, relaxed south. It was some kind of anti-mine wheeled armoured personnel carrier. Two impressive machine guns protruded from turrets on the roof, and the crew were fatigued, 'wired' and aggressive. They put me in the front of the vehicle with a pair of binoculars and told me to keep a lookout. The reasons why soon become clear. Anbar was still in the grip of the insurgency at that time and attacks were very frequent. As we travelled along Route Mobile, south of Camp Fallujah, I noticed black scars on the road, which occurred so frequently that in places the road looked like a giant zebra crossing. Every mark was from a previous IED attack. Later I realized that the front of the vehicle is the most likely to be destroyed in a detonation, so the least useful team member is put there. One of our SUV convoys was IED'ed on the same road a while later, and our team had to run up the road to another vehicle under fire. There was something about contracting that made events like this appear mundane. The IED blew one wheel off, forcing the air-conditioning unit to fall into the lap of one young contractor. His reaction was simply to tut loudly. ... I am often asked if it was frightening. It wasn't, exactly, but a near miss always felt very tiring, like a bad day in the office at home. Still, the team who got IED'ed enjoyed watching themselves being attacked on Liveleak [a video-sharing website] later on. As usual, the terrorists who uploaded the footage claimed that they had killed all the target. In reality the teams were unhurt.

IDF was a constant threat wherever we were. From being rocketed occasionally in Baghdad, I got used to being rocketed every night in the COB [British Army's Contingency Operating Base] in Basra. The rockets there were noisy, but most of the airfield was sand or mud depending on the season, so they didn't do much damage. Fallujah was another big dustbowl. The camp was effectively under siege all the time due to the strength of the insurgency in the surrounding area, but as a siege it was fairly ineffectual. Mortar rounds would occasionally be fired over the perimeter, but like the COB, the camp was vast and there was little chance of them hitting anything. The USMC was also very keen on returning fire, and would send artillery rounds or rockets from its MLRS [multiple-launch rocket system] batteries back towards the firing point. I was sometimes in their headquarters while the Marines were returning fire, and they really did talk as though they were on a ship: 'Broadside Fallujah guns, starboard! Fire!'

IDF was most dangerous when Iraqis were working on camps, as the militias would invariably infiltrate spotters among the workmen. The day after work stopped on a perimeter trench at 1st Cavalry Division's HQ in Camp Victory [5km (3.1 miles) from Baghdad International Airport], three rockets were fired directly at the building. I was inside at the time, and conversations were briefly interrupted by the buzzing noise and vibration as remotely operated chain guns took out the encroaching missiles. Little was said about the matter. The attitude to IDF depended on where you were. In Fallujah and Victory, little notice was taken of it because it was usually ineffective. At Basra, the Brits spent excessive amounts of time sitting about waiting for the all-clear to sound, although the pattern of attacks was identical each night. When I initially moved to the IZ, I was still pretty blasé about IDF until the first rockets came in. As the alert system, the C-RAM [counter-rocket, artillery and mortar], sounded I was mooching along with my hands in my pockets, when suddenly I realized that I was now alone on a formerly crowded concourse. IDF in the IZ was much more dangerous. For one thing, it was highly accurate because of the number of Iraqis working there. For another, the rockets and mortars themselves were more lethal. They were landing on concrete and the shrapnel would fly out to a far greater distance than if they were hitting sand. I used to work in a tower that the JAM [Jaish al-Mahdi – the Mahdi Army] used as an aiming point for rocket attacks from home turf in Sadr City [in Baghdad] and once saw the flare as a rocket hurtled past, heading for our compound.

Contractors probably take this kind of thing less seriously than regular troops because we see so much of it. There were different C-RAMs at the various locations, but everyone's favourite was the one in the IZ. It sounded almost exactly like the beeping when a truck backs up: three blasts, followed by a crazed-sounding American voice saying, 'Incoming! Incoming! Incoming!' One of the boys managed to record it during an attack and had it on his mobile phone. I was envious and tried to do the same, but was never quick enough. There was a downside to devising a warning signal that sounds almost exactly like something else. Every Tuesday morning at 07.00 hours, the Iraqi shitwagon came to clean out the portaloos. When it backed up it sounded exactly like the C-RAM. So every Tuesday morning I, and probably the rest of the camp, woke up with that dreaded IDF feeling deep in the pits of our stomachs. Also, when the attacks are happening, you get that adrenalin buzz that makes it very difficult to go back to sleep....

The one really close call I had was in the IZ as well. This was when the attacks on the IZ were making the news on a daily basis, and people were getting killed. I remember seeing the city from afar on Sky TV, with a big black plume rising from where our generator unit had been set on fire. One morning I was still in bed when the attacks started … When I looked out I could see that a rocket had detonated in between the building where I lived and the one next door. One of the guy's rooms downstairs was close to the blast. His door had been blown off and he himself had been injured. I wasn't sure whether to run down and help him, as I could hear other rounds coming in. As I was agonizing, a group of British Gurkha guards ran across the compound and into the guy's room and started administering first aid. As other impacts were occurring, I thought I had better wind my neck in and think about getting some armour on. Later I went to look at the blast impact and was surprised how little damage it had done. We were lucky that the JAM had chosen to use the smallest kind of rocket. They had used some much bigger rockets at other times and caused a lot more fatalities and damage. I was also particularly fortunate that I had changed shifts the day before. If I had been working the early shift I would have been close to where the rocket had landed, and would probably have been shredded. A couple of hours later I went to work as normal. It was just another day at the office.[12]

Notes

1   Permission of Nat Helms
2   Used with permission from *Stars and Stripes*. © 2005–2009 *Stars and Stripes*
3   Vermont Public Radio, June 2006
4   ibid
5   ibid
6   ibid
7   Permission of Lara Yacus Chapman
8   Courtesy of the *University of Virginia Magazine*
9   www.vetvoice.com
10 *Independent*, 5 September 2007
11 *New York Times*, 31 March 2008
12 Permission of Graham Cushway

Afghanistan
(2001–10)

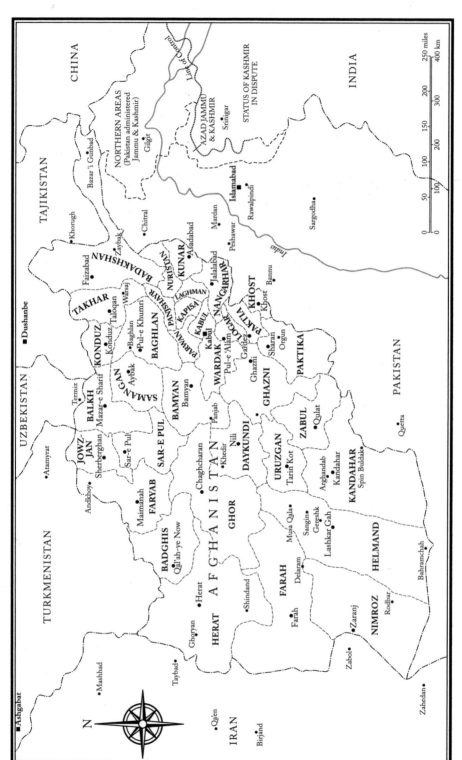

Afghanistan, its provinces, major towns and cities

Afghanistan – an introduction

The population of Afghanistan is around 30 million, made up of the following ethnic groups: Tajiks (around Herat and in the northeast), Uzbeks (in the north), Turkmen (along the Turkmenistan border), Hazaras (who occupy the central mountains), Pashtuns (the country's largest ethnic group located in the east and south-central part of the country), and Balochs (in the extreme south). Almost all of the population is Muslim. The majority are Sunnis, with some 2.5 million Shi'as (mostly Hazaras), forming the minority.

The country's economy is mainly agricultural, though the conflicts of the late 20th and early 21st centuries have resulted in exports dwindling to a minimum, with the exception of the lucrative, and illegal, opium and hashish trades. The capital Kabul was once a major trade hub, but has been ravaged by recent conflicts. As a result, its industry has largely disappeared.

Afghanistan was neutral in both World Wars and during the Cold War (until the late 1970s), receiving aid from both the US and the USSR. However, severe economic problems, most notably a serious drought in the centre and north of the country, led to the overthrow of King Muhammad Zahir Shah (1914–2007, ruled from 1933–73) by a group of army officers in 1973. Muhammed Daoud Khan (1909–78, ruled from 1973–78) became president and prime minister, but was himself deposed and killed in 1978 by a group led by Noor Muhammad Taraki (1913–79, president from 1978–79), who introduced Marxist reforms and allied Afghanistan more closely to the Soviet Union. In 1979, Taraki was killed and replaced by Hafizullah Amin (1929–79, president in 1979), but in December of that year, the Soviet Union sent troops into the country, deposed and killed Amin, and installed the Soviet puppet Babrak Karmal (1929–96, president from 1979–86).

The Soviet invasion of the country was the catalyst for a full-scale civil war waged between the Afghan government and its Moscow backers and opposition guerrilla forces, called mujahedeen (Islamic warriors). The war devastated the country and the economy. In 1986, Karmal resigned and was replaced by Mohammad Najibullah (1947–96, president from 1986–92), but the government lost ground when the Soviets withdrew in 1989 and the mujahedeen captured Kabul in 1992. They set up a new government made up of a 50-member ruling council. But the guerrillas proved unable to unite, and Afghanistan became divided into independent zones.

During this time, a movement of mujahedeen and Pashtun tribesmen who had spent time in Pakistani madrassas (Islamic religious schools) began to challenge for power in Afghanistan. This group was called the Taliban. Its leaders followed Wahhabism, an orthodox form of Sunni Islam similar to that practised in Saudi Arabia. By 1994, the Taliban had a foothold in the southern city of Kandahar; two years later, they captured Kabul and took control of the national government.

Taliban rule was characterized by the rigid interpretation of Islamic law. This resulted in the public execution of criminals (they hanged the former president Najibullah from a tower outside the presidential palace), the banning of television, the enforcement of head-to-toe veils for women, and jailing men whose beards were thought to be too short. Islamic law was enforced by the dreaded Ministry for the Promotion of Virtue and Suppression of Vice. Never recognized by the United Nations, the Taliban nevertheless controlled 90 per cent of the country. Only Saudi Arabia, Pakistan and the United Arab Emirates supported and gave aid to the Taliban. Saudi and Pakistan aid ceased, at least officially, after the terrorist attacks on the World Trade Center in September 2001.

The UN invasion of Afghanistan in 2001 ousted the Taliban from power, but did not destroy the group. Indeed, by 2007 it was estimated that the Taliban maintained a permanent presence in over 50 per cent of Afghanistan. Despite its rigid application of Sharia law, the Taliban did have some support among ordinary Afghans. For one thing, it cracked down on the widespread corruption that had characterized successive Afghan governments. The Taliban also brought a welcome degree of stability to the country after decades of violence had resulted in nothing but death and dislocation for the civilian population. That said, the Taliban is merciless to those it regards as enemies, whether real or imagined, and it rejects all notions of compromise and negotiation with its adversaries.

The following accounts from the conflicts in Afghanistan range from experiences during Operation Enduring Freedom, which began shortly after the attack on the World Trade Center in 2001, to the ongoing NATO operations that continue in Helmand Province and other hotspots within this troubled country.

Operation Enduring Freedom

Following al-Qaeda's attack on the World Trade Center on 11 September 2001, the US launched an offensive in Afghanistan to destroy al-Qaeda's bases in the country and topple the Taliban regime, which harboured Osama bin Laden and his followers. The operation was codenamed Enduring Freedom. As in Iraq, US military technology proved irresistible and overwhelming against a poorly armed adversary. The Americans enlisted the help of a motley group of anti-Taliban forces called the Northern Alliance. The latter, made up of Tajiks, Uzbeks and Hazara Shi'as, captured the northern Afghan city of Mazar-i-Sharif on 9 November 2001. This success meant that the Americans and Northern Alliance had a forward base inside Afghanistan.

After Mazar-i-Sharif, Northern Alliance forces pushed south towards the capital, Kabul. Taliban troops and their allies – Arabs, Pakistanis, Chechens and others – were rushed to the city to prevent the Northern Alliance advance, but with US air support they had little chance of success. By 13 November, the Northern Alliance controlled 40 per cent of Afghanistan. On the ground, US and British troops worked with Northern Alliance forces as Kabul was captured. The Taliban fled south.

By the end of November 2001, the city of Kandahar was the last Taliban stronghold in Afghanistan. By 7 December, the city had been captured, and Taliban rule in Afghanistan had collapsed. However, unfortunately for the US–British Coalition, the Taliban still retained the ability to wage guerrilla war.

In early December 2001, the Central Intelligence Agency (CIA) believed that Osama bin Laden and around 1,000 Taliban and al-Qaeda fighters were holed up in the Tora Bora cave complex in the White Mountains of eastern Afghanistan. Northern Alliance troops, advised by US Green Berets and given massive air support, attacked the Tora Bora complex. By 17 December, Tora Bora was captured, but bin Laden (if he was ever there) escaped into Pakistan.

In 2002, a major concentration of insurgent forces entrenched themselves in the Shah-i-Kot Valley, in Paktia Province of Afghanistan. To destroy these forces, the Americans and Afghan government forces launched Operation Anaconda. Once again, Coalition air power was overwhelming. The operation was launched on 1 March, and by 5 March over 450 bombs had been dropped on the Taliban and al-Qaeda. By the end of March, nearly 3,500 bombs had been dropped on the enemy, resulting in 500 insurgent dead. US casualties were eight dead and 82 wounded. But the insurgent war in Afghanistan, far from being over, was only just beginning.

Gary Berntsen

Central Intelligence Agency (CIA) operative Berntsen commanded a team of CIA and US Special Forces during the war in Afghanistan in 2001.

First off, I think that [it was] very savage up in Mazar-i-Sharif. The BLU-82s [bombs] that they used – they dropped two of them up there to break the frontlines. That was pretty savage. BLU-82 is a 'Daisy Cutter' [bomb that detonates above ground], a 6,818 kg [15,000 lb] device. It's the largest bomb in our inventory shy of a nuclear weapon. It's got a long fuse on it so that when it hits the ground, it doesn't fill the crater, and the blast goes way out. It was initially constructed to cut landing zones in jungles. We use[d] two of those up there on the frontlines. Just shattered their will. It was pretty savage. Similarly, what people don't understand is down in Kandahar, that team that went in there ... literally landed on a leaf in a lily pond full of Taliban and al-Qaeda. These guys entered into an area, and there were thousands of people hunting them. You're talking about the band on the run. Holy cow, that was very dangerous.

I was lucky. I was up in an area where I had a very large team, working with the Northern Alliance on the frontline. It was a more traditional frontline. It was like World War I where we were. We were outnumbered. We probably had 6,000 or 7,000 and they had 15,000. My concern was that they would just overwhelm us, overrun us. So the danger for us was different, but it was sizeable. The Special Forces teams with us did great work. They kept the Taliban from initiating an offensive against us. Had they conducted a full offensive, they'd [have] overrun the Northern Alliance, probably captured and killed all of us.

While I [was] there, we [did] no interrogations; any individuals that were captured I turned over to the US military. Just like [slain CIA operative] Mike Spann and the other officer did. They'd go through, 'Do you want to talk to us?' They'd give a prisoner a couple of minutes. They were looking for someone that would step forward and volunteer information.

I was not happy, because I was trying to save hostages. We had planned to seize the city [Kabul] two days later. We were going to drop a BLU-82 and then launch an offensive on 14 [November]. The city fell, I believe, on the 12th. I was very troubled entering, because I was afraid that I was going to find the hostages ... had their throats slit, even though I had paid a source on the other side to save them. Turned out to be lucky, and the man we had paid had turned them over to people that had let them go. But I was very, very concerned about them ... because I didn't want them to be turned over to bin Laden and used as human shields.

It doesn't feel like victory, no, because I'm looking for bin Laden right away, because I want to start killing him and his people immediately. So almost immediately we find out he's fled into Nangarhar Province. I assemble a team; I send them down ... Well, first off, I'm trying to get the Northern Alliance to send a team with me. They don't want to; it's not their homeland. I ask Special Forces if they'll send people in. They say, 'No, we're not going down there. It's unstable. You don't have a reliable ally.' I understand, because ... the bar is higher for them, because the American public, if you lose the lives of soldiers ... there's significant criticism. To be honest, you lose CIA officers, [the] American public isn't as concerned.

So I send my eight guys down there. Four of them are agency; three of them are JSOC officers (Joint Special Operations Command). They came to help us with the hostages, rescue the hostages ... and then without telling anyone, I [sent] them down to Nangarhar Province. They were thrilled to do it. They go down; they link up with a warlord. Then with that warlord, we'd collect intelligence. I received intelligence from the Northern Alliance that bin Laden had fallen back into the mountains, so then we drive down to the foot of the White Mountains [a region near Tora Bora]. We put a four-man team up in the mountains alone. We have them inserted. Based on intelligence that we have, bin Laden is down to about 1,000 people. And then we come upon his camp ... at Melowah. And then four guides, two CIA officers and two JSOC with about 10 Afghan guards call in the first 56 hours of air strikes against the motherload of al-Qaeda down below them. It was a nice beginning to what would be about a 16-day battle.

We didn't do a body count. Of course, we threw a BLU-82 in there as well, which just blows things to bits. You have to go in there with Q-tips [cotton swabs] to get samples, literally; that's how devastating that thing is. It just vaporizes things that are close to the centre. You're not going to find bodies. The US military, CENTCOM [Central Command], was very generous with air power. Really, really pounded them.

We pick up a radio off a dead body, and we're listening to bin Laden speak to his men. We're listening to him pray with them. We're listening to them talk about him. He gets away, gets out. I even asked that we put American soldiers on the back side [of the mountains], but the Pakistani frontier force comes up, captures 130 of them. But bin Laden is able to vector off and evade capture. I understood that once that happened, it was going to be a big problem capturing him after that, and that's proved to be very difficult.[1]

Nelson G. Kraft

Captain Kraft commanded Company C, 1st Battalion, 87th Infantry Regiment (1-87th Infantry), US Army, for 18 months. Task Force 1-87th Infantry deployed to Karsi Khanabad Airfield, Uzbekistan, on 5 October 2001 in support of Operation Enduring Freedom as one of the first conventional units in theatre. During November 2001, Task Force 1-87th Infantry deployed to Bagram Airfield, Afghanistan, to provide security and support for combat missions. The Task Force actively participated in Operation Anaconda in March 2002, conducting combat operations in the Shah-i-Kot Valley, Afghanistan.

On 26 February 2002, I received an operations order from the Task Force 1-87 (TF Rakkasan) staff to conduct combat operations in the Shah-i-Kot Valley of southeastern Afghanistan. As the task force main effort, my company was to establish platoon-blocking positions (BPs) Heather and Ginger, south of the village of Marzak, along likely enemy exfiltration routes Chrysler and Jeep.

The big picture of this operation was for the Rakkasans [Japanese phrase for 'falling-down umbrella men', the nickname for the 187th Regiment] – 3rd Brigade, 101st Airborne Division (Air Assault) – to establish blocking positions along the eastern and southern ridges of the Shah-i-Kot Valley to block escaping al-Qaeda and Taliban forces, while Anti-Taliban Forces (ATFs) and Special Operations Forces moved from Gardez and cleared the Shah-i-Kot Valley, which contained the villages of

Serkhankhel, Babulkhel and Marzak. The weather was supposed to be good for the air assault, and the enemy had the advantage of terrain. The enemy situation was described as minimal. As we set up our blocking positions along with the rest of the task force, it was anticipated that Afghani civilians and mixed al-Qaeda and Taliban forces would try to evacuate the Shah-i-Kot Valley through our blocking positions ... The key tasks of my intent were to conduct a successful air assault, quickly establish the blocking position, block the enemy exfiltration routes, protect the force, and destroy the enemy ... My decisive point was the destruction of al-Qaeda on route Chrysler. I chose this decisive point because I believed it was the most trafficable route out of the Shah-i-Kot Valley.

My plan to mass overwhelming combat power at the decisive point was to place ... my most combat-experienced platoon at that location. 1st Platoon had priority of everything and was tasked to destroy al-Qaeda forces on route Chrysler with the purpose of facilitating al-Qaeda's destruction by anti-Taliban forces. 2nd Platoon, supporting effort number one, was tasked with blocking al-Qaeda forces on route Jeep to allow their destruction on route Chrysler by the company main effort. 3rd Platoon, supporting effort number two, was tasked to block enemy forces to prevent the envelopment of the company main effort from the south. The purpose of fires was to disrupt enemy movement along route Chrysler.

After numerous rehearsals at both task force and company levels, the company felt well prepared for this mission ... Almost immediately after the CH-47s [Chinook helicopters] departed, we came under enemy direct fire from a ridgeline to the east. The company command post (CP) and the battalion tactical command post (BN TAC) were accompanying 1st Platoon, the company main effort. 1st Platoon continued movement to establish Heather, and the command and control elements from both battalion and the company followed.

After a minute or two, the enemy's fire increased, and they engaged with rocket-propelled grenades (RPGs). 1st Platoon took immediate action by suppressing the enemy, while the rest of Lift I took cover. We quickly moved out and established the CP in a draw approximately 75 metres [244 ft] away from the BN TAC.

While 1st Platoon continued to bound back and suppress, 2nd Platoon established communications from LZ 13. They too were under heavy enemy direct and RPG fire. Also at 2nd Platoon's location was the battalion mortar platoon. I ordered 2nd Platoon to return fire, seek cover, and look for a route to establish blocking position Ginger. Meanwhile,

1st Platoon established Heather and began receiving direct fire from a ridgeline in the west. I reported to the BN TAC that Heather was established and that unless the enemy was destroyed in the east, it would be difficult to set up Ginger. The platoon forward observers from 1st and 2nd Platoon were calling for both indirect fire and CAS [close air-support] as their respective platoons moved into position.

We began to receive heavy enemy mortar fire at both locations. The enemy accurately adjusted the indirect fire and one round impacted directly on BP Heather, injuring the platoon leader, platoon sergeant, forward observer and radio-telephone operator. The remainder of 1st Platoon was able to collect casualties and start movement to the company casualty collection point (CCP). While 1st Platoon moved to the CCP, another round impacted, resulting in more casualties.

Our strongpoint was established with darkness about five hours away. Although Heather and Ginger were not established, the strongpoint was in such a location that we were able to accomplish our mission of blocking enemy exfiltration routes Chrysler and Jeep.

We continued to receive enemy fire from the north, west and east for the remainder of daylight. We engaged the enemy with everything we had – small arms, M203 HE [grenade launchers], M240 [machine guns], 120mm mortars, CAS and Apaches.

Although the enemy owned the high ground and surrounded us on three sides, the battle during daylight was at a stalemate. Once darkness fell, we dominated the fight. After 30 minutes of no enemy contact, the medevac helicopters were called in to evacuate our casualties. As the helicopters started to land, the enemy began to fire again. We immediately returned fire, and the aircraft safely departed.

… The firefight lasted 18 hours and, although Company C sustained 19 casualties, the enemy was defeated. Numerous company-level lessons were learned and confirmed from previous battles during this operation. Ensure that everyone in your unit is trained to assume the next-higher duty position. In our battalion, the battalion command sergeant-major rigidly enforces the training of the 'fall-out-one drill'. This is a drill where a leader or holder of a key position is wounded or killed, and the soldier next in line steps up and assumes those duties.

This training could not have proved more valuable than on 2 March 2002. Shortly after setting up their platoon-blocking position, 1st Platoon was hit with two 82mm mortar rounds, wounding the platoon leader and platoon sergeant. Without hesitation, the 3rd Squad leader assumed command of the platoon and flawlessly led it through the rest of the firefight. Nothing surprised this young staff sergeant, because he had trained for this scenario on numerous occasions.

Every soldier in the unit must be combat-lifesaver qualified. During this 18-hour firefight, Company C sustained 19 casualties. At this writing, every one of those casualties is back at work. Although the medical personnel attached to the company for this operation did an excellent job, it was the combat lifesaver who made the difference. Before Operation Anaconda, 1st Battalion, 87th Infantry, combat-lifesaver certified every soldier in the battalion. There were no delays in delivering immediate treatment to every casualty sustained.

Having your higher headquarters co-located with you during an operation can be useful. The battalion TAC was co-located with Company C during this first firefight, and the leaders could not have asked for a better command relationship. There were no delays in any requests for guidance, and the experience alone that the members of the TAC brought to the fight was superb. The actions and demeanour of the battalion commander, command sergeant major and operations officer set the example for the less-experienced company leadership to follow.

Light-infantry units must stay light. Our soldiers went into Operation Anaconda with two standard uniforms and one standard load. When we were moving or the weather was warm, we wore Gortex pants and the Army PT T-shirt under our Gortex jacket. This uniform worked well. The Army PT T-shirt is the only short-sleeved shirt in the Army's inventory that wicks the moisture away from the body. When we were static and it was cold, we wore polypropylene tops and bottoms with our Gortex. For both uniforms, we wore the issued 'Matterhorn-type' cold-weather boots. The rucksack load was very simple: ammunition, batteries, water, chow and warming gear (chiefly for casualties). Every ounce counts.

Full dress rehearsals are critical. The only aircraft Company C used for troop transport was the CH-47, loading on both the seats and the floor. This was something completely new for our troops. Not only had we never used CH-47s in training back at home station, we never used aircraft without everyone sitting in a seat ... with soldiers entering combat for the first time, it is important to employ any measures that can be taken to reduce the number of new procedures for the soldiers. Knowing the soldiers' inexperience with CH-47s and floor loading, the chain of command scheduled a full-dress ... rehearsal, which paid huge dividends and helped remove any uncertainty from the soldiers' minds.

When operating at high altitudes with extreme changes in temperatures, soldiers must have some sort of heating source or agent available to warm beverages. This is by no means a showstopper, but it does improve the soldiers' motivation, which in turn improves the soldiers' combat performance. Company C used heat tablets and stoves that the United Kingdom was more than happy to share with us. I am not sure whether the Army has such an item in its supply inventory, but if it does, I've never seen it. Whatever the case, if you find that you are about to lead your soldiers in a similar environment, order or purchase some sort of heat source for your soldiers.

Leaders must retain the decision authority of whether rucksacks are dropped during enemy contact. When an infantry unit makes enemy contact, the element in contact drops rucksacks, seeks cover and returns fire, while the elements not in contact manoeuvre to an assault position, drop rucksacks, and destroy the enemy. What about when your entire unit is in contact with an enemy that has you surrounded from three directions on higher ground? As Company C came under enemy fire after exiting the aircraft, many rucksacks were dropped and the unit sought cover to return fire. This decision did not affect the battle until approximately the sixth hour, after casualties had been sustained, the temperature dropped and re-supply was needed. Never did we imagine that the battle would last for 18 hours. Company C was able to recover many of the rucksacks and needed supplies without any further casualties, but having a plan in place for the worst-case scenario could have made the situation much easier to deal with. There is no cookie-cutter solution to this issue, but the next time my unit is faced with a similar situation, there will be a load plan where one or two members of each squad or fire team will be packed for the worst and under no circumstances will drop their loads.

Sensitive items must always be kept on the soldier, not in an assault pack or rucksack. One lesson learned in Somalia was that no matter what time of day, when going into an operation, all soldiers must have their sensitive items, such as night-vision devices. Company C followed this lesson learned, but now it needs to be taken to the next level. Where should night-vision devices be stored? Do your soldiers sight out their night vision when they are going out to the local training for daylight-battle drill training? They should. Many units carry their night-vision devices around their necks at all times, but all too often, the equipment gets banged up or broken when the soldiers conduct individual movement techniques. The same goes when it is stored in a butt pack. Then there's the assault pack.

These work great for storing sensitive items when training at home station, but the truth of the matter is – unless you are on a QRF [quick reaction force] mission or part of a unit that is going to blaze into battle quickly and exit the same – the rucksack is needed to carry the infantryman combat load. Maybe the new MOLLE (modular lightweight load-carrying equipment) system will solve our problem. Although I have not used this system, I've been told that you can drop your main load and keep the assault pack on your back. When Company C landed in the Shah-i-Kot Valley on 2 March 2002, the sun had just come up. Night-vision equipment was not going to be needed for at least 12 hours after landing. Some of the company stored their night-vision equipment in their rucksacks. Because the company was forced to drop rucksacks early on in the firefight, many soldiers were forced to move under enemy fire to retrieve their night-vision devices. No matter what time of the day it is when a unit is operating in a combat area, all sensitive items must be kept on the soldier at all times.

Infantrymen must remain flexible and prepared to execute any type of mission that surfaces. Prior to Operation Anaconda, apart from securing valuable airfields, the missions Company C took part in were very far from the norm for which we had trained for back at Fort Drum [New York State]. 1st Platoon was selected to be the QRF for Special Operations Forces [SOF] conducting missions in Afghanistan. Training for this mission was facilitated through the battalion leaders' former experiences in SOF and Ranger assignments. 1st Platoon's first test of its QRF training came with a prison uprising in Qala-i-Jangi, Afghanistan. The platoon performed magnificently. Within days of 1st Platoon's success, a second QRF mission came down: 3d Platoon flew into Mazar-i-Sharif, Afghanistan, to secure a landing zone and evacuate casualties. Again, another superb execution.

The final mission the company executed prior to Operation Anaconda was a detainee-screening mission at an Anti-Taliban Forces prison in Sherberghan, Afghanistan. The concept … consisted of Company C securing the prison and routes to and from the detainee extraction point and a company of military police screening the detainees. Again, a mission that has never come close to making the company's mission-essential task list was executed flawlessly. How do you train your unit to prepare for these unusual missions? Continue to focus on the basics. An infantry unit that is expert at physical training, marksmanship, combat lifesaving and battle drills can adapt and execute any mission as well as … destroy the enemy.[2]

Brandon Friedman

Brandon Friedman served as an infantry officer in the US Army's 101st Airborne Division in Afghanistan and Iraq. In March 2002, he led a rifle platoon into Afghanistan's Shah-i-Kot Valley in order to engage Taliban and al-Qaeda fighters as part of Operation Anaconda. A year later Brandon commanded a heavy weapons platoon during the invasion of Iraq.

I was 23 years old when I led a rifle platoon into the Shah-i-Kot Valley. And while I was prepared for combat to some extent, no one ever tells you what massive bombing several hundred yards away looks or feels like. And that's what we were witnessing when we first approached our blocking position.

My first thought was: that's a big fucking mountain. My second was: it's on fire. There were trees with branches burning all along the north face of Takhur Gar. I'm not sure if Captain K. consciously decided to stop, was ordered to stop, or just did it instinctively, but we did. I took a knee with Taylor at my side. Just then a bomb hit the side of the mountain, lighting up the entire sky. I had never before seen anything like that. I had never witnessed a shot fired in anger, much less a bomb fall on people. When the bomb hit, the sound was deafening. It made the air vibrate. For the split second in which the mountainside was alight from the explosion, I could see trees swaying from the shockwave. I could see embers blowing off branches and into the snow. Kneeling, I watched as two more bombs struck the mountain in quick succession, causing the same set of effects. It was then that I noticed Sergeant Collins had moved forward from the back of the column. He was kneeling next to me. When he saw me looking at him through my night vision, he pointed to the mountain. Then he whispered, measuring out each word carefully, 'A man's got to know his limitations.'

Around three in the morning, with teeth working like little off-white jackhammers, I give up on trying to rest. I start pacing in small circles on the rocky, snow-covered, and now muddy ground. I notice that this has become the first quiet night of the operation. There is no crackle of machine-gun fire in the distance; there is no Spectre gunship on station searching for enemy positions with its infrared beam. All has gone silent in the snowfall.

A few minutes later Sergeant Pascoe joins me. He is doing the same thing. It is simply too cold to sleep or even to sit still. We stand there conversing in whispers until the sky begins to lighten. We talk for several hours, though now I can't recall a word that was said. We are technically in combat, but in reality we are just two shivering guys standing on a mountain, talking about life and wondering if it will end soon.[3]

Richard D. Schleckser

Staff Sergeant Schleckser, 19th Air Support Operations Squadron, US Air Force, was on the ground during Operation Anaconda, directing air strikes. This account is part of an post-action report written by Richard Schleckser. The task of the 19th was to provide air support for the 101st Airborne Division (Air Assault) and the 5th Special Forces Group (Airborne).

We moved with C Company to the north to a bowl where we took mortar, sniper and machine-gun (DShK) fire. We moved from ridge to ridge trying to avoid the bad situation. We kept just in front of their rounds. While this was happening, the TAC [tactical air control] was unsuccessful in knocking out the mortar fire. So I told my partner to stay and request aircraft. I took his plugger [GPS receiver] and the laser range finder. I went to the top of the hill and got the exact grid to the mortar position. We did all this while mortar fire was coming down on and around our position. An aircraft was diverted to our position almost instantaneously. We gave them the coordinates and they dropped bombs, knocking out the mortar position. We did the exact same for the Dishka [DShK machine gun] as they dropped more bombs. The last target was the mortar position to our southeast, on a ridge. We called for another aircraft and had the B-52s drop bombs on the ridge. That night the TAC sent the battle captain to get us and move us to the Bn [battalion] TOC [Fire Base Raider]. We rucked [hiked carrying rucksacks] to their position, met with the battalion commander and rucked with him all night long to link up with the battalion being air assaulted in the morning.[4]

Martin Wallace

Operation Anaconda also involved troops from Australia, Canada, Denmark, France, Germany and Norway. Wallace was an Australian Special Air Service (SAS) signalman who fought alongside US troops. He and another Australian were part of an 82-man team that was ambushed during the operation.

It was the first time we took it to the hardline al-Qaeda, who weren't prepared to flee or run and hide in Pakistan. These guys were definitely committed … they were there to fight to the death, and we accommodated them. We landed in the middle of a valley, and then, off to my right shoulder, I noticed a flash … I recognized it as danger, so we started running for cover. There was an RPG round that was fired at us from about 300 metres [330 yds] away. The round hit the ground and slid through the mud, basically chasing us up the hill as we ran from it. It just lay there steaming in the ground as we scrambled for cover. I was just lying there watching out of the corner of my eye, and about five or six of them disappeared in a puff of grey smoke. It was basically a direct hit on the American mortar from the al-Qaeda mortar.

We had guys with chest injuries, there [were] open fractures, basically fragmentation wounds, some of them over, you know, their entire bodies.

I asked Clint if he wanted me to establish communications. He said yep, so I ripped out my antenna. First call, I got back into our headquarters at Bagram and told them we were in a bit of a shit-fight. (I was later told by the young fellow who was on the radio [that] one of the other officers behind was asking what I meant by a 'shit-fight'.)

I was lying on my back, watching the B-52 come overhead, and you could see the bomb-bay doors open and the bombs as they started to fall. You're just hoping that they're going to be on target and not on your position. When you're dropping things from 9,000 metres [30,000 ft] and they're not laser-guided, then, yeah, there's definitely a recipe for disaster.

When they hit, you get the initial shockwave, which moves both you and the earth, and then you get the noise that follows, and then all the shrapnel comes sniffling in overhead.

I think it took them [al-Qaeda] a little bit to regroup, maybe 15 or 20 minutes, but then they started putting more mortar rounds and small-arms fire down into us. I was just thinking of how I'm going to get out of here and how I'm not going to bloody die in this valley. [Apache helicopters were called in.] The entire hillside basically opened up with small-arms fire and that was the last we saw of the Apaches.[5]

Greg Darling

During Anaconda, Lieutenant Darling, 10th Mountain Infantry Division, US Army, led a group of 30 soldiers who were among several platoons dropped along a 5 km (3 mile) ridgeline known as 'the Whaleback' to block any Taliban or al-Qaeda fighters attempting to escape.

> The [al-Qaeda fighters] had a vantage point from one hilltop, and the actual objective was the hilltop itself. So I pulled two of my AT-4s – that's an anti-tank weapon – over to the vantage point, and I pulled my guns over there, and we initiated fire onto the objective for probably a good minute. And then I brought my other two squads around to the side, and we had these guys cease fire. And as we came up, we threw a frag [fragmentation grenade] into the first opening we came to, and my first squad went up and encountered one enemy [fighter].
>
> He was actually the only one we found living. He was pretty shell-shocked from being hit by two anti-tank weapons, so they took him down [killed him]. We didn't give him a chance. That's our rules of engagement. We were told everyone on the Whaleback was hostile.[6]

Matthew F. Bogdanos

After several years in the Reserves, Colonel Bogdanos, US Marine Corps, returned to active duty following the terrorist attacks of 11 September 2001. In 2003, when the National Museum of Iraq was looted, he was chosen to lead the investigation. In 2005, Bogdanos received a National Humanities Medal for his leadership in recovering the stolen artefacts. In March 2002, Bogdanos was at Bagram, Afghanistan. His words illustrate that the conflict in Afghanistan, far from being won, was only just beginning.

> You do what you must to get through the day. Every bend in the road is a potential ambush site. Every shadow hides an Arab or Chechen fighter. Every person you meet is suspect until proven otherwise. Competing against this necessary paranoia (remember, just because you are paranoid does not mean they are not out to get you) is the overwhelming affection you feel for the Afghan people. They are all (Pashtun, Tajik, Hazara and Uzbek) warm and (when not trying to kill you) very friendly people. We live with the Afghans, and I am invited at least once a day for the traditional tea, almonds and raisins. To refuse this invitation in such a guest culture is an unforgivable insult. Nor does it matter if the tea is being served in the only room with a roof, where the remainder of the mud-brick house is bombed-out rubble. Most of the houses I have seen outside of

Kabul are mud-brick, but every one has a guest room with their best carpet and, sometimes, pillows.

I have an interpreter, and the conversations over tea are priceless. Many Afghans have blue eyes, which they attribute to Sikander. We call him Alexander the Great, but Afghans, like Persians, could not pronounce his name, so they call him Sikander. He is still revered. We argue about the routes Sikander travelled and his use of cavalry. They always ask why President Bill Clinton abandoned them when the Taliban took over and if we are going to do the same. I tell them that I hope not, but that I am low on the food chain. Actually, what I told Matobwadeen (a 23-year-old Tajik with a heart of gold and an artificial right leg) is, 'I'm not the Madam, just one of the whores.' It translates well, and now he repeats it in English half-a-dozen times a day – always followed by a laugh.

It is during tea that you hear about the real horrors, things done by the Taliban and al-Qaeda that you find impossible to believe – until you walk outside and see how many people are missing body parts. Matobwadeen is not alone. You also see the despair, the hunger and the poverty, and you know they are telling you the truth without embellishment or exaggeration. You feel uncontrollable rage, softened by the children laughing and playing – even if they are playing across the road from a minefield. That is my favourite part – the children, not the minefield. They love chocolate. So I always make sure to carry around enough in my pockets. I show them the chocolate first and then make them eat the delicious meals (ready-to-eat) before I give them the chocolate.[7]

Notes

1 Permission of Gary Berntsen
2 Nelson G. Kraft , 'Lessons learned from a light infantry company during Operation Anaconda', *Infantry Magazine*, Summer 2002
3 www.vetvoice.com
4 'Operation Anaconda (March 2002) After-Action Report', US Air Force February 2005
5 www.defencetalk.com
6 Radio Free Europe, 20 March 2002
7 www.leatherneck.com

NATO's war

Between 2003 and 2005, the Taliban began to fight back against North Atlantic Treaty Organization (NATO) forces in Afghanistan. The apparent victory of 2001–02 was revealed to be a myth as Taliban forces simply melted away to towns and villages on both sides of the Afghan–Pakistan border when faced with Coalition offensives, only to re-assemble once the danger had passed. NATO forces were faced with an additional problem: that of needing to provide sufficient security assistance to the new Afghan government of Hamid Karzai (b. 1957, interim leader and then president 2001–). Simply stated, NATO didn't have enough boots on the ground, and Coalition forces began to alienate many Afghans when large-scale firepower – especially air strikes – was used indiscriminately against target areas, resulting in an unacceptable number of civilian casualties.

From January 2006, a NATO International Security Assistance Forces (ISAF) contingent began to replace US troops in southern Afghanistan. The British 16th Air Assault Brigade was the core of this force, supported by troops from Australia, Canada and the Netherlands. ISAF operations began promisingly, with Operation Mountain Thrust opening on 17 May 2006. More than 1,000 Taliban fighters were killed and 400 wounded during the six-week operation. In Operation Medusa in July 2006, NATO forces killed a further 500 Taliban fighters. But tactical victories did not translate into strategic success, and NATO was forced to deploy more troops to Afghanistan. By the end of 2006, there were over 32,000 NATO troops in the country. The largest contingent was from the US (11,800), with Britain in second place (6,000), then Germany (2,700), Canada (2,500) and the Netherlands (2,000).

NATO forces continued to fight the Taliban in 2007 and 2008, in a war that showed no signs of ending. In individual battles, the training and firepower of NATO forces was often overwhelming, but on a countrywide scale, the Taliban was proving to be remarkably resilient. The US National Security Council concluded that the 2007 war effort in Afghanistan had not met the strategic goals set by the US military. And while US- and NATO-led troops had been successful in individual military battles against the Taliban, the militants still appeared able to recruit large numbers of fighters. These included many foreigners, especially Pakistanis, though the main source of new recruits was unhappy Afghans.

The war in 2008 and 2009 followed the usual pattern: success in individual battles, but strategic stalemate. At the end of 2008, a Taliban field commander in Kandahar province, whose men had fought hit-and-run battles with Canadian and British forces during the summer, stated, 'In all, we feel that things are going very, very well for us. And what is more, time is on our side.' More worryingly for NATO, Abdul Qadoos, a businessman and tribal leader in Kandahar Province, lamented, 'Once, people would look to the government for justice. Now they go to the Taliban.'

These views were seemingly echoed by US President Barack Obama, who at the end of March 2009 called the situation in Afghanistan 'increasingly perilous' and pledged more troops to fight the Taliban and al-Qaeda. On 13 February 2010, NATO forces launched Operation Moshtarak (meaning 'together' or 'shared'), designed to liberate parts of Helmand from Taliban control. Around 15,000 troops, mostly US, British and Afghan, began sweeping through Marjah and Nad Ali, to 'break the back' of the Taliban in Helmand Province.

Fariba Ahmadi Kakar

Fariba Ahmadi Kakar is an Afghan member of parliament (elected in October 2005 along with several other female representatives) and the government representative for Kandahar, the southern province that has witnessed some of the fiercest clashes between Taliban fighters and NATO troops.

NATO's role needs to be made clear. Its presence is a good thing for our country, but if they continue as they have – with bombings that have destroyed people's homes and killed their families – then there is no doubt that ordinary people will rise up against them. With each civilian attack, they create enmity. The solution to our present security situation lies in negotiation, forgiveness and reconciliation. The Taliban should receive a share in the government. We have gone through this process with other Taliban and other government opponents. Jihad leaders are present at all levels of the government today. Inviting the Taliban to discussions is the best way to solve the problem.[1]

Kevin Patterson

Kevin Patterson is a Canadian doctor who served for six weeks in Kandahar
Field Hospital. During his service he recorded his experiences. The following
was written during February 2007.

About two-thirds of our patients are Afghans: Taliban and Afghan
National Army (ANA) personnel and civilians. The rest are Coalition
soldiers. The Coalition folks generally do well; their body armour is very
effective, and the amount of penetrating chest and abdominal trauma is
limited. Not so with the Afghans. They often don't have body armour, and
they aren't eligible for evacuation. When we received news that a mass
casualty was en route with severe burns, we were told not to intubate
Afghans with burns over more than 50 per cent of their bodies – because
in the absence of a burns unit, such a patient requiring life support rarely
survives – but that we should do everything possible for Coalition
personnel because they would be evacuated to Germany or Dubai and then
to places like Brooke Army Medical Center in San Antonio, where the
burns care is the best in the world. Any temptation to protest the different
valuation of life explicit in the order was stalled by the briefest survey of
the country around us. What else is new?

Ten thousand soldiers and civilians work and live at Kandahar Airfield.
The civilians mostly work for KBR [Kellogg Brown & Root, an American
engineering and construction company], the former Halliburton subsidiary
that runs the dining facilities and maintains the miles of prefabricated,
pressed-metal barracks. The contractors speak with midwestern and
southern accents mostly, chatting merrily with soldiers like neighbours
leaning over a fence. The few other civilians include a handful of
physicians, some foreign-service personnel, and – judging from the
haircuts and eyewear – some CIA types. It becomes a game to spot Special
Forces soldiers, who do not wear uniforms, but are revealed by their
shoulders, exuberant beards and sun-wrinkled eyes.

In the dining halls, Australian, New Zealand and Jordanian soldiers eat
alongside soldiers from NATO countries, one polyglot mass of blinking
and farting martial vigour. Viewed from the entrance, the long rows of
tables appear as a kind of fabric mosaic: the Americans and Canadians in
their pixilated browns and greys, the Australians in their bunny-ear-
patterned beige, the British streaked by sawgrass-coloured fronds, and the
Romanians in yellowish-brown uniforms and floppy hats – currently the

trend in military millinery; the Canadians, Dutch, and British all sport variants – looking rather like lifeguards in mufti.

Soldiers may not be fed if they are unarmed – though neither are they permitted entry if they are carrying a bag of any sort. I ask a soldier waiting in line with me for breakfast why this is. 'In case a Taliban in disguise,' he nods towards one of the Jordanians, 'wants to blow us up.' He suggests I stuff my camera bag in a jacket pocket. In line ahead of us is an American private from the perpetually deployed 10th Mountain Division carrying an M203 grenade launcher; in front of him the Jordanians stand in jungle-green fatigues, AK-47s slung casually over their shoulders, magazines jutting from their pockets.

The Romanians, who help provide airfield security, have quickly acquired a reputation for both aggressive patrolling and a certain erratic quality to their response times. Opinions vary over which characteristic predominates. Again and again, I try and fail to engage Romanian soldiers in conversation, but they keep to themselves. They've built a little church that appears to have been lifted whole from the shore of the Black Sea. On New Year's Day, Romania joined the European Union, and their presence in Kandahar can be explained both by the application to join and the expectation that it would be accepted. Everyone comments on how much the Romanians eat – great, heaping mounds of chicken and potatoes and steaks stacked like flapjacks. Still, their comparatively gaunt faces seem half the size of their corn-fed brethren, dark eyes under shaven heads gazing around at such foreignness. And all the food you can eat.

I am standing at the memorial to the 43 dead Canadian soldiers when the first rocket flies into the camp. A granite slab with Captain Nichola Goddard's picture etched into it smiles out from among the others. She was an artillery officer from Shilo, my old regiment, working as a forward observation officer (who directs the fall of artillery shells) when she was killed by a rocket-propelled grenade (RPG). Orthopaedic surgeon Steve Masseours – we'd both been captains in Ottawa a dozen years earlier – is standing beside me. He's a major now, and was on duty when Goddard came into the hospital, in May 2006. 'She had terrible luck,' he says. 'Fragment of shrapnel flew in under her helmet, over her armour, at just the wrong angle, and went into her head.' She was the first female Canadian soldier killed in action in Afghanistan. Twenty-six years old. Horsey, good-natured grin. Almost beautiful. Beautiful, in fact. 'We started to resuscitate her, but it was pretty clear it was hopeless,' Steve says.

Just then, a rocket whistles overhead, a short, thin stream of red light trailing behind it. Steve is already ducking low when it explodes in the military police compound, 90 metres [100 yds] away. A fraction of a second later, another. As the attack siren goes off, we lie on the concrete pad among the pictures of the fallen – smiling, large-toothed men, and one woman, self-conscious in their posed portraits – the common elements: shoulders and acne. After a few minutes, we scurry over to the nearest bunker, joined by a nervous clot of newbie soldiers from Canada and Holland, and Americans, who do 12- to 15-month tours and were long ago inured to such attacks. 'That's the helicopters going up,' one lanky Texan says, to the thumping sound filling the air. When it is next possible to be heard, he adds, 'Give them 30, 45 minutes and y'all can go back to work.' The Texan describes how the rockets are triggered when a block of ice holding down the release lever melts – leaving the Taliban time to get many miles away before the helicopters find the launch site. I nod more times than is necessary. He is entertained. The all-clear signal rings out and we walk quickly to the hospital. There is only one wounded – an American MP who was picked up and tossed by the explosion.

A little later, we eat with Major Sanjay Acharya, an anaesthetist of Gujarati stock by way of Newfoundland, who speaks with the rolling lilt of that island, almost Irish in its gregarious musicality. 'What this represents, gentlemen,' he declares, indicating the salmon on his plate, 'is creeping mediocrity.' Island peoples have high standards for fish, but Acharya also allows he's rattled by the rocket attack. 'Bastards are probably off giggling like it's some fucking game of Knock Knock Ginger.'

At home, in Ottawa, Acharya keeps workaholic hours – more than 120 on-call nights a year in critical care and anaesthesia. Here, he sleeps heroically when the wounded are not coming. When upright, he lays out his plans: to start a cult modelled on Scientology – 'I've already got that Eastern mystic-yogi-guru thing down' – to attend law school, to leave the military as soon as he's eligible for his pension. In an organization committed to the cultivation of zeal, he has proved barren land. He tells us he once dodged a court-martial (he had irritated his superior into apoplexy) by simply failing to cooperate, give a statement, or use the military-appointed lawyer. The functionaries, it is plain, would only ever be baffled by him. The nameplate on his room reads 'G. Assman'.

By Valentine's Day spring is unfolding; this is pleasant, in that the rain has stopped and one can sit in the sun and read, but it causes some foreboding. Musa Qala, about 160 km[100 miles] northwest of Kandahar in Helmand Province, has recently been seized by Taliban forces in defiance of a mutual-withdrawal agreement made earlier with the British. Today the British killed the Taliban commander with an aerial strike. Helmand looks to be this year's hot spot, where the British have just launched Operation Kryptonite, aimed at seizing control of Kajaki Dam, a major power source that has been off-line since 2003. There have been hundreds of Taliban casualties in the previous six weeks – a fact we can learn from Google News. But the bed censuses at the Coalition hospitals tell the story just as well: the British-run Camp Bastion field hospital in Helmand is constantly in condition red, and the overflow … com[es] to us.

Administered with the help of the Red Cross, the Mirwais Hospital in Kandahar City will take any civilian or Afghan National Police (ANP) officer initially treated by us, but it won't take Afghan soldiers. The Taliban have threatened Mirwais doctors who've come to our base for clinical mentoring, and they worry that if they assist ANA soldiers, their hospital will be attacked. [T]he Afghan military base Shir Zai, a facility the US military built to be the provincial ANA hospital, has been sitting empty, much to the frustration of a US naval officer who's been labouring to open it. Unused crates of equipment and CT scanners sit in the building, she says. We meet with the Afghan brigade surgeon responsible for the Shir Zai hospital, an educated and committed man who has watched his physicians and nurses desert one after another, afraid and demoralized. 'No one from the north, where it is safe and where their families are, wants to come here,' he tells us. 'Kandahar has always been like this, far from Kabul and hostile to anyone from any other place.' He spots Acharya among us and addresses him in Dari. Acharya replies that he speaks only Gujarati. There is a moment of what I take to be silent commiseration: South Asians surrounded by 'farangis', which in both languages means foreigners.

Like every Saturday, today local merchants line up at the base gates before dawn and submit to body searches. By mid-morning they've set up a bazaar to hawk food, rugs, hookahs and the relics of previous conflicts: piles of ancient British Enfield rotating-bolt rifles (the Colonial Army left behind thousands) and Soviet Army uniforms, many with carefully patched bullet holes. The object lesson could not be more clear.

Genuinely multinational combat armies are uncommon. Historically, one nation dominates an effort, and bit players stand around for show. Yet 37 nations compose the ISAF, each with its own generals and political masters. Aberrations in codes and procedures can lead to friendly fire, though the US military prefers the 'blue-on-blue' appellation. Twice, Canadian infantry have been fatally attacked by American aircraft. But far more common is Coalition personnel firing on Afghan allies. A few days ago, an Afghan soldier riding in a truck approached a Canadian military convoy from behind; he was recognized as ANA by the rear vehicle and waved forward. This was not communicated to those in the lead vehicle, who opened fire, killing the driver and sending six rounds into the passenger's evidently robust body armour and another into his right arm, breaking the bone and severing the ulnar nerve. We grafted his nerves, and in six months or so (peripheral nerves grow a millimetre a day) it will be possible to know if the surgery was successful.

Can doctors tell if fire is friendly or not? The infantry believes it should be easy to know: NATO countries use 5.56mm ammunition, while the AK-47 favoured by the Taliban uses 7.62mm. Except local allied forces – the ANA, ANP – use AK-47s too, as do the forces of the former Warsaw Pact – the Romanians, the Estonians – and anyway, when bullets strike bone they can shatter, spraying shards of metal through the body like a satellite breaking up on re-entry. More often the full-metal-jacketed rounds go through and through, as they were designed to do. We can't necessarily tell whether a wounded person was shot by his confederates or by an antagonist, except by what is claimed. Probably, more times than we could guess, we wouldn't want to know the answer.

When an aeromedical team tells us they're bringing in an ANA soldier shot in the thorax, we wonder why they're bothering – such patients usually die en route. But the shooter must have been at an extreme distance, for the bullet is palpable just under the skin over the sternum and excised under local anaesthesia by Lieutenant-Colonel Reeuvers, a Dutch surgeon. When he plucks out the AK-47 bullet, Reeuvers and his patient exchange amused grins. Reeuvers tells him to buy lottery tickets. A translator tries, but both he and the patient look puzzled. 'Go to the casino,' Reeuvers tries again. Still only baffled nods. Then the Afghan soldier leaves our base for his own, the question of who shot him unasked, unanswerable.[2]

Stephen Grey

Stephen Grey is the author of *Ghost Plane: The True Story of the CIA's Rendition and Torture Program.* He is an award-winning investigative reporter who has written for the *New York Times*, BBC, PBS and ABC News among others. He made the following report on 13 December 2007 while embedded with NATO troops in Afghanistan.

Afghanistan's government flag was raised Wednesday on what had been one of the biggest strongholds of the Taliban and al-Qaeda in Afghanistan and a leading world centre of heroin production.

The town of about 45,000 people was secured at about 09.30 hours as Afghan troops, steered by British soldiers and US Green Berets, drove out remnants of the Taliban resistance from Musa Qala in the opium poppy region of northern Helmand.

As the only journalist to join NATO forces entering the town, I found it a ghost town abandoned by both the Taliban and its residents at the end of an eight-day Coalition operation. The offensive was one of NATO's biggest in the country since Operation Anaconda in 2002.

Embedded with a team of British troops and a detachment/A-team of US Special Forces, I watched the Taliban being pounded these last few days with overwhelming force – vapour trails circled in the clear blue sky over the Helmand desert as B-1 and B-52 bombers, backed by A-10 tank busters, F-16s, Apache helicopters and Specter gunships, were used to kill hundreds of Taliban fighters.

The operation was launched last Tuesday with an attack across the Helmand River by British Royal Marine Commandos, a thrust from the west by light armour of the UK Household Cavalry Regiment; all this, however, was a feint for the main airborne landing from the north of a battalion of soldiers of Task Force Fury from the 82nd Airborne [Division].

Faced with a full brigade of NATO forces, a brigade of Afghan government fighters and the defection of a key Taliban commander, the Taliban chose not to flee at first but to fight a desperate battle.

I joined one feint attack of Afghan soldiers last Friday that came under fierce Taliban fire in a village on the outskirts of Musa Qala – AK-47s and heavy machine-gun fire opened up on us as we advanced across open ground. The British and Afghans counterattacked backed by US Special Forces, who opened up with 50-calibre fire and by calling three F-16 strikes and a B-1 bomber strike.

On Sunday, as the 82nd Airborne advanced to take positions north, east and south of the town, I watched the sky being lit with large explosions from heavy ordnance dropped from the air to support the US advance. US forces believe the Taliban were backed by a large strength of foreign fighters, including those linked to al-Qaeda. Soldiers who I accompanied found one dead fighter whose notebook revealed he was from Pakistan. While hundreds of Taliban are believed to have been killed, two

British soldiers and one American soldier lost their lives. All the deaths, however, resulted from vehicles striking mines left not, it is believed, by the Taliban but by Soviet forces in the 1980s.

On Monday, after days of fierce fighting – more ferocious than NATO commanders had expected – the Taliban called it quits and fled the town. Afghan troops entered the town on Tuesday and completed their occupation on Wednesday after only token further resistance.

NATO forces now hope to launch a programme of reconstruction that will persuade the local population to turn their backs on the Taliban.

In a controversial move, Musa Qala had been abandoned the previous year after British troops lost seven lives defending a base ... from waves of Taliban attacks. Although handed over, in theory, to the elders of the town last October, it was taken over by the Taliban by February and became one of the few major places in Afghanistan where the Taliban could operate in the open, trying to set up their own local government and courts. Last year's British-backed deal was criticized openly by US commanders and the recapture of the town heals an open wound that undermined claims by NATO that the Taliban were being defeated militarily.[3]

Ray Wiss

Captain Ray Wiss, an emergency physician from Sudbury, Canada, treated soldiers in the critical moments after their injuries as the lead medic of an armoured ambulance crew. On 18 December 2007, he was 'on the road'.

This was my last day at Forward Operating Base Lynx ... I was asked yesterday to cover another base (FOB Leopard, northeast of FOB Lynx) for the next month, to give the senior medic there a break (he had been at the base since August).

The distance between the two bases is less than 10 km [6 miles], so helicopter transport was not going to happen. That meant I would have to join a convoy and go by road. This is a lot worse than going cross-country on an attack, since improvised explosive devices (IEDs) are almost never placed out in open fields – they are almost always placed where there is a high probability of a vehicle passing over them ... The seriously wounded soldiers I have treated were all injured by IED strikes on vehicles. While waiting to board my LAV [light armoured vehicle], I kept seeing their severe leg wounds, some of which had led to amputations ...

We left FOB Lynx right after breakfast … For most of the trip we were in flat, open terrain … The road to the outpost took us by a Taliban cemetery. Everyone lying there had been put in the ground by us. I was happy they were dead, but you can't help but reflect on the wastefulness of war in places like this.

We spent an hour at the outpost, resupplying the troops there. We then went back the way we came, past the turn-off to FOB Lynx and on to the east. As we got close to the village beside FOB Leopard, the scene became a cliché: heavily armed Western troops in armoured vehicles riding through an area crawling with kids, all of them dirt-poor and begging for handouts … We didn't stop to interact with the children, nor did we give them anything … On 18 September 2006, a soldier from Espanola, Private David Byers, [had been] killed not far from here. He died, along with three other Canadians, when a Taliban suicide bomber on a bicycle drove into them while they were feeding Afghan children. There were 27 Afghan casualties that day, most of them children.[4]

Jesse Murphree

Army Specialist Jesse Murphree, D Company, 2nd Battalion, 503rd Infantry Regiment (Airborne), US Army, lost both legs to a roadside bomb on 27 December 2007 in northeastern Afghanistan. He was a gunner on an up-armoured Humvee. His platoon was overwatching another platoon in the Korengal Valley near Ali Abad; as his convoy prepared to move, his vehicle struck an improvised explosive device. He was awarded the Purple Heart.

Every day we were getting shot at. [Y]ou hear about other people in Iraq, they got shot at a couple of times. We're like, we've been shot at every day.

You start thinking you're fighting a forgotten war, like no one's paying attention. I went home on R&R [rest and recuperation] before I got hurt, and people were coming up to me, they're like, at least you're not in Iraq and stuff, and I was looking at them, and I was like, what? And they'd say, you don't do – they called it 'battle' – they're like, you don't do battle anymore? And I'm like, are you kidding me? Like, yeah, I do.

I know the area our unit's at is definitely hot and definitely feels they're forgotten about, like the people think that Afghanistan is really not a big deal or nothing's really going on. We still [have] people that are dying, we still [have] people that are getting hurt.[5]

Dan Kearney

Captain Kearney, 173rd Airborne Brigade Combat Team, US Army, in the Korengal River Valley in the northeastern province of Kunar, February 2008.

The Korengal is like a tough Los Angeles neighbourhood and we're the LAPD [Los Angeles Police Department] kicking in the door, arresting guys, demanding information about the gangs, and slowly the people say, 'No, we don't know anything, because that guy in the gang, he's with my sister, and that other guy, he's my uncle's cousin.' Now, we've angered them for so many years that they've decided, 'I'm gonna stick with the ACM – anti-Coalition militants – who are my brothers, and I'm not gonna rat them out.'

My guys would tell me they didn't know which houses they're shooting from, and I'd tell them they can't shoot back into the villages. They hated me.

We saw people moving weapons around. I tried everything. I fired mortars to the back side to get the kids to run out the front. I shot to the left, to the right. The Apache – an attack helicopter – got shot at and left. I kept asking for a bomb drop, but no one wanted to sign off on the collateral damage of dropping a bomb on a house. Finally, we shot a Javelin and a TOW – both armour-piercing missiles. I didn't get shot at from there for two months. I ended up killing that woman and that kid.

The only reason anyone's listening to me in this valley right now is 'cause I'm dropping bombs on them. Still, I wasn't going to let myself shoot at houses every time this unit took fire: I'd just create more people that hate me.[6]

David Haight

Colonel Haight, 3rd Brigade Combat Team, 10th Mountain Division, US Army. In March 2009, he was at Forward Operating Base Airborne, Afghanistan. The base is near Highway 1, the road linking the capital Kabul to Kandahar in the south, and faces two valleys, Jalrez and Nerkh, that are crowded with Taliban fighters.

It's hard to find a good, old-fashioned combat fight in Afghanistan right now – even here, surrounded by the battle-hardened, well-armed infantry and artillery troops of the 10th Mountain Division's 3rd Brigade Combat Team. I can, in an instant, become someone's worst enemy. But that's not really the main reason that I'm here. I'm here to try to help the people.

It's an economic war. The enemy here – he's just looking for a job. He's going to make $100 from the Taliban to carry a [rocket-propelled grenade launcher], or maybe we can pay him $150 to work on a road – put a shovel in his hand instead of an RPG.

He [the enemy] either has to choose to fight us – and if he does then we can either kill or capture him and that's good – or he chooses to leave, and that's good also, because it separates him from the people and then the people can get on with running their lives. Quite honestly, putting a man on the moon is easier than getting water running in Afghanistan.

We're not getting outfought here in Afghanistan by the enemy. We're getting out-governed. These people [locals] who are fence-sitters are being pushed over with a feather. It isn't as hard as I anticipated it might be. But if people come to believe in the government, they will have eliminated most of the insurgency. If they achieve that, that's going to be a high enough quality of life that the enemy's alternative [won't be] acceptable to them. It's too oppressive.[7]

Notes

1   Copyright © 1995–2009 WGBH educational foundation
2   www.motherjones.com
3   Permission of Stephen Grey
4   *Sudbury Star,* 18 December 2007
5   *NBC Field Notes,* 31 March 2008
6   *New York Times Magazine,* 24 February 2008
7   American Forces Press Service, March 2009

Helmand Province

'We don't care about the future of Afghanistan. We don't care about
democracy, clean water, schools for girls or the political overview.
All we care about is each other and making sure that our
mates get out of this alive.'
—anonymous British soldier during Operation Panther's Claw,
Helmand Province, July 2009

The War on Terror is predominantly an American affair. The world's premier
superpower has committed more troops, more resources and spilled more blood
in Iraq and Afghanistan than any other member of the so-called 'Coalition of
the willing'. Yet, as the focus of the War on Terror switched from Iraq to
Afghanistan in late 2008, the southern Afghan province of Helmand assumed
centre-stage in the struggle against al-Qaeda and the Taliban. And it wasn't
the Americans who were in the frontline in this fight – it was the men and
women of Britain's armed forces.

In January 2006, the British government announced that its troops would
be replacing US forces in Helmand Province as part of Operation Herrick. The
British 16 Air Assault Brigade formed the core of this force, which started to
arrive in April. The fighting that followed in the subsequent months and years
would be the most brutal and unrelenting that the British Army had been
involved in since the Korean War (1950–53). In Helmand, the Taliban were
determined to take and hold ground against NATO and Afghan Army troops.

Helmand is one of 34 provinces in Afghanistan. It has a population of
740,000 and an area of 58,584 sq km (22,619 sq miles). The province is mainly
desert, though the River Helmand provides water for irrigation. Most of the
population is Pashtun, with Hazara, Baloch, Brahui and Tajik minorities
mainly resident in the capital, Lashkar Gah. Helmand has a southern border
with the Balochistan province of Pakistan, which is very porous with regards to

the comings and goings of the Taliban. The province is the heartland of the Taliban, and it is also the world's largest opium-producing region, responsible for a staggering 42 per cent of the world's total production. Many of Helmand's tribal groups are heavily involved in the lucrative opium trade and do not take kindly to the presence of NATO forces. The tribes often form loose alliances with the Taliban to combat UN efforts to bring peace to the province or more accurately to interfere with the lucrative narcotics trafficking.

The British quickly established bases in the towns of Sangin, Lashkar Gah and Gereshk, but the main base is Camp Bastion. Situated on a plateau northwest of Lashkar Gah, surrounded by miles of desert, it has its own runway, water supply, sewage, electricity and hospital. Its garrison of 2,000–3,000 troops is very much in the middle of enemy territory, at the forefront of the effort to win the War on Terror. For only victory in Helmand can defeat the Taliban and perhaps deal a mortal blow to al-Qaeda itself. NATO is fortunate to have in its arsenal a force such as the British Army, whose ranks are staffed with some of the most professional troops in the world. But the price in British blood is high.

Danny Groves

Corporal Groves, mortar section commander with the 3rd Battalion, The Parachute Regiment. In August 2006, Groves was sent to the town of Musa Qala in northern Helmand. The Paras' job was to defend the isolated British base nicknamed the Alamo, which was a rundown police station surrounded by thick mud walls and an old prison tower in the centre.

14 August
World War III. Woken around 07.30 hours by the usual rocket-propelled grenade (RPG) alarm clock from our friendly Taliban neighbours. We can tell from the continuous crack and thumps, however, that this is no hit-and-run.

The Taliban fan out in the field to the east and prepare for an all-out sustained assault. We are down to 33 rounds per barrel on the 81mm mortar with no sign of a re-supply. One Taliban fighter attempts to fire an RPG at us three times. Unknown to us, our intelligence is listening in and monitoring this fighter's transmissions. His commander says, 'Pull back, you will surely be killed!' and the guy says, 'No! No! The infidels murdered my brother.' This explains his determination. The fourth time turns out to be his last. One of our deadly mortar rounds crashes down, bringing his campaign to an end.

26 August

The attacks increase – sometimes there are eight a day. Our fresh ammo will be lucky to last 10 days. At 19.00 hours, we are hit by a massive explosion. It becomes obvious we are surrounded as the click-click-click of incoming rounds intensifies.

Everyone is firing, and all you can see is the friendly red tracer – the standard used by NATO forces – going out, and the enemy green tracer, the colour used by [former] Soviet bloc countries, flying in and bouncing everywhere as the Taliban aim and fire at us. It is madness. This is the heaviest, closest attack we've sustained so far. [*In February 2007, the Taliban retook Musa Qala and held it until December, when NATO mounted an operation to retake it. After three days of heavy fighting with casualties on both sides, the Taliban withdrew and Coalition moved in.*][1]

Jason Conway

Staff Sergeant Conway was also a member of the 3rd Battalion, Parachute Regiment. In October 2006, he was under heavy Taliban fire at the Sangin base.

I've never been in an environment like Sangin, where the threat was real. It was mentally draining. Part of you wanted to grieve [for fallen comrades], but then part of you knew that you, especially me – in a position of command, had to rally the lads. It does grind you down, when you're going out, day after day.... For young guys, to be involved in something, come back in, probably get a few hours' sleep, having thought about what's just happened, then get the kit back on and go back out into the same environment ... it is a test. One of our colleagues was involved in a mine strike last week. He was a young man, [with a] young fiancée, baby due; severe head injuries, and he lost both his legs in a mine strike. You know, you can't weigh that up. You try and put it at the back of your mind.

I don't know whether it's from boredom, I don't know whether it's because they've [the Taliban] got nothing else, so the honour of jihad would be in some way an escape for them, to get away, you know. Half past four, the mosques are crying out, ready for prayers, and then by six, you see the young boys now: they're in the fields doing hard labour.[2]

Jamie Loden

Major Loden was the commander of A Company, 3rd Battalion, The Parachute Regiment, at Sangin in October 2006.

People have said to me in the past, before deployments, 'Do you want to go?' Can you imagine being a doctor, doing seven years of medical school, and never performing an operation? Our regimental history [has] an ethos of producing incredible fights when the odds are not in our favour, so even if we were in that sort of position, we would be absolutely revelling in it.[3]

Hugo Farmer

Lieutenant Farmer was one of Loden's platoon commanders (A Company's 1st Platoon) at Sangin in October 2006.

For what must have been two weeks, we were being attacked as many as five, six times a day. The majority of the contacts were at night, so it was like a light show, the tracer rounds coming over, the noise of being fired at – it's a bit like somebody getting a wooden ruler and slapping it on the table, and then somebody standing next to them with a couple of boules balls and clicking those together. It's a very odd sound … when it's really close, you'll hear a snap and a ricochet.[4]

Rory Bruce

Lieutenant-Colonel Rory Bruce, Royal Marines Reserve, spokesman for the United Kingdom Task Force (UKTF).

Operation Glacier 4 marks the continuation of our recent operations in and around Garmsir to reach out and strike at legitimate Taliban targets and command centres. With the first use of Afghan artillery, it also marks a significant step towards enabling full combat capability for the ANA [Afghan National Army] and ultimately to Afghans being able to provide security for themselves. Operation Glacier 4 is part of our ongoing offensive to disrupt their command chain, their lines of communication and their ability to re-supply and re-arm.[5]

Charlie Mayo

The Taliban are nothing if not resilient. In March 2007, NATO launched Operation Achilles, which consisted of approximately two brigades of troops from US, British, Afghan, Dutch and Canadian units – around 5,500 soldiers in all. Lieutenant-Colonel Charlie Mayo, UK spokesman in Afghanistan at the time, was upbeat at the beginning of Achilles, as this following account illustrates.

We know that the senior Taliban leadership is made up of fighters from outside of the area who have coerced and intimidated the local people of Sangin into fighting for them. As ISAF has advanced and put pressure on the Taliban, there is strong evidence to suggest that this leadership has chosen to flee rather than fight.

Prior to the operation, we informed the local population of our intentions through the governor of Helmand and also by means of radio broadcasts, letters and word of mouth. We asked the people of Sangin just to stay away from the fighting so that we could defeat the Taliban quickly.

This operation is not directed against the ordinary people of Sangin, but against the hardcore Taliban and foreign fighters who have forced the people to live under a regime of intimidation and cruelty.

Part of the role of ISAF is to mentor the Afghan National Army, who will gradually assume responsibility for the security of Sangin over the coming days and weeks. That will then allow the government of Afghanistan to deliver the services that the people of Sangin deserve and require. It is critical for the long-term success of this operation and to maintain security in Sangin that the local people support the government of Afghanistan and its own security forces.

In October 2007, Lieutenant-Colonel Mayo's opinions seemed to have undergone a change. He was more realistic in his assessment of the situation in Helmand Province and also more realistic about the difficulties faced by the troops on the ground.

It is a bloody nightmare. To be brutally honest, in places, it is like fighting in the jungle. Forget the idea that they [British troops] are engaging at 100–200 metres [110–220 yds] and opening fire, they are being ambushed at 10 metres [33 ft], and on many occasions they are fixing bayonets before going into the fight.[6]

John Allen

Lieutenant Allen was Troop Commander with 26 Regiment, Royal Artillery, British Army. During Operation Achilles the regiment was firing up to 500 rounds of high-explosive shells a day from its 105mm light guns in support of 29 Commando Regiment, Royal Artillery (29 Commando Regiment is the Close Support Artillery Regiment that supports 3 Commando Brigade, Royal Marines).

When we first moved into the area, the district centre was receiving mortar and rocket attacks every night. During the two months there we made significant progress, with an area of a diameter of 3 km [2 miles] surrounding the centre being virtually cleared of the Taliban.

As a command post officer at Garmsir (about 195 km [120 miles] from the Pakistan border), it was my job to ensure that data for the guns was passed on for the various fire missions.

Our guys had to convert from working with their larger 155mm mobile AS90 guns to the smaller and lighter guns. Fortunately the drills were similar. We worked as mobile outreach groups to support operations wherever they were.

We were supporting Zulu Company. The remainder of our group were at the Forward Operating Base Robinson covering a 7 km [4.5 mile] area of the southwest Sangin Valley. Of the four gun troops, they were the busiest. It was a Taliban focal point, and they had four or five missions a day, under constant mortar and rocket attack.

It was great experience to work with the tempo full on. There was a massive responsibility put on you. It was a great way to get such good operational experience. It was a challenge on a number of fronts, particularly with the area being so barren and so hot.[7]

Folarin Kuku

Second Lieutenant Kuku made history in 2007 when he joined the 1st Battalion, Grenadier Guards, British Army, becoming the first black officer in the regiment's 350 years of service. But to the Taliban, he was just another enemy soldier. In May 2007, Lieutenant Kuku was fighting Taliban extremists around the Helmand town of Gereshk. The town has a population of around 44,000 and is about 120 km (75 miles) northwest of Kandahar.

We stepped off quite early in the morning. The ANA [Afghan National Army] were doing what they were instructed to do, which was to search compounds and detain any suspects that were harbouring, or indeed were, Taliban. They arrested three men in total. However, they let two go free once they questioned them.

Once we got within one or two kilometres from there, that's when it started to get tasty. We pushed forward to clear that position and we spotted a mortar barrel, but couldn't get clear identification of it, so we were not happy to use our heavy weapons.

We are not here to level the place; we are here to specifically target the Taliban. We found in one or two compounds there were women, children and older men taking refuge in there, who were caught up in the fighting and didn't have time to flee. Our company commander got into a wagon loaded with men and went after them, as most people would in his situation. He then got ambushed by a superior force and cut off from us.

The Taliban are gutsy fighters; they stood up in the open even though they were getting engaged at close quarters with small arms. When we came under accurate mortar fire, I took the decision to retire southwards into a different area of operation, which belonged to our Brigade Recce [Reconnaissance] Force. We made contact with them and called in heavy weapons to take out the mortar barrel, at which point the enemy broke off contact and the company commander was able to extract himself.[8]

Chris Holmes

Sergeant Holmes was serving with the 1st Battalion, the Royal Anglian Regiment (known as the 'Vikings'), British Army, when the unit was deployed on operations in Helmand in 2007. The regiment's troops experienced some of the most intense fighting the British Army has seen since World War II.

A lot of lads didn't know what to expect, but we knew there was enemy waiting. In Nawzad, we went out on patrol looking for Taliban positions when my platoon was ambushed. Straightaway we had to find the enemy, but it's extremely difficult when you're hit with rocket-propelled grenades (RPGs) in dug-out positions. Our vision was only 20 per cent and we carried 36 kg [80 lb] on our back. We extracted back to a wall, then radioed for mortars. Initially we were in shock, but within 10 seconds everyone stepped up a rank. By now the whole company was surrounded by Taliban and we fought our way back to base, under contact from every angle. It took two and a half hours. I've been to Iraq, but nothing comes close to it.

I've got no remorse for the Taliban. They started the fight that day and we finished it. At the time, my wife was heavily pregnant, and Katie was born while I was on an op. I found out over the radio afterwards, which was weird and I felt tearful. When I came back on R&R, my wife was at Brize [RAF Brize Norton airbase] waiting to meet me with our new baby. It was very emotional.[9]

Bill Drinkwater

Lance-Corporal Drinkwater was also fighting with the 1st Battalion, the Royal Anglian Regiment, British Army, in Helmand in 2007.

We went to Putay, north of Sangin, to clear a village and win hearts and minds. But as we walked towards a ditch, all hell broke loose. We got ambushed and there was a ferocious amount of fire. As we lay in a ditch, I could see RPGs overhead. I was looking out for my blokes, but at the same time, you've got to get fire down to make sure they can't give it back.

The worst bit was trying to cross open ground. The Taliban hid in a maize field and were firing from within. We peppered the field, but it was mayhem. One bloke fell and we were just about to go and get him when he suddenly darted across. As we got out, we got hit again. But this time, we took cover in a big ditch. We radioed for close air-support and American A-10s flew in, which allowed us freedom to move. In the wagon on the way back, you say to yourself, 'Thank God, I'm still alive.'[10]

Muhammad Khan

Private Khan was another soldier of the Royal Anglian Regiment (the 'Vikings'), British Army, who was battling for his life in Helmand in 2007.

My main memory of Afghanistan is of rockets flying into base. My role was as the 'eyes and ears' at the front of patrol, with my section commander just behind. The heat was always intense, and the weight of our kit and our body armour when we're doing Ks after Ks [kilometres] is exhausting. Most contacts take place during the day. The Taliban don't really fight at

Corporal Garrett Jones, 2nd Battalion, 7th Marine Regiment,
1st US Marine Division, was blown up by a booby trap while on patrol in Iraq.
He has continued his military career.

Captain Lara Chapman, US Army, served in Iraq between January and December 2006, one of the thousands of women who have served in the conflict.

Roshan Khadivi was a United Nations Children's Fund (UNICEF) External Relations Officer in Kabul, serving a two-year assignment beginning in 2002.

A US Marine dog handler with Alpha Company, Task Force Raider, walks with Pinkie, a bomb-detector dog working in Helmand Province, Afghanistan.

US Marines fire on Taliban positions during a firefight in Nawa District, Helmand Province in October 2009. The battle began when Taliban fighters opened up with assault rifles and machine guns on a Marine patrol.

Flags fly at half-mast at the main British Operations Base at Lashkar Gah,
Afghanistan, in November 2009 to honour troops killed in recent operations.

US Marines come under Taliban small-arms fire in Nawa District, Helmand Province, Afghanistan, on 4 October 2009.

US Marines carry a young Afghan gunshot victim to a waiting Army Black Hawk helicopter during a medevac operation in Helmand Province, Afghanistan, in October 2009.

British Royal Naval Reservist Leading Hand Richard Byrne was in Afghanistan in 2009, where he was using his agricultural expertise to advise Helmand's farmers.

Christopher Campbell was the Chief Air Mobility Liaison Officer,
XVIII Airborne Corps, US Army between 2002 and 2004.
He is pictured here with Afghani children in Kabul.

Royal Marines from 45 Command patrol Sangin,
Helmand Province in November 2009.

US troops firing a 105mm light gun from FOB (forward operating base) Dwyer in Helmand Province in November 2009.

night, when muzzle-flash would easily give their positions away. There was only one contact when I identified a suspicious sighting on high ground. We engaged when they opened up on us, and they definitely took a few casualties that day.

Out on patrol, the locals were fine with us, but when the Taliban infiltrate villages, they fear for their lives and move out, which is a combat indicator. On the news, all you hear about are the deaths of troops, but blokes lose limbs and it doesn't get even mentioned.[11]

Kev Walker

Corporal Walker, 1st Battalion, Royal Electrical & Mechanical Engineers (REME), British Army, was in Camp Bastion in January 2008, repairing and servicing the All Terrain Protected Vehicles called Vikings.

[Viking armoured all-terrain vehicles] are extremely good for rocking up and scaring the shit out of the Taliban. They really don't like it. We provide equipment support, offering quick engineering decisions, repairs and advice to the Royal Marines on what they can and can't do on the Vikings. We take our tools with us and try to keep the Vikings 100 per cent available. Keeping on top of faults and on top of mobility, simple maintenance, checking the tracks and keeping 100 per cent availability of the Vikings for the troops. The Royal Marines trust our guys to fix the kit.

I think they're doing a fantastic job. They're awesome vehicles for what they do. The teething problems were down to the terrain. If you put any vehicle across that terrain, which is mountainous, rocky, dusty and sandy and has everything that will knacker up gears, it will have trouble with it.

They make a massive difference to the operation. We were working closely with the Gurkhas and the Royal Welsh [The Royal Welch Fusiliers] and you could see the relief on their faces when the Viking turns up. The Royal Welsh got contacted by an anti-aircraft gun. My troop went in with the Vikings to create a screen, allowing them to get out. We put down heavy fire from the Viking's general-purpose machine gun (it is also fitted with 350-calibre guns), and before we left, having taken no casualties, it looked like all the Taliban had left. If we didn't have something like the Viking it wouldn't have been such a happy ending. It was pretty heavy terrain too, and I'm not sure any other vehicle could have got in there.

They can cope with the terrain because they have track mobility, which is much better than wheeled vehicles and get bogged down less. We know the Taliban don't like them. They're pretty much unstoppable.[12]

Matthew Croucher

Lance-Corporal Matthew Croucher of Britain's 40 Commando Group's Commando Reconnaissance Force, was operating from Forward Operating Base Robinson (in Helmand Province, located next to the Helmand River, near the town of Heyderabad) on 9 February 2008. His subsequent heroism won him the George Cross. His Citation read: 'As the team moved silently through the still darkened compound, Lance-Corporal Croucher felt a wire go tight against his legs, just below knee height. This was a trip-wire connected to a grenade booby-trap, positioned to kill or maim intruders in the compound. He heard the fly-off lever eject and the grenade, now armed, fell onto the ground immediately beside him.'

I automatically sensed an extreme fear when I looked down at the ground and realized that there was a grenade with the pin pulled at my feet. It was one of those where I had a split-second decision what to do. I had a quick look around and realized that there was no real place to take cover.

There were two guys initially right behind me and a third just a bit further back, so I felt a bit guilty for setting the device off. I thought that the best course of action for everyone, including myself, was to lie right next to the grenade, point my body armour towards it with my day sack and take the brunt of the explosion and see what happens from there.

I was more or less alongside of it to create a barrier, and when I was on the ground I was just gritting my teeth waiting for the explosion, and I had that deep gut feeling of, this is going to hurt, or I'm in serious trouble now.

It felt like someone had run up to me and kicked me in the back really hard, along with a loss of hearing, ears in extreme pain and a throbbing head. Then my body started aching and there was a smell of burning. Total disorientation.

The battery [in the day sack] took the brunt of the shrapnel which came from the grenade. It was blown about 10 metres [33 ft] away or so and started flaming furiously, so we all thought it was a secondary device that had gone off in the compound. So everyone took cover again, looking at this battery that was flaming away. It's lucky that the battery was blown off me, otherwise I would have had serious burns from that as well.

A couple of hours later I was happy to stay on the ground, kind of got my head together. Although I had a lack of hearing and my head was throbbing, it was an ideal situation to try to catch any Taliban in the area. Obviously, Taliban in the area on hearing an explosion would automatically think that we were on the back foot with casualties, so it would be an ideal time to attack us.

We lay in wait in a ditch and over the next couple of hours there were various people who came out of compounds, so there were various teams waiting to pop up and arrest people or initiate contact if that happened. Unbeknown to me, when I was in a ditch, one of the lads spotted a Taliban soldier approaching with an AK-47 … he spotted us and raised his AK-47 to fire some rounds off, so we returned fire at him before he could get any rounds up at us and took him out.

Every day in Afghanistan you're in gun battles and you finish the day thinking, 'Lucky it wasn't me who was injured.' On numerous occasions, guys were injured in combat situations that I was in over there, so it's a relief when it's not you, but then you feel sorry for the guy who's been badly injured from it. You have to deal with these things every day, really.[13]

Tom Charles

At the beginning of March 2008, Major Charles of the Welsh Guards, British Army, was operating in the so-called 'green zone' of Helmand Province (the narrow strip of lush vegetation that cuts through the desert along the River Helmand).

When we arrived in the consolidation phase, we had to create a degree of security and persuade people to move back in and start living their lives without the Taliban interfering. Over the time we have been here, the number of locals has definitely increased and that is because they see ISAF [International Security Assistance Force] as a force for good.

I think they understand that we are here to help them and to support the Afghan government. Because this is such a remote area, the government's tentacles are yet to reach out here, but in the meantime, we are trying to meet the problems they encounter.

They absolutely crave security. This is the number one issue to all locals. Unfortunately, this means we have to fight much of the time, but locals understand why and are prepared to be inconvenienced for security. We do anything we can to help them practise their religion because it's a good way of winning their consent, and that's why we gave them the mosque equipment. This area is not ready for a school, because the Taliban would bomb it and probably kill the teacher, but we have bought some equipment – blackboards, notebooks, pens, pencils – and in the meantime we are going to try and get a teacher in once a week.

Straight after we took over, the Taliban hit to test our tactics and see what firepower we had available. We were attacked four or five times at this location. That happened for about a week, but they kept on getting hit with our more substantial firepower. After that we got into a routine of normal patrolling to dominate the ground and disrupt the Taliban's movement.

It is a game of cat-and-mouse, with us both trying to find each other. What we are now encountering is small pockets of enemy, using insurgency-type tactics that hit and leave quickly. They are very agile and know the ground, which makes it difficult to pin them down.

During the rain, the irrigation ditches filled with water and got wider and wider. It became an ambush paradise, but because there's no high ground, the only way to get through it is to clear through on foot.[14]

Christian Wildsmith-Gleave

As in Iraq, air power is crucial to the war effort in Afghanistan. Squadron Leader Wildsmith-Gleave was a Harrier pilot and Executive Officer on No IV (Army Cooperation) Squadron, a mixed force of British Royal Navy and RAF pilots comprising 130 aircrew, engineers and mission support staff. In April 2008, he was flying his Harrier over Helmand.

With the Harrier's increased technology, we have become the premier choice for Coalition ground forces and can provide a scalable and escalating choice of weaponry.

The level of teamwork, throughout theatre, and the camaraderie I experience is unrivalled in any other aspect of life. Hearing the relief and seeing the emotion from the guys on the ground after we have successfully delivered weapons on their behalf has been the most rewarding aspect of my entire career. Basically, to land knowing you have saved someone's life is a remarkable experience. A group of Gurkhas had been ambushed on a road north of Sangin whilst re-supplying an FOB [forward operating base]. Their convoy had been hit by an IED [improvised explosive device], RPG [rocket-propelled grenade] and small-arms fire from insurgents hidden in a nearby wood.

I was called in by the Joint Tactical Air Controller attached to the convoy. I established where the enemy was and what threat they were to our guys, and then, having weighed up all the options, delivered two pods of rockets and a single air-burst bomb onto the wood-line. It looks like it did the trick as there was no more incoming fire and the Gurkhas recovered the vehicles.

There is always a risk that mistakes can be made and that my weapons could injure or kill friendly forces or innocent locals. The time between release and impact are the longest seconds imaginable.[15]

David Robertson

In May 2008, Lieutenant Robertson, B Company, 4th Battalion, Royal Regiment of Scotland (Highlanders), British Army, serving with the Helmand Task Force Warrior Company, was supporting an Afghan National Army (ANA) advance on a Taliban position in the countryside around Musa Qala.

We were advancing on an old graveyard, up on some high ground. There were some trees after a small village. As I crested the last hill before the trees, several RPGs were fired at us. I just saw this one coming head on. [The RPG bounced off Robertson's body and detonated nearby, leaving him with injuries to his arm and side.]

I didn't get my life flashing in front of me, but it did slow down. The thing split into three parts, bouncing off and then detonating. It must have just skiffed off me and went to my left and detonated on the fully open gunner's hatch. I was knocked backwards; I hit the back of the turret pretty hard. I remember a big bang and a heat wave and then felt burning in my arm and side. I radioed back to report what had happened and then we started to extract some of the ANA casualties who had been injured.

One of my lads took a look at my arm, which was stinging and felt hot and sore. He whacked a dressing on it and we carried on. We went forward again with the wagon and brought back another ANA casualty and then supported them with fire support. In the end an air strike was called in. At the time I was just cheesed off that I was being extracted. Last night I was just constantly replaying it and thinking how incredibly lucky we were.[16]

Alli Shields

Captain Shields, Royal Logistic Corps, British Army, was discovering that nowhere was safe in Helmand. She joined the Royal Logistics Corps in the 1980s when women were classified as non-combatants. In her 21 years of service she served two six-month tours in Iraq and also served in Northern Ireland, as well as being deployed in Helmand.

It doesn't matter whether women are allowed to join the infantry or not. Girls are fighting the enemy in one way or another every day. It really annoys me when you see people on television talking about the frontline in Afghanistan. Everybody is at risk, even the chef inside a base, whether it's from a bullet, a landmine or a bomb.

Vehicles would get stuck in the sand; the temperature was 50°C [122°F]. At the time there was fighting all over the Sangin Valley. [Three times her convoy came across deadly roadside explosives.] The desert is covered with them. They are all over the place and that really preyed on your mind.[17]

Jacq McKinnon

Flight Sergeant McKinnon, Senior Nurse in charge of Kandahar Airfield's Royal Air Force Aeromedical Evacuation Team (AET), April 2008.

The majority of patients are still [British] troops, but we also treat Afghan National Army, local civilians and, of course, troops from other Coalition nations.

Last month [March 2008], a suicide bomber detonated himself in Kandahar City. Over 200 civilians were killed and injured. After the Mass Casualty Alarm sounded, we all reported to the Aeromedical Cell. Some of us were tasked to support the doctors in the Role 3 Hospital Facility, whilst the rest of us prepared to move the casualties to other medical facilities in theatre. We ended up moving four badly wounded men to Bastion that day.

It makes you realize what we ask of our young nurses and medics, most of whom are 'first tourists' and have not experienced anything like this before. I was immensely proud of how they responded to what was an extremely traumatic incident. They worked flat out for over nine hours and undoubtedly saved lives. Although we have lots of reasons to be sad, due to all the traumatic injuries we see, the morale of the team is always high due to the close bond we have formed and the support we give each other.[18]

Amy Thomas

Lance-Corporal Thomas, serving with 114 Provost Company, 5th Regiment Royal Military Police (RMP), British Army, deployed to Afghanistan in October 2008. In 2009 she became the first British female soldier to fire a weapon on the frontline during a firefight with Taliban insurgents in Helmand.

I was just myself – I just got on with it because you have to, really. At first I thought I wouldn't be able to because I'm quite a girly girl, but once I was out, the training just kicked in.

The [Royal] Marines did not treat me any differently as a girl and I felt like one of the lads when I was out with them. Obviously, I found it hard being the only female because we were living out in the open at times, away from the bases. It was hard for washing and going to the toilet.

Everything they did, I'd be doing. We would be yomping for 7 km [4.5 miles] at any one time; much longer over the course of the whole day and night. Sometimes we would be out for four days at a time. I'd be carrying up to 48 hours of rations, at least six litres [1.6 gallons] of water a day, all my detainee-handling and evidence-gathering kit, my personal kit, spare ammunition, helmet and body armour – it was heavy.

It was also difficult because, as I was Military Police, anything they found on the ground I'd be carrying. If they found evidence, I'd be carrying it – ammunition, weapons, parts that could potentially be used in improvised explosive devices. If we captured detainees they would also have to be escorted, usually under the supervision of me and the other Military Police soldiers.

We were doing a night move and we'd just left the compound, and after about 185 metres [200 yards] we were crossing an irrigation ditch, and I just fell in. I'm quite tall, but I couldn't touch the bottom and I went right under – it was at night so I couldn't see anything. My kit was soaked, but when I got out we still had to yomp 7 km [4.5 miles] to a village to surprise the enemy, and when we arrived we came under fire straightaway.

20 March 2009 [Operation Aabi Toorah against one of the final Taliban strongholds of Marjah, to the west of Lashkar Gah]

I always get nervous before deploying on a new op, but I was excited, too. But this was the worst place I've ever been. We came under contact in Marjah and it was just non-stop all day and all night, incoming small-arms fire and mortars and 107 rockets.

As soon as we left the helicopters, the company came under fire, and then it was non-stop. There were loads of Taliban in the area. I identified one of them running with a weapon and indicated him to the lads. They didn't see him, so I took the shot. It went on all day and all night. We had to keep moving location through the village, moving from compound to compound. At the time I've never been so scared in all my life, but I don't think that I was the only one. Sometimes they could see I was nervous, and they [the Royal Marines] would constantly be checking that I was okay and looking out for me. On that day, two of our guys got shot, and I found that quite hard, but they were all right – as long as we haven't lost anyone, that is the main thing.

A lot of people don't believe that I'm in the Army, so it's hard to tell them about what I've been doing. I've really enjoyed it, and I'd definitely like to come on another tour. I am really happy that I got to work with the Royal Marines because they are easy to get on with and some I would now count as very good friends.[19]

David 'Tommo' Thompson

Sergeant Thompson, 8 Troop, Y Company, 45 Commando Group, Royal Marines took part in a raid in January 2009 on compounds in the area of Mazak, north of Forward Operating Base Inkerman, in the Upper Sangin Valley. Inkerman's strategic position at the head of the Sangin Valley means that it is a bulwark against Taliban attacks.

Before entering any compounds, we are always aware of the threat of booby traps, IEDs and the enemy within. Unless we are confident that the enemy are inside, then the entry will always be what we call a 'soft knock' – minimal force and maximum care is adopted. Special care is taken to respect those housed within, initially making sure they do not pose any threat, whilst also taking into account the cultural and tribal sensitivities. This undoubtedly puts a lot of stress on younger lads throughout the patrol. For the members of the troop [some straight from training, aged as young as 18], this is a part of a daily routine that has to become the norm.[20]

Jack Lopresti

In January 2009, Gunner Lopresti, 266 Battery, 100 Regiment Royal Artillery (Territorial Army), British Army, was providing force protection on the Medical Emergency Response Team (MERT) Chinook helicopter at Camp Bastion, Helmand Province.

[W]e dropped off our patient and immediately took off again. We had to land somewhere in the middle of the desert, and so, with our Apache helicopter as escort, I thought things might get a bit hairy. As we got nearer we found out more details; it was a mine strike, three Americans: one dead, two injured.

We landed, and I and the other troops got out of the Chinook and fanned out to give protection as the injured were loaded onto the helo. Once back on the Chinook, it was a hive of activity, with the doctors and nurses frantically working on the two casualties. I helped by passing the medical team things and holding up the drip and lightly squeezing the bag as instructed. When we got back to Bastion, I then helped carry the stretcher to one of the waiting ambulances.

As I got back on the Chinook, they were cleaning out the helicopter – it was a brutal demonstration of the grim reality of the conflict out here and the daily sacrifices being made. I thought of the families of those boys, the heartache and the calls they were going to get in the next few hours.

And still we weren't finished! Another call had come in, out to another FOB; a poor lad had been injured by mortar fragments. There was a lighter moment on the way back, though; he was stable, conscious and laid out on a stretcher. I don't know whether it was the morphine which did it or not, but he started to hug and cuddle one of the nurses; we didn't blame him, as she was actually very pretty! She was very nice to him and chatted all the way back to the hospital; no mean feat in a noisy helicopter. All this happened in a single morning. It was a hell of an introduction to the heroic work of the aircrew and medical teams who do these duties 24/7.[21]

Gordon Messenger

In a stand-up fight with the Taliban, the superior training and equipment of the British Army will always win. In February 2009, the British launched Operation Diesel, a raid by 700 troops from the Royal Marines' 45 Commando,

42 Commando and 3 Commando Brigade's Reconnaissance Force, plus armoured infantry and close reconnaissance from the 1st Battalion, Princess of Wales's Royal Regiment (1 PWRR). The target was a Taliban drugs factory and arms stronghold in the Upper Sangin Valley in Helmand. Brigadier Messenger, Royal Marines, was the commander of Task Force Helmand.

> The links between the Taliban and the drugs trade are well proven, and we know that the revenue from narcotics production directly funds the insurgency ... Operation Diesel was a clinical precision strike, supported by strong intelligence, which has had a powerful disruptive effect on known insurgent and narcotics networks in the area.
>
> The success of the operation is a significant boost to the Afghan authorities in their fight against the drugs trade. As a combined ISAF [International Security Assistance Force]/Afghan team, we will continue to take every opportunity to strike at the linkage between the narcotics trade and the Taliban, the product of which brings so much misery to the Afghan people.[22]

Matthew Webb

Marine Webb was a sniper with 9 Troop, Yankee Company, 45 Commando Group, during Operation Diesel.

> Once Yankee started their move towards the eastern objective, we were up on the high ground giving them cover. We got contacted first – RPGs soaring over our heads and a bit of AK fire – we always expect this, so it wasn't anything too new. We just got on with picking out enemy forces as they moved – appearing in breaks in the tree line or when they moved from the compounds ... We were picking targets from about 1,500 metres [1,640 yards], and, for those further out where we were not able to clearly identify them as enemy, we were providing the information to the Apaches which have better optics at those distances. We were always checking to make sure they were enemy.[23]

Duncan Phimister

In May 2009, at Camp Bastion field hospital, Territorial Army personnel from the Midlands region of England were treating the wounded. Their commanding officer was Lieutenant-Colonel Duncan Phimister, who in civilian life worked at the George Eliot Hospital in Nuneaton, Warwickshire, England.

... There is no typical day here. The activity fluctuates wildly. Some days you can have 20 casualties, some days four or five. It could be minor – a heat-related illness – or it could be the fallout of a suicide bomb. The other week we had three [suicide bombers] in one day. To get people with their limbs blown off – double amputees – you don't see that back home. But that is what it is like here, there is severe trauma.

Last week was extremely bad. We lost six soldiers, four in one day.[24]

Anthony Matthews

Trooper Matthews of the Light Dragoons, British Army, was hit by a rocket-propelled grenade during Operation Panther's Claw in Helmand Province in July 2009 (the operation to clear territory of Taliban insurgents prior to the Afghan elections in August 2009). The Light Dragoons were based near Lashkar Gah, the provincial capital. During the early hours of 7 July, his platoon stepped into an ambush. A grenade seriously wounded Matthews and his friend Trooper Aaron Bradley. Matthews described how he applied a tourniquet to his leg wound and to that of his injured comrade as he returned gunfire. After treatment, he was flown to Birmingham's Selly Oak Hospital, where an operation sealed a deep wound across the back of his left leg.

There aren't many people [who] can tell the tale of getting hit by a grenade. I've just been very lucky. We came out of the compound we had taken over, and there was a tree line that we used as cover. My mates were beside me at either side, and then all I remember is hearing a massive bang.

There was dirt all over their faces and they were screaming. It was like a scene out of [the movie] *Saving Private Ryan*. My ears had gone, and I looked at my friend and I could see he had been hit badly. I turned and looked down at my leg and my pants were all broken. I put a tourniquet on while I was still shooting.

When the bullets are whizzing past, it's terrifying. They sound like bees flying past your ears, and then you hear them land and it sounds like someone clapping their hands ... It was just adrenaline. I didn't feel anything [after being hit]. I stabbed myself with morphine and held on until the helicopters came. They got us back to Camp Bastion in four minutes … No one was killed or even injured badly that time, amazingly. A team came out to clear the area and make sure it wasn't a 'daisy chain', where a number of bombs are linked to a single command-and-control wire. It's proper war out there. One time it took us from first light until last light just to move 800 metres [874 yds]. We were in constant contact with the enemy.[25]

Al Steele

Major Steele, the commander of B Company, Black Watch Regiment, British Army, also took part in Operation Panther's Claw.

There is nothing worse for soldiers' morale than suffering casualties without being able to inflict them on the enemy. I never use mortars – they are good for raising the morale of the troops, but you risk injuring civilians. When, later, we meet the village elder of the family of a child that we have killed, it just sours everything and undermines everything we are trying to do … Running around, getting into fights and killing a few enemy is all very well and good, but my main concern at the moment is that we haven't talked to any local nationals or really got out our main message to the community that this time we are here to stay.

I was in the Upper Sangin Valley recently, where there was heavy fighting, and there were several occasions when I had the opportunity to kill enemies of the peace, and some I did kill because they are not friends of Islam, but others we could not because there was a danger that we would hurt innocent civilians.[26]

Christian Cabaniss

In July 2009, Lieutenant-Colonel Cabaniss arrived in southern Helmand with 4,000 US Marines from the 2nd Marine Expeditionary Brigade for Operation Khanjar ('Strike of the Sword'). Their mission – the first major military operation ordered by the new US President Barack Obama – was to oust the Taliban from the region and then stay in every area cleared in order to win the trust of the local population ahead of the Afghan presidential elections in August 2009.

By wintertime [2009], the Taliban are going to be on their heels, sitting in Pakistan, wondering what to do next. And we'll have the people. Once the people decide they won't tolerate the Taliban's presence, there's no way they can stay.

The Brits had a good understanding of what was going on down here, but they never had enough combat power to do what they would like to do and then sustain it over time. My battalion is taking over, we're obviously just a little bit larger; we've been able to position forces all over the central Helmand River Valley and really get out amongst the people. They just didn't have the capability to do it right.

What I told the Marines before they went out was – this isn't going to happen overnight. My hope is that by Eid we will have really cemented relationships with the local population, built that trust.

The Marine battalions in al-Anbar [Province] in Iraq had already come to the same conclusion: that working closely with the local population and building relationships with them had a greater impact on security than just going from street to street shooting did. We learnt that the hard way in Iraq, and we're starting the right way in Afghanistan.[27]

Alan Strain

Territorial Army volunteer Lance-Corporal Strain from Northern Ireland was attached to 4 Squadron Combat Support Logistic Corps, British Army. In August 2009, he was delivering supplies to British military outposts across Helmand Province, and came in close contact with the Taliban on numerous occasions.

It was a bit of a shock for my fiancée when I said I was coming out here, but she's coping really well. She would speak to her friends about how much she is afraid. She doesn't say too much about it to me because she wants me to keep my head straight. We have four kids, and so they, and planning for the wedding, are keeping her going. Hopefully she'll have everything organized by the time I get home, so that all I'll have to do is put on my uniform and say, 'I do.' She had said about getting married before I went on tour, but I preferred to wait until I got back. It's something that will keep you going.

You'll always get days when you want to lift your bags and walk away from it. But all the guys round you help. Everyone knows how everyone feels, so you get each other through it. I have had a few encounters with the Taliban, but the worst was when I was down in a place called Patrol Base Minden [south of Musa Qala], where they were building a new forward operations base.

My job was driving down to a wadi, which is a dried-up river, to collect stones and sand to fill the Hesco bags [big sand- or rock-filled bags that provide a safety barrier]. I did five wadi runs and was contacted [attacked by the Taliban] every time, but the worst was when I was sitting in the driver's seat. I was shattered and exhausted, and was waiting on the guy filling the container behind me, when I heard these two rounds whizzing past the window. I just ducked out of the way and the next thing a mortar came in and landed about 9 metres [30 ft] from the truck. It was very close.[28]

Eddie Scott

TA corporal in the 1st Battalion, The Royal Regiment of Scotland, British Army, in January 2010, Eddie Scott was the Section Commander in 4 Platoon of the battalion's B Company. He and his men were protecting a resupply convoy in Sangin, Helmand Province, when they were attacked by the Taliban.

Getting supplies around Helmand by land is a dangerous business. The locals who drive the trucks and the British troops who protect the convoys don't get half as much recognition as they deserve. My men and I were watching a convoy only recently and unfortunately this situation was no different. No sooner had we 'got eyes-on' the vehicles, than they were contacted by insurgents.

Rocket-propelled grenades [RPGs] and small arms were directed at the convoy but the enemy were not expecting us to be waiting in the wings. We identified their firing position and engaged them. To say that they were surprised when we started firing at them would be an understatement. The result of our action was that they turned their attention away from the convoy and started to concentrate their fire on our position.

Three RPGs later, the wall behind which the guys and I were firing had taken a pounding. However, we were soon back in position on top of the crumbling wall, returning fire with our own 66 [rocket launcher] and another burst on the machine gun. This seemed to do the trick and I called ceasefire. [29]

Notes

1   *Daily Mail*, 11 June 2008
2   *Guardian*, 14 October 2006
3   ibid
4   ibid
5   *Defence News*, 20 February 2007
6   *Defence News*, 10 April 2007
7   *Defence News*, 26 April 2007
8   *Defence News*, 21 May 2007
9   *Defence News*, 4 July 2008
10   ibid
11   ibid
12   *Defence News*, 28 January 2008
13   *Defence News*, 25 July 2008
14   *Defence News*, 3 March 2008
15   *Defence News*, 1 May 2008
16   *Defence News*, 13 May 2008
17   *Observer*, 22 June 2008
18   *Defence News*, 29 April 2008
19   *Defence News*, 29 April 2009
20   *Defence News*, 26 January 2009
21   *Defence News*, 27 January 2009
22   *Defence News*, 18 February 2009
23   ibid
24   *Guardian*, 31 May 2009
25   *Guardian*, 15 July 2009
26   *Guardian*, 25 July 2009
27   *BBC News*, 19 August 2009
28   *Belfast Telegraph*, 28 August 2009
29   *Defence News*, 4 January 2010

Winning hearts and minds

Defeating the Taliban and al-Qaeda forms only a part of the Coalition strategy in Afghanistan. Battlefield success means nothing if the underlying problems of the country are not addressed. The North Atlantic Treaty Organization's (NATO's) role, as stated by the organization itself, is 'to assist the Afghan government in exercising and extending its authority and influence across the country, paving the way for reconstruction and effective governance. It does this predominantly through its UN-mandated International Security Assistance Force.' This translates into 85,795 troops (as of February 2010) sourced from 43 countries, including all 28 NATO members.

Afghanistan's problems are indeed huge. To this end, both the UN and NATO have established large-scale aid programmes to assist the Afghan government in its efforts to rebuild the country. But the scale of the resources required to achieve this is truly daunting.

According to the UN, nearly 40 per cent of children under the age of three are moderately or severely underweight, and more than 50 per cent of children in that age group are moderately or severely stunted. The literacy rate for 15–24-year-old Afghans is 34 per cent, with 50 per cent for men and only 18 per cent for women. The infant and under-five mortality rates in Afghanistan are among the highest in the world. They are only higher in Angola, Liberia and Sierra Leone. Only one in three Afghans in urban areas has access to improved sanitation. In rural areas, this figure is one in ten.

Not only is the infrastructure of the country badly damaged, unlike Iraq, Afghanistan has no access to oil revenues to assist with redevelopment projects. In addition, one of the most lucrative forms of income – the opium trade – is being targeted by NATO offensives. On its own, therefore, the government has almost no hope of rebuilding the country. With international aid, though, Afghanistan has a chance. But the sums required are vast: between 2001 and 2008, the US alone provided $26 billion in aid to Afghanistan. In 2008, international pledges amounted to a further $15 billion, with the US providing

$10 billion of that figure. Whether all the aid donated actually reaches its intended targets is a moot point, but what is not debatable is that by the end of 2009, 42 per cent of Afghanistan's 30 million inhabitants were still living on less than a dollar a day, and life expectancy was only 45 years.

Roshan Khadivi

Roshan Khadivi, a United Nations Children's Fund (UNICEF) External Relations Officer in Kabul, arrived in Afghanistan in 2001. In January 2007, she reflected on the progress she had seen regarding the welfare of children in the country since her first assignment there more than five years previously.

Prior to my first trip to Afghanistan in 2001, I remember a time when the horrible pictures of group killings in Kabul football stadiums reached the rest of the world. News reports spoke of oppressive restrictions and daily torture of innocent people. Worldwide, many wondered how things would turn out here.

I came to this country in late 2001 on a short assessment mission, followed by a two-year assignment beginning in 2002. I have been back in Afghanistan for about a month, and this most recent visit has been a real opportunity to see how things have changed ... Kabul is still one of the main hubs for the journalists. There are the many regulars and then there are the 'firefighters', the reporters who come and go on three-day visits. The stories that seem to get the most media coverage are those about security in the southern and eastern parts of the country.

There is no doubt about the security and access problems here, but there also has been significant progress on the ground. Somehow, stories of these extraordinary works hardly make it to the main news bulletins around the globe ... For example, more than 4.89 million children in Afghanistan are going to school and 48,000 women, even in remote villages, attend 1,782 literacy centres – astounding for a country where just a few years ago, education was banned and any progress for youth seemed unattainable ... My friends who live outside Afghanistan always seem amazed when I talk about UNICEF's support of literacy courses for women in Kandahar Province, where over 4,000 individuals will learn basic reading and writing skills and gain access to vocational training this year alone. This is because to outsiders, Kandahar is a place described in dire terms on the evening news, a place filled with insurgents. They have no idea that despite the efforts of those who try to intimidate people through the burning of schools or attacks on civilians, communities are more than eager to send their children to school or attend literacy classes in order to improve their lives.

The universal saying that it is always easier to destroy something than to repair it applies very much in this case – especially after so many years of war and destruction of infrastructure and morale. Afghans know from real experience that war and fear do not work. They have seen destruction on a daily basis and have experienced the pain of losing loved ones. They know that when people in a community become strong by educating themselves, negative forces can no longer use fear or violence to stop them.

From what I have seen, despite the daily challenges, people in Afghanistan are more determined than ever to move forward. They know that by educating their children, they are building a foundation for a country that is based on progress and peace, not the destruction of the past.

In 2007, with support from local communities, UNICEF staff members are planning to immunize Afghan children against polio in hitherto inaccessible areas. They plan to reach out to ensure that over 400,000 girls will be enrolled in schools. They aim to improve the quality of education, in part through the building of 200 cost-effective schools around the country. In addition, over 62,500 women of all ages will be enrolled in literacy courses.

Extraordinary things do and will continue to take place in this country. Since my first visit to Afghanistan, extraordinary changes have taken place – this despite the attacks of those who fear peace and progress in a nation whose children are as deserving as those in the rest of the world.[1]

Barry Pitcher

Provincial Reconstruction Teams (PRTs) were first established by the Americans in Afghanistan in 2002. Comprising military personnel, diplomats and civilian specialists, their aim is to support reconstruction efforts in unstable states. There are currently around 26 PRTs operating in Afghanistan. In March 2007, Corporal Pitcher of the Royal Canadian Military Police arrived from Canada to undertake PRT duties in Afghanistan

The latest Civilian Police (CIVPOL) contingent for Afghanistan, comprised of three Royal Canadian Military Police (RCMP) and one

Medicine Hat [a city located in Alberta] police officer, recently left Ottawa for the Kandahar Provincial Reconstruction Team. Prior to leaving, we underwent two weeks of training to prepare for the mission. Classes included improvised explosive device (IED) and booby-trap recognition, cultural awareness, and weapons testing. We also spent a few days at CFB [Canadian Forces' Base] Kingston, where we received a refresher on military patrol drills and the latest intelligence briefs from Afghanistan.

With the training fresh in our minds, we began the journey from chilly Ottawa on 16 February. After routing though various airports around the globe, we finally clambered aboard a C-130 Hercules for the final approach into Kandahar Airfield on February 20. We were expecting blistering desert heat, but it was raining when we arrived. We linked up with our luggage in an old hangar that we were told was the Taliban's 'last stand' when Coalition forces seized the airport in early 2002. Craters were all around, as were hundreds of bullet holes in the walls. What strikes you immediately is how vast and busy the airfield actually is. Helicopters and fighter jets from various countries were coming and going, and there is a real sense of urgency in movement. Right away, we started to gain an appreciation of the conflict that this country has seen in years past.

We linked up with Superintendent Dave Fudge, our contingent commander, and we were soon off to our new home via military convoy. Our accommodations at Camp Nathan Smith house the PRT, which also comprises a large military component as well as representatives from Foreign Affairs. Over the next two weeks, we learn to settle into camp life and get to know all the military partners that make things happen.

From the issuing of blankets to getting our ammunition, everything was on a strict schedule. Of course, in the middle of all this, is the fact that many of us have yet to adjust to time change. There is also the telltale rattle of gunfire, helicopters and artillery going off at all hours. It is not uncommon for us to now wake at 04.00 hours, ready to start the day. We are told that like many things, it will take a few weeks for the body to adjust to being here …

Kandahar, Afghanistan. Just in from the Zhare district, west of Kandahar, where I spent the last few weeks with the Royal Canadian Regiment Battle Group. Since we were in the 'birthplace' of the Taliban movement (Sangasar), things would occasionally get testy. It was interesting watching our Afghan police brothers break off training for combat; now there's something we don't see at division headquarters every day. It was amazing to see these guys take off, 12 to a Toyota pick-up, loaded down with rocket-propelled grenades (RPGs). They fight the Taliban in a skirmish, come back to have a bite of bread, reload the RPGs, then back out across the grape fields again. One commander told me he has been fighting the Taliban for 12 years and that is all he knows how to do. Make no mistake, these men are perhaps the bravest and fiercest fighters I have ever seen. Many of them have nothing but a grey uniform and sandals, yet they sprint across open ground faster than a deer. When I head out to the field, I often take a 'goody bag' of small flashlights, pins and traffic vests for the Afghan National Police (ANP) as a reward for training.

Unlike a traditional police force, the ANP are referred to as police 'soldiers', as it is a more honourable title. Here, a police officer who is static is seen as less than honourable. Combat for these men is the highest form of glory, and you can see it when they return from a fight; they are as excited and giddy as schoolchildren. We shake hands and hug them as they come back to us after an engagement, because they seek our approval in a sort of 'big brother' way.

5 June marked the official opening of one of the first Provincial Reconstruction Team (PRT)-sponsored police stations in Kandahar. The official name was ANP Sub Station No 9, and its white walls clearly stood out against the surrounding hilltops in which it is nestled.

In cooperation with military engineers and CIMIC (Civilian Military Cooperation) officials from Camp Nathan Smith, the civilian police (CIVPOL) contingent has overseen the construction and staffing of this, the first of ten modern police stations in the city. As a result of an ever-increasing security risk for police forces in Kandahar, the PRT sought to assist the ANP in developing more secure bases of operation so they could move more freely on patrol. This started back in 2006 during the last rotation of CIVPOL officers here.

The design chosen is something akin to a French fort in the Arabian Desert; high concrete walls, guard towers, barbed wire and steel-reinforced gates. It may sound somewhat daunting, considering it is a police station, but let's not forget what a local police officer faces on a daily basis in this environment. Recent statistics from the Afghan Ministry of the Interior put the Afghan police-to-army casualty rate at 27:1. [T]here is a valid reason for this level of protection. The walls are constructed in layers of stone and concrete so that it can withstand a close IED strike or rocket-propelled grenade attack.

The location of the building itself was very strategic. This particular station sits guarding one of the main northern approach routes into the city from the nearby mountains. This has traditionally been an infiltration route for insurgent activity and has seen many forces pass though there, including the Soviet armoured battalions of the 1980s. Accompanying the construction of the station itself is a concrete observation post on a nearby mountaintop that provides a view to the approach routes. From there, you can see the city in its entirety.[2]

Hélène Le Scelleur

Captain Le Scelleur, Deputy Commandant, Health Services Support Company, Joint Task Force – Afghanistan, is part of Canada's humanitarian aid effort in Afghanistan.

At nine o'clock in the morning of 15 January 2008, we finally opened the doors of the District Joint Coordination Centre in Spin Buldak, ready to welcome everyone who wanted free medical care. This much-anticipated moment was the beginning of a Village Medical Outreach (VMO) visit, a project close to my heart since I first set foot on Afghan soil.

The need for health care is great in Kandahar Province, but Afghans have limited access to services. Security problems make development agencies hesitate to invest time and money in this area. To help bridge the gap, I proposed a VMO programme to help people in desperate need of health services, although the Health Support Services Unit at Kandahar Airfield had not conducted one since July 2006.

… Despite the popular belief that they are part of a 'hearts-and-minds' campaign, VMO visits are actually conducted to gather and confirm information about the health of the population of a given area. Statistics and epidemiological studies are sadly out of date. A secondary goal is to find children who need specialized clinical care and to register them – through our CIMIC [civil-military cooperation] section – with Afghan Trust Funds Assistance, a granting organization that ensures children receive the care they need to recover fully.

Escorted by a Reconnaissance Squadron (commanded by Major Pierre Huet), we drove from the forward operating base near Spin Buldak to the District Joint Coordination Centre, a convenient location for potential patients that was made available to us by the District Leader of Spin Buldak. With a platoon of infantry for perimeter security and two full medical teams (one male, one female), our clinic offered care to more than 260 patients, both children and adults, in six intense hours of clinical work.

… We saw people with a wide variety of troubles ranging from trivial to terrible: dehydration, malnutrition, musculo-skeletal problems, upper respiratory infections, cancer and congenital deformities. With no testing facilities or opportunity for follow-up, we could give only primary care, referring the most serious cases to the hospital in Spin Buldak. Everyone was grateful for what we had to offer, even if it was just a listening ear. An embrace, a handshake, a smile from the children: all day that was what we got. For once in their lives, these people felt recognized, which matters when you're sick.

At three o'clock, when the doors were shut, we told ourselves, 'Mission accomplished!' All went well, adding a little glow to the growing collaboration between Afghan and Canadian medical teams. We returned to the forward operating base knowing that we had done a little good for Afghans living in difficult circumstances. No, we didn't improve the general health of the population, but Rome wasn't built in a day. In winning the trust of the Afghan people, we will be able to introduce preventive measures along lines as simple as hygiene, which over the long term will help relieve Afghanistan of the burden of infectious disease.

We do not pretend to be the solution to the challenge of health care in Kandahar, but it's a sure thing that action speaks louder than words.[3]

Fraser Clark

Canada assumed responsibility for the Kandahar Provincial Reconstruction Team (KPRT) in August 2005. The KPRT numbers around 300 and has diplomats, corrections experts, development specialists, the Canadian police and the military within its setup. Captain Clark, the KPRT's Public Affairs Officer, made this report in April 2008.

As our tiny convoy lumbered into a village in central Kandahar City, the mid-morning sun began to strengthen and the temperature climbed to over 35°C [95°F]. Dozens of small children swarmed around our hefty, olive-coloured LAV IIIs [light armoured vehicles], jockeying for position to greet the soldiers as they climbed out of the vehicles. As we halted amid the entrepreneurial chaos of an Afghan market on this Friday morning – the official day of rest in Afghanistan – shop-owners gazed from their mud hovels over displays of colourful pashminas, trinkets and other goods typical of a Third World bazaar. Meanwhile, young Pashtuns leapt about, blurting 'Bic!' as they madly scribbled with invisible markers in their palms; they wanted pens.

Normally, Canadian convoys stop in neighbourhoods like this to meet the locals, see how they're getting on, and let them know ISAF hasn't forgotten them. But this patrol had a different reason. We regularly drive through these villages during our patrols. And as kids will inevitably be kids, some in this area have taken to throwing rocks at our vehicles – not unlike kids at home throwing snowballs at passing cars; the same thing is happening here. We really want to curb this trend, though, as on a couple of occasions these rocks have broken mirrors on our vehicles. We're conducting this patrol in an effort both to gain some positive face-time with the kids and to ask them to stop throwing rocks.

But what started out as a routine patrol to pass some information on to the locals suddenly turned into a parade.

Dozens of boys and girls, uninhibited by any cultural norms and obviously not intimidated by our weapons or body armour, welcomed us into their enclave. Many cheered with excitement while others shook our hands vigorously. And in the midst of this youthful melee, our patrol commander sought out village elders to engage them in conversation and pass along our message: Please don't throw stones at us.

The youthful owner of a pharmacy – educated in Pakistan, he speaks English so well it could be his mother tongue – blamed homeless Afghan children for these mishaps. 'They are the ones who throw the rocks,' he asserted. 'The kids with families here are good, we don't have any problems with them. But the ones without parents, they are the ones who get into trouble.'

As the patrol slithered through the city, hundreds of kids couldn't wait to speak to the Canadians, even if most couldn't speak a speck of English – or even French. (One kid came out with 'Bonjour!' so our Quebec-based predecessors of Roto 4 must have made quite an impression.)

To our surprise, several children confidently asked us questions in dramatic, lilting tones. 'How are you?' 'How old are you?' many demanded, while others inquired, 'What is your name?' and 'Where are you from?' As they asked their questions, others rushed in, wide-eyed and smiling, and tried to teach us some of their expressions. In our best Pashtun, we said 'Salam-alaykum' – peace be with you. Encouraged, the kids continued walking with us, teaching snippets of their language along the way ...

Their innocence and inquisitiveness couldn't help but move the hardest of our soldiers; the seemingly impenetrable icy gaze set in place by months of training and (in some cases) combat suddenly melted into broad smiles and laughter. It was a cultural exchange only these influential young diplomats could pull off.

One child who couldn't have been any more than eight years old approached me and extended his hand with a disarming smile. Instinctively, I took my hand off my rifle and put it in his hand, sealing a fleeting bond of friendship. My light-hearted companion kept pace with our patrol as we sauntered along the great canal bisecting the city, smiling at us the entire time. As we made our way from village to village, he carried on a conversation with me in Pashto – I couldn't speak a stitch, but this didn't seem to matter to him – while cleverly rolling a bicycle tire with a little piece of stick, apparently strutting his stuff for our entertainment. It was a truly surreal experience.

This foot patrol was designed to stop children from throwing rocks at our vehicles, but I think it achieved much more – a bit of friendship, faith, trust and hope. It is often said that tanks, troops and guns cannot win the hearts and minds of ordinary Afghans. Where I sit, it looks like the children of Afghanistan are winning the hearts and minds of Canada's soldiers.[4]

Joe McAllister

In October 2008, Superintendent McAllister was in Afghanistan as part of the Canadian civilian police (CIVPOL) first deployed to the Kandahar Provincial Reconstruction Team (PRT).

Last week I went to the Dhala Dam – one of Canada's signature projects. It's an amazing site north of Arghandab. The dam holds back the Arghandab River, which is the irrigation system that feeds this entire area. It has been left to deteriorate for over 50 years, so Canada is helping to rejuvenate this system. I was there to work with the local police to provide infrastructure and systems improvements, so that the dam workers would have some security. The police have two mud huts, a couple of machine guns, rocket-propelled grenades and AK-47s. They have nothing else, so offering them upgrades is pretty easy. One of the first projects is to build a road and bridge that can hold the weight of construction equipment, so the work trucks can get in. From there the building will begin.

A new thing I learned up there was how Afghans treat their animals. Up on a mountain checkpoint we had to hike to, I encountered local police and their two dogs. They were mangy beasts, but being a dog-owner and lover, and wanting to just chat with these police, I asked the normal question, 'What's your dog's name?' To which they replied, 'It's a dog, why would we give it a name?' And I said, 'Well, because it's your pet and you should name him.' They all laughed and said, 'They are dogs, we call them dogs.' At least they don't eat them like in East Timor.[5]

Donald Cullison

US Army Lieutenant-Colonel Cullison was the head of the civil affairs efforts for the Paktia Provincial Reconstruction Team in Paktia, and the executive officer for the 80-person team based at Forward Operating Base (FOB) Gardez. The FOB sits nearly 2,347 metres (7,700 ft) above sea level, and snow and ice cover much of the area. The base sits just outside of Gardez, in Paktia Province, about 72 km (45 miles) from the Afghanistan–Pakistan border. The rural province is home to nearly 500,000 people. In February 2009, Cullison held a meeting in Gardez with local government officials.

In this fight, dollars are bullets. Development is just as important as security. You can't have security without development, and you can't have development without security. It goes to different degrees. But you can't have them exclusive.

It has nothing to do with going out there and being nice and giving people things, or being the Peace Corps of the Army. Why do we do everything that we do? Because I want the people to jump on the side of [the Afghanistan government] and the Coalition.

Our ultimate goal is to separate the populace from the insurgency. The insurgency isn't all the people. There are quite a few out there that just want to go about their lives and live peacefully. Right now the Afghan people are not sure. Are we going to stay? Is their government going to work? That's why the insurgency is allowed to operate within Afghanistan, because the Afghan people are still not sure which way this government is going to go and which way the Coalition forces are going to go.

Corruption is in every element of everything that is done here. It's the cost of doing business here in Afghanistan. We don't cut corners. We don't make promises that are going to benefit a [particular] Afghan official. We don't award projects based on a kickback or somebody benefiting. We do things because it's the right thing to do.

I think that they're beginning to see that when everybody trusts that the system is fair and is transparent, that everybody benefits.

You defeat an insurgency by influencing – convincing people that it's more advantageous for them to support their government. The way the PRT is fighting this war is the way the insurgency is going to be defeated.[6]

Richard Byrne

In February 2009, British Royal Naval Reservist Leading Hand Richard Byrne was in Afghanistan, where he was putting his expertise in agricultural development to work for the benefit of Helmand's farmers.

I joined the Royal Navy Reserves with the vague idea of sailing to various exotic ports around the globe. Five years later, I find myself in the middle of the Afghan desert, living in various not-so-glamorous locations.

I was mobilized from my civilian job as a senior lecturer at Harper Adams in April last year, and had six months of pre-deployment training in the UK and Germany, where I basically morphed from being a sailor into a soldier.

I'm now part of a MSST team (the military love abbreviations) – that's a Military Stabilization Support Team. I work with a STABAD (Stabilization Advisor) who is a civilian, and live in a FOB (forward operating base) where there is a galley (that's a cookhouse to non-naval types) and usually hot water.

I work out of Musa Qala, in the north of Helmand, and live in part of an old Russian hotel, which at least is dry. When I go on patrol, I stay in a PB (patrol base) which is usually based around a local compound, and I live off ration packs, with hot water from solar showers or puffing-billy boilers. This gives a real opportunity to see how the locals live and [to] appreciate how well built and warm their mud-brick compounds are. Living is pretty basic in the PBs – particularly the toilets, where daily duties involve burning the 'output'. It can be fun as well, and I'm lucky to be based with the Gurkhas, who produce fantastic curries out of ration packs.

My main role has been to look at the agriculture and opportunities to develop it, particularly as a way of drawing people away from growing opium poppies. The only way of doing this is to get out among the locals and see what they are doing, and try and understand why as well. The only way of doing this is on patrol, either on foot or by vehicle – usually a Snatch (Land Rover).

Patrols last a few hours and can take you into bazaars or into the open countryside. Going out is inherently dangerous, although staying in can be equally hazardous, as FOBs and PBs are attacked regularly with rockets and mortars, as well as small-arms fire. Out on patrol, the main danger comes from small-arms contacts and IEDs (improvised explosive devices). These are now unfortunately part of the Helmand landscape.

Patrolling in such an environment is both nerve-racking and thrilling, particularly in stunning mountainous landscapes. Reality bites, though, when you hear a shot or an explosion – and then things become a little less aesthetic and a little more dramatic. I often think it's a bit like a movie, with the helicopters, air strikes, smoke and noise. I also wonder – quite often – why I'm here, when I could be in my nice office in Harper Adams working on a paper or tutoring a student, but such is life. Unlike in the movies, where patrols just happen, in reality they take lots of planning and briefing – to keep us and the local population safe.[7]

Dave Bergman

During their occupation of Afghanistan, the Soviets littered the country with many thousands of mines, which continue to kill and maim Afghan civilians. Between 2002 and 2008, for example, 1,034 Afghans were killed by mines or explosive remnants of war (ERW), with a further 5,001 injured. Part of the Coalition effort in the country involves clearing the mines. To give an indication of the scale of this work, between January and April 2009 alone, 10,254 anti-personnel mines, 246 anti-tank mines and 365,987 ERW were destroyed in Afghanistan. Major Bergman, an Australian Army combat engineer from Melbourne, is the officer in charge of the Mine Action Centre, a detachment of mainly US military personnel focused on de-mining operations in and around the massive Bagram Air Base in northern Afghanistan.

Over the past six years, more than 200,000 landmines have been cleared in and around the base, but it is a slow, tedious, dirty and dangerous job. People wandering through the minefields present a danger to the de-miners as well as themselves. I know of one man who has been blown up four times and now has a prosthetic leg, simply from gathering scrap metal in the minefields in order to make enough money to feed his family.

Hemaya Brothers International Demining Company has established a demilitarization programme which recycles munitions from the minefields in a safe and secure manner, as well as a carpentry programme that teaches new skills and provides products for the community. The demilitarization programme employs five people. Three qualified carpenters are employed in the carpentry programme to teach up to ten locals, who all have a mine-related disability. It's wonderful to see an Afghan-owned company empowered and successful enough to be taking the lead and finding solutions to help the citizens of this country in such a way.

Personally, being able to bring about influence for the better by implementing programmes that help the Afghan people is extremely rewarding. More than 72,000 displaced civilians have so far been able to return home as a result of landmines being removed, and we're reducing the risk faced by those who would otherwise scavenge in the minefields.

Professionally, it is a huge responsibility to lead and put soldiers from another nation at risk, but the opportunity for Australia to provide the officer in charge of the Mine Action Centre allows us to wield influence in the community and the international Coalition. In turn, the Army and Australian Defence Force is gaining invaluable knowledge and experience in this type of work.[8]

Christopher Campbell

Christopher Campbell was the Chief Air Mobility Liaison Officer, XVIII Airborne Corps, US Army, between 2002 and 2004. In 2002, he was in Afghanistan and had first-hand experience concerning the problems of mines scattered throughout the country.

At the one intersection we come to, we turn southeast, taking the less populated route to Kabul. For miles as we leave the area of the base, the roads are lined with rocks every 6 metres [20 ft] or so. Red and white each rock is painted. White side to the road, red to the fields ... the minefields.

Only a week before I came here, one of the drivers of one of the fuel trucks waiting outside the gate had resisted the call of nature for as long as he could. The inspection of each truck is thorough, and the line that day was long. He stepped off the road, the road we've just come along, and walked a few paces in order to relieve himself. In that field, he left the contents of his bladder, a good bit of his blood, and the shards of bone and flesh that had once been one of his feet. One of his fellow truck drivers walked into that same field and carried him out. 'He was my friend. He was crying out for help. What else could I do?'

I had been told before coming here that this was the most heavily mined corner of the Earth. But if the engineers' slides are to be trusted, that's not so. At a mere 40 mines per square mile [2.6 sq km], this land ranks behind Iraq, Egypt, Croatia, Cambodia (reported by some sources to have more amputees per capita than any other country in the world), and finally Bosnia. For Bosnia, the tally is nearly 150 mines deployed per square mile. We once feared nuclear winter as a horrible possibility. But a worse decimation of the land has already set in, in some places.

Imagine standing on the edge of our national forests and looking in, but knowing that to venture there was to take your life in your hands. Imagine the Appalachian Trail not marked with discreet cairns, but with red and white painted stones every 3 metres [10 ft] or so. Irregular stone bobbers to mark out the territory belonging to another sort of fishers of men. 150 mines per square mile. One-quarter as dense as the placement of poles in De Maria's *Lightning Field* [a land-art installation in New Mexico consisting of 400 stainless steel poles inserted over an area measuring one mile by one kilometre], if they were evenly distributed. They're not. Stroll across such a field to buy your lottery ticket, and your odds of losing on the way far exceed your odds of winning, if you get there at all.[9]

Sameer Ahmad Tahseen

Sameer Tahseen, a Kabul University student, was at his home in Kunduz Province when 90 people were killed by a NATO air strike on 4 September 2009. (NATO aircraft blew up two fuel tankers hijacked by Taliban fighters. Unfortunately, the tankers were surrounded by civilians.) His comments illustrate the tightrope NATO treads in Afghanistan – trying to rebuild the country and foster good relations with the population, while attempting to destroy the Taliban and al-Qaeda. When mistakes happen, they can inflict serious damage on the campaign to win the hearts and minds of the locals.

I heard about the incident in the mosque. But the reports were all confused and it wasn't clear what exactly happened. Later on I learned more details from my father, who is the editor-in-chief of a local newspaper. I went to the main hospital in Kunduz straightaway. The security was tight; they were not letting anyone in – only close relatives of the injured. There were many villagers from the village where the strike happened. There must have been around 60 to 80 people gathered there. When I asked them about the number of injured people, they said there were around 20 people with severe burns.

People around here think that the civilians killed did know the insurgents. They are believed to be relatives, friends or neighbours of the Taliban. It is said that some of the victims received phone calls to let them know about the opportunity to get free oil. There is a rumour that 18 members of one family were killed in the attack – all from the same village. Several other families lost many family members, too.

It's really disturbing, especially that this happened during the holy month of Ramadan. Ordinary people are really angry because they believe that most victims are villagers. The Taliban will use this as an opportunity to gather wider support in the area. Kunduz has a high number of Taliban sympathizers anyway, and it will probably see an increase in Taliban activities. This is bad news for us as Kunduz is already becoming the Helmand of the north in terms of Taliban influence.

This was a sheer act of stupidity and arrogance by NATO. Why didn't they communicate with the local police department? This attack would have been successful only if they had managed to avoid civilian casualties. The issue of civilian casualties makes every Afghan angry, including myself. They are going down the same route as the Soviet troops. It is a very effective way to spread hatred among ordinary people and to give the Taliban the opportunity to recruit more people.[10]

John Agoglia

In 2010 Colonel Agoglia (US Army) was the Director of the Counter-insurgency Training Center, Afghanistan, at Camp Dubs outside Kabul. His comments indicate that, after nine years of war, NATO is still struggling to implement an effective hearts-and-minds campaign in Afghanistan.

In Afghanistan we've been focused on counter-terrorism, not governance. That's stupid shit. We've been trying to implement a comprehensive integrated approach when we in the alliance don't know what that is. We're learning. The key is to to get the best match of capabilities to address three key issues: security, governance, development. You have to look at it in a holistic way. You have to change the mindset. It's about understanding, leading to respect, leading to trust. You need awareness, you need to take time to go out and learn.

We're acting like police in many areas. We use the old British police mantra – 'look, listen, touch'. You've got to study the environment, understand the culture and the ethics, then listen to the population to gain information, in that order. And you've got to keep reviewing what you do. For example, ask yourself: 'have we alienated or attracted people this week? What have we done about corruption?' We try to isolate the hardline guys, win over the majority who are moderates. The insurgents we deal with in two ways. We turn them or we kill them.[11]

Notes

1 Permission of Roshan Khadivi
2 Public Works and Government Services Canada
3 ibid
4 ibid
5 ibid
6 US Department of Defense
7 This article was first published on *Farmers Weekly's* Field Day' blog at www.fwi.co.uk/fieldday. Many thanks to Richard Byrne.
8 Permission of the Commonwealth Copyright Administration
9 Permission of Christopher Campbell
10 BBC News 7 September 2009
11 *Guardian*, 5 January 2010

Casualties of war

The currency of war is blood. However much Western politicians and generals talk about surgical operations, minimal casualties, and regardless of how they encase their troops in body armour and inside armoured vehicles, when the fighting begins, men and women die. They die from bullets, shrapnel and shells. They get burned to death inside vehicles that have been hit by rocket-propelled grenades (RPGs). They get blown up by improvised explosive devices (IEDs), roadside bombs and suicide bombers. They die in accidents during training exercises, and can be killed by their own side, in so-called 'blue-on-blue' incidents. Each death is a human tragedy that leaves a deep and lasting scar on the dead individual's family and friends. The soldiers, sailors and airmen and women who have died in Iraq and Afghanistan, and continue to fall in the latter country, are invariably young, mostly in their twenties (some even teenagers), cruelly cut down in their prime. This is the reality of war.

There is also another grim reality of conflict: the wounded. Bombs, shells and bullets can sever limbs, shred flesh and bone and deform bodies hideously. And the number of bodies that have been torn apart in Iraq and Afghanistan runs into the thousands. In Iraq, between 2003 and mid-2009, at least 31,446 US troops were wounded in action (Pentagon figures), and in Afghanistan, 3,304 US personnel were wounded in action between 2001 and mid-2009.

Between 1 January 2006 and 30 June 2009 in Iraq, 315 British military and civilian personnel were admitted to UK field hospitals and categorized as 'wounded in action', including as a result of hostile action. In Afghanistan, during the same period, 696 British military and civilian personnel were admitted to UK field hospitals categorized as 'wounded in action'. Shattered bodies, shattered lives, shattered families. Those who are wounded are 'lucky', in the sense that their doctors have access to the best modern surgical techniques and equipment and advanced medicines. A soldier wounded in Afghanistan can, if his or her wounds are serious enough, be back in a hospital in Britain or the United States in a matter of hours. And during the flight, the aircraft transporting them can be turned into an airborne intensive care unit. Once back on home soil, the process of repairing shattered bodies and lives can begin, but for the patient, the road to recovery is long and often painful.

It would be impossible to list accounts from even a small percentage of those who have been wounded in either Iraq since 1990 or Afghanistan since 2001. Therefore this chapter lists just four accounts from soldiers who were wounded, four individuals who became casualties of war. We must always remember and honour the dead and the ultimate sacrifice they have made, but we must also never forget the wounded.

Garrett S. Jones

Corporal Jones, 2nd Battalion, 7th Marine Regiment, 1st US Marine Division, was blown up by a booby trap while on patrol in Iraq. He was 23 years old when he suffered life-threatening wounds.

It sounded like I was whispering, and because of the explosion, I couldn't catch my breath. [The next thing he knew, he was onboard a helicopter flight headed for the Landstuhl Regional Medical Centre in Germany. He was strapped into a gurney with a military chaplain hovering over him.] The chaplain asked me if I wanted to pray. We prayed. Then the doctor told me my left leg would be amputated above the knee.

[He awoke a couple days later, after surgery.] I just remember talking to my family. I remember saying, 'I hear they make really good prosthetics.' [He was then flown to the National Naval Medical Center in Bethesda, Maryland, where his wounds were cleansed and torn flesh was removed from his body.] It seemed like forever. I had a bunch of tubes stuck in me. I was so drugged up I didn't feel much of anything. I don't remember much, but I do remember that one of my buddies who was shot by a sniper was also on the same flight. I didn't know what happened to him, I just saw that he had a bunch of tubes stuck in his chest. [Jones was then transferred to Naval Medical Center San Diego (NMCSD) for further treatment.]

I went from about 73 kg [160 lb] to 54 kg [120 lb]. I was in the bed almost all the time. The only time I got up was to do stretching and go to the bathroom. If I wasn't in my bed, I was in a wheelchair.

[*During his recovery, Jones had a total of 17 surgerical proceedures to clean the infected area in his left leg. He was treated for third-degree burns and shrapnel that peppered his left shoulder and both legs. In November 2007, he finally linked up with a prosthetist, who would help him become familiar with the functions of prosthetics. The prosthetist fit Jones for a total of six walking prosthetics and one snowboarding prosthetic – he was a keen fan of the sport.*]

The first day, I was able to make it down the mountain. As the days progressed, I got stronger and more confident on my snowboard. Once I knew I could snowboard again, I realized I was going to be able to do a lot more than just snowboard. I was like, 'If I could snowboard, who knows what else I can do?' It kind of opened my mind up to all the other possibilities. I just kept thinking about my next snowboard trip and getting back to 2/7 [the battalion] ASAP. I asked to come back to 2/7 … and, a couple of days later, I had orders back to 2/7. I was so excited I almost didn't believe it. [*Although Jones couldn't return to the infantry, he was able to serve in other sections within the battalion and was subsequently assigned to the intelligence section.*]

At first I didn't know what I was able to do. It's good to be able to do something that will keep Marines safe. Although I can't be out there with them, I get to directly help them. It wasn't just a hook-up [a favour]. I had to do all the training all other Marines do. My leg popped off a couple of times in the Humvee scenario, and once when I was leaving a range. I thought it was funny because how many guys walk around with combat loads and have a leg fall off? I still did it to prove that I could deploy as an amputee … I love being with the guys, the same people. I really do. If it wasn't for the guys in this unit, I wouldn't be here. It's an honour to serve with them and be in a place where many Marines don't get a chance to go.

A lot of people were sceptical of me because I'm a new amputee. It's been a little bit of a challenge for me, mentally, at first. People were saying, 'It's going to be hard and [you] can't do it.' So, being out here [Afghanistan] was a confidence builder. [*The career retention specialist (CRS) has even submitted a permanent limited duty (PLD) package so Jones can continue his military career.*]

Everyone here has been supportive in helping me get this re-enlistment package started. The CRS submitted a PLD package for me back in March 2008. We are still waiting on that to be finished. A lot of people are like family here. I guess that's partly why I'm so happy to be here. [*He meets with new amputees to show them there is 'light at the end of the "canal".'*]

I've told them to keep their head up. I want to show them that if I can do it, they can do it. I want to set the example for other amputees. I want to show them that a bad thing might happen, but you can still make good of bad circumstances ... Just because you have an injury, it doesn't mean you have to leave the Marine Corps. You just have to work hard. I want to let those guys know back in the States that there is a place for you. I plan on being one of those examples.[1]

Stuart Pearson

Sergeant Pearson, 3rd Parachute Battalion, 16 Air Assault Brigade, British Army, lost his leg when he stepped on a mine in Afghanistan.

I lost my left leg in Helmand on 6 September 2006. Moments earlier, my friend Corporal Stuart Hill had stood on a mine and been badly injured. While I was looking for a helicopter landing site so we could evacuate him, I stood on a second mine. I also suffered massive blast injuries to my right leg, which was saved, thanks to the skills of the medics.

I remember thinking, 'Oh shit, not me!' I couldn't believe it. I injected myself with morphine straight away, and my mate Andy Barlow applied a tourniquet to my stump. In the chaos that followed, there were two further explosions and, again, I was caught by the blast. Eventually a US Black Hawk helicopter winched us out of the minefield and took us to meet a Chinook that had medics aboard.

On our journey to the field hospital at Camp Bastion, Corporal Mark Wright, who had also been injured in the minefield, died. I spent two days in the field hospital undergoing further amputation to stop gangrene, and doctors opened up my stomach, fearing internal injuries. Luckily, none were found.

From there, I was flown on an Aeromed C-17 to Birmingham Airport. An ambulance then whisked me straight to Selly Oak Hospital in Birmingham. Staff cleaned my wounds and applied skin grafts to my right leg, using skin from my right thigh. My right ankle was smashed, but by the end of October, doctors had managed to save my foot.

Being treated with other military patients in the same ward definitely helped. Only other military patients truly understand what we'd been through. When my best friend Peter visited, he bought me a toy parrot, an eye-patch and a copy of *Runners Weekly*. That was good. When my mates visited, we'd often go to the pub next door. That was just two-and-a-half weeks after I got hit, but my surgeon was all for it. Banter was a big help. Military patients joke that if you lose a lower leg, it's just a scratch. However, mine's a 'proper amputation' – above the knee.

My Commanding Officer visited me as soon as he got back from Helmand. I felt guilty, but he stopped me in my tracks and said, 'Look, that's wrong. You made the correct decisions.' … I've also seen a counsellor at Headley Court, where I was fitted for my prosthetic leg … there is always at least one patient worse off than you. Camaraderie is very strong and we can share our experiences with others who've lost limbs.

Immediately, I was fitted for my prosthetic leg; I felt more independent. Without a shadow of a doubt, the doctors and nurses got me through it. You don't think about walking when you've got two legs, but now I need to think about it a lot more. I get phantom tingling all the time, which, according to the experts, is common following a shock amputation. It's so weird getting a cramp when I know there is nothing there.

When I took my first steps I used crutches, but as soon as my physio Kate came back carrying walking sticks, my eyes lit up. That was so different, and I was dead chuffed. By Easter, I was down to just one walking stick, but now I don't need any.

I never feared my career was over, and I vowed to crack on. I've only got eight years of my career left and I'd rather see them through. There is a chance that I could go back to Afghanistan, but nothing is confirmed. If I do, it won't be frontline duty. I'll be stuck behind a desk. It's going to be different from being in the thick of it with the Taliban, but at the end of the day, I've had my fun, my own little war.

I do get down sometimes, but I try not to let it happen too often. A positive attitude is essential, because I know that my leg's not going to grow back. I've got to live with it and make the most of what I've still got.[2]

Alvin Shell

Captain Shell, 16th Military Police Brigade (Airborne), US Army, arrived in Iraq in January 2004. He endured some of the toughest battles in Iraq, including the Battle of Fallujah, before ultimately being injured.

When we went to Fallujah, we all did a fair share of fighting. Fallujah was the toughest time. [I]f Fallujah didn't get me, nothing would get me. The entire company and platoon made it through pretty well; we didn't have any casualties, and we did an awesome job. After those four months in Fallujah, they ... sent us [to] Camp Victory. [T]o us, it was like a vacation, [but] that was actually where I happened to get hurt out on a patrol.

When the IED exploded and hit the semi-truck, the shrapnel actually ripped through the gas tank and it spilled the gasoline all the way down the MSR [military supply route]. The truck was immobilized, the convoy still had to keep going, and if you know anything about being hit, you ride until the wheels fall off.

You have to also imagine that the gas [fuel] was still running out of this truck, as we are pulling it off, and right when they got the winch hooked up, a [rocket-propelled grenade] came over my left shoulder. I could feel the heat from it ... it hit a Humvee and just a spark from the RPG ignited the road. The entire road caught on fire. I remember the gas still pouring down, and I remember the fire almost chasing the gasoline down the MSR. I remember looking through the fire and ... seeing Sergeant Spaid on fire ... As I saw the gas coming my way, I jumped back on the MSR, and ran through the gas and the fire.

[*Shell said he went to rescue Staff Sergeant Wesley Spaid, who was confused and believed he had little hope, and asked Shell to shoot him.*] I yelled at him and said if I would have shot you, I would have done it over there, out of the fire. [*After rolling him on the ground and covering him with dirt, Spaid was able to retreat out of the fire.*]

I had to make a choice, I ... put my left hand on my face, and my right hand on my rifle and when I ran through, I lit up like a Christmas tree because I was pretty much soaked in the diesel fuel from my boots to my pants, and when I ran through the other side of the fire, I lit up ... I just remember being on fire and I rolled and couldn't get the fire out. I remember running to the vehicle to get the fire extinguisher. [*But they had been used on a previous mission. He saw a ditch, jumped in, and extinguished the flames.*]

I remember when I got out of the ditch, I still thought I had my weapon in my hand. I looked down, but my weapon wasn't there. It got so hot that it melted the skin in my hand and my weapon fell on the ground. [*Shell would subsequently endure 18 months of rehabilitation and therapy and more than 30 surgical proceedures.*]

My father retired and actually came up and lived with me when I got hurt; he was there constantly. My wife was there constantly. They pretty much moved to Texas and took care of me 24 hours a day. I think my family and my friends were pivotal; I couldn't have recovered to the point I am right now. I think I would have healed, my wounds would have healed and scabbed over, but when you talk about actual recovery or you reach a point of wellness, I don't think I would be that person today. I admire my wife [Danielle] because she is tough as nails. [*Shell currently works full-time at the Department of Homeland Security.*] I don't think that it is in me to accept my 100 per cent disability and not go to work. I could have accepted that 100 per cent disability cheque and my wife would have gone to work and would have never complained, but my parents didn't teach me any other way but to work.[3]

David Bradley

In August 2004, Major Bradley was commanding B Company, the Princess of Wales's Royal Regiment (PWRR), a group of 120 men attached to the Cheshire Regiment, British Army. He and his men were operating from the Shatt al-Arab Hotel, Basra, a large British military base. He was badly wounded during fighting against a radical Shi'a militia group known as the Mahdi Army (see page 105 for Bradley's account of getting wounded). After being treated in Iraq, he was flown back to the UK for life-saving treatment.

They brought me out of the induced coma on Friday, 13 August 2004. I was in intensive care, but I didn't know it at the time. Waking up was a strange experience because I didn't think that I was that badly wounded. I thought I had some shrapnel damage to the right-hand side of my face, and obviously my right hand was injured. I had no idea how long I had been under or where I was. I knew I had been hit by an RPG round. I was massively sedated; there was no pain. Morphine is what they use and that's what caused the hallucinations.

Coming round, my wife and father were there – I remember hearing their voices. I don't know what they were saying, but they were talking to me. However, I was on a breathing apparatus with a tube stuck down my throat and couldn't speak. They asked if I needed anything because I was obviously agitated. I remember trying to spell the word 'doctor' using my fingers: one, two, three, four fingers for 'D' and so on. I got to 'DOC', but for some reason it was coming out as 'DOG'. They looked puzzled. You want a dog? We haven't got a dog. I was thinking, obviously it is 'doctor'. Why would I ask for a dog? It was the morphine, I didn't know what I was doing. I couldn't get across what I needed. They were talking to me and telling me that I was fine, but everything was just a blur.

Through that first night, the drugs were reducing as they were bringing me out of unconsciousness. The night-time intensive-care doctor came to see me and he took the decision to take the breathing system out, I remember that. He wasn't the consultant, he was just the on-duty care doctor. He must have talked to me, as I wanted it out because it tickled me and was uncomfortable. My oxygen levels were good enough, so they took the tube out. It's like having your lungs ripped out. It was a strange feeling, a really horrid feeling … Then they stuck a thing on my nose to provide additional oxygen. I am then semi-conscious and I can see my surroundings.

The worst aspect of being so heavily sedated was the persecution complex – I thought the intensive-care nurse was trying to kill me. I was lying there, and both my hands were elevated (they had had to cut my innominate vein) to stop blood pissing out of them. I had the feeling of weakness and vulnerability. On one finger was a little CO_2 [carbon dioxide] measure, and my finger kept slipping out of it, and I had drips everywhere on my body and was attached to all sorts of bleepy things.

I remember my finger slipping out of this CO_2 sensor and the Filipino nurse had to come back and put it back on again, and at one point I thought he was leaning over and saying, 'Don't let that slip out again, because if you let it slip out again, you won't see your family.' I'm thinking: I don't believe it. They are going to kill me. I need to get away. Can I get myself off this bed and crawl out? Because he is going to kill me. I've made it all the way back from Iraq, and I am going to die here in hospital. I remember a bag being shaken behind me and I was utterly … terrified.

The sister came over and I told her that the nurse was trying to kill me; I also told the doctor. It was a side effect of the drugs, you see. They assured me that no one was going to kill me – I didn't believe them. It was a horrific night, though; I was absolutely terrified.

The nights are the worst, because you don't sleep. I was incredibly uncomfortable; not in pain, but just the feeling that nothing was right with my body, which it wasn't. My chest had been opened up, I had 13 drains in me, I was connected to all these sort of things, and I had a catheter inserted. I was utterly weak in this drug-induced haze, attached to things that you don't understand and don't want to be attached to.

Then the morning came, and my father and wife turned up. I was really pleased to see them, but agitated, and said that the nurse tried to kill me last night. I don't want that nurse again and please can you stay with me. So my poor wife, until I felt strong enough … slept next to me in a chair … I was in intensive care for two weeks. I had suspected MRSA and confirmed *Acinetobacter*, which are both superbugs. The latter was a superbug that many of us brought back from Iraq because of all the crap that was blown into our bodies, especially into open wounds. The filthy dust of Iraq is made up of, among other things, raw sewage which has dried. It was disgusting – open sewers and no rubbish collections – so you can imagine the filth. So an explosion blowing dust and crap into you is bad news, and so I had this serious superbug, which meant I had to have enormous amounts of antibiotics fed through a drip. They also had to feed me through a tube into my throat, which was horrid. You can't taste it and I was throwing up continually past my feeding tube; it would come back up at various stages.

It was like being a baby, being rolled over to be washed and being rolled back carefully by the intensive-care nurses. It was a revelation that someone's job for 12 hours was to stand next to a bed with a PC monitor, keeping me alive. The pressure on them must have been immense. They would not let the same people have the same patient. You wouldn't have the same day nurse time and time again, for the reason that you couldn't establish an attachment to a particular individual, even though we as patients wanted to build a personal attachment.

I remember the hallucinations clearly. Each day I woke up for the first five days, I would be in a different, strange world. One day, for example, I was in a Southeast Asian paddy field and the nurse would walk over a little canal into my paddy field, to my bed, which was on a little island in the middle. The people were real, what they did to me was real, but the world around was not.

It was in intensive care when I actually found out what was wrong with me. I had been hit by two RPG rounds. One had hit my rifle and had cut my right hand in half between the index finger and the middle finger. I had such bad damage that they had had to remove the whole index finger and rebuild my hand. The blast had blown out the lens in my right eye and had shredded the cornea. They weren't sure I would get the sight back in my right eye (the wound had been left open for 24 hours in the field; they put a patch on it before sending me back). Shrapnel had entered through my shoulder, travelled down into my chest and cut my innominate vein. If it had cut an artery I would have been dead. I also had a really nasty shrapnel wound to my chin.

They had to do a lot of operations on my shoulder. I remember the chest surgeon was discussing whether he needed to get back into my chest or not and whether I was recovering from all the chest surgery. The plastic surgeon was discussing what he needed to do to my shoulder and my hand. At that point they hadn't rebuilt my hand. They had to 'de-glove' it: cut away all the damaged skin back to good skin to prevent infection and then work out how they [were] going to rebuild it. They made a big cut into my shoulder, taking out 80 per cent of the muscle, back to good flesh.

Tim Graham was my chest surgeon and Mr Peart was my plastic surgeon. They had a healthy sort of military banter, taking the mickey out of each other. It reminded me of how you take the mickey out of each other in the Army, which gave me a bit of confidence. Both were in fact civilians, but they were very talented men. They respected each other, but they just took the mickey a bit.

Mr Peart unwrapped my hand, which was in a massive bandage. I couldn't feel anything as they had given me an extra dose of morphine before they did it, but I couldn't bear to look at my hand as they examined it. They decided they were going to remove the index finger, take off all the damaged flesh and do a skin-flap transfer, which is more than a skin graft. Basically they cut a flap of skin from my stomach and put my hand underneath it and sewed the flap on to my hand. In this way, my hand could be fed with blood. I had to have my hand attached to my stomach for three weeks while that took. You think how having the flu is being ill, but at this stage I was just incredibly weak.

I had 16 operations during my time in Selly Oak, and I was there in intensive care for two weeks. I had another six weeks on the ward and subsequently had another six operations, so that's 16 operations in all. There were operations to rebuild my hand, take the drains out, sew the eye up and so on. After I left hospital, they had to give me a corneal graft, a new eye lens, and then they took the stitches out. Then it was back to my hand. They reattached a tendon to my thumb to give me more function.

With both wounds, they had to leave periods in between operations to work out whether they had worked before they went back in again. My last hand operation, for example, was in 2006. After an operation on the eye, they didn't touch it again for 12 months to give it time to calm down and recover. So the eye was a very long, drawn-out process to work out what they could and couldn't do.

Being moved from intensive care was a worrying time, but I wanted to get on with it. I wanted to get better. I still felt I had time to get back out there [Iraq] and finish the tour. To me it was rational. It takes time to understand how badly you are wounded. During my period in hospital, of course I began to realize that I wasn't going to be able to get back to Iraq, but I thought I will be able to get back to Tidworth [base of the Princess of Wales's Royal Regiment] to meet the lads when they come back, then I will rejoin them and I will take over my company. I was company commander; a brilliant job. I loved it. I wanted to finish my time and stay in the Army. I thought I would go back in January [2005], but as you realize the seriousness of your wounds, your horizons stretch. You understand that it's a long process, and actually you won't get back straightaway. Then you realize you won't go back at all.

For me, though, there was always hope because of the nature of my wounds, i.e. that the next operation might be the one that fixes everything. With my right hand, I have got no real dexterity, but I thought that would come back if I keep working on it at Headley Court [Defence Medical Rehabilitation Centre]. But then you realize that you are not going to get that dexterity back. The damage to my hand, the bits that have been taken out, and the damage to the rest of it, is such that you have got back what you are going to get back.

With regard to the sight in my eye, I am never going to get full vision back. I wear a contact lens, which helps quite a bit, but I don't have perfect vision in it. In addition, a corneal graft is very vulnerable, there is always a chance of rejection.

I was discharged from [Selly Oak] hospital after eight weeks, and the transition of going home was a difficult move, but I knew I needed Headley Court. I knew if I was going to get back to my company – I couldn't do anything with my right hand or shoulder; could hardly move the fingers – I needed to get some physio on it. So I went to my local military medical centre, which referred me to Headley Court. I had a brilliant physiotherapist at the local medical centre, and started working every day for long periods to try and get my hand working again, and waited for my referral to Headley Court. I went there at the beginning of December [2004]. In my mind, I was Major Bradley again.

I was a soldier and I had been wounded and it was just good to be a soldier again. My time at Headley Court was a great moment. It was really important and arrived at the right time. I went on the ward, which was mixed ranks, where you have nurses to look after you. There were a lot of road-traffic accident victims in a terrible state, and that puts your injuries into perspective. You realize that you might have been wounded on operations, but that poor 20-year-old who got knocked off his bike with severe spinal injuries and head injuries is in a much worse state. So that was a good experience in putting my injuries into context. Then I got moved to the upper limbs course. It is a fantastic place, but there was no magic bullet. It is just common sense: great skill on the part of the doctors, physiotherapists and the military PTIs [physical training instructors] and hard work from you. The combination of the two means you get great results. They were working on really just getting my fingers to move and to get some movement back in my shoulder. My shoulder was fixed, so they were trying to get it to move. So day after day for nearly four weeks that's what we worked at. I couldn't do much of the other exercises, such as press-ups, so I just concentrated on trying to close my hand into a fist, which I couldn't move more than an inch at first. Week by week, you gradually get a little bit further, having physio to try to get it to close.

It was good being part of a group. It was all first-name terms, but the banter was great. You are in a military environment and it is just good fun. You go back to the mess, you have a drink and you make friends. You stand at the bar and you take the piss out of each other – black, military humour. On my course there was a sergeant from the Black Watch who had been wounded a few days after me by a roadside bomb that had killed his driver and wounded him in his hand, so he was there getting his hand to work. That was good because we could talk about Basra and what had been going on. He could tell me what had happened a few days after I got hit, so I could piece together what had been going on after I had been wounded.

Over the subsequent four years, I had five more trips, six in total. After four weeks at Headley Court, you need to go back home because it is pretty intensive and hard work. I would go back, see the family and work at the regional rehab unit for three months. Then it was back to Headley Court. [It's] a very positive place. I miss going there because it was a real shot in the arm. When you went there, you came out better physically than when you went in, and [felt] strengthened mentally and physically. Enriched, I would say, though that sounds a bit 'wet' and unmilitary.

I needed to get back and do something, so in September 2005, I got a job as a staff officer at the Army HQ in Salisbury. I wanted to get back working, so they found me a job. It was an interesting job that I enjoyed doing and I did it for two years.

I left the Army in September 2008. I have no resentment towards the Army for discharging me. It was the right thing to do. It's a fit man's game and I am no longer a fit man. I can't take my place in the frontline. I could have stayed behind a desk, but that's not why I joined. That's not the Army that I wished to be a part of. Other wounded do want to stay in, and I understand their decision, but it wasn't for me. Better to move on. I was a soldier and I got blown up. I have to live with that. It is time for a new challenge. If I stayed in, it would not have been a challenge. If I stayed in, I would have resented it. I would have done less interesting jobs and that would have galled me. So I got out at the right time. Move on, new challenge.

For a long time I had feelings of regret of being taken away from my company. I was a company commander, leading a brilliant company of my lads, you know, fighting in Iraq. It was just what I wanted to be doing, 120 blokes with Warriors [armoured vehicles]. I wouldn't have been anywhere else than where I was at that time. I wouldn't change anything, although I got wounded; but at the same time, I wish I hadn't been. So that just eats away at you. But it's a shouting-at-the-moon sort of rage: why me, why couldn't I finish my time? I did four months, but the majority of the fighting actually took place after I left, and I wasn't there to lead them. One of my soldiers was killed [Private Lee O'Callaghan] in the same battle that I was wounded in. I couldn't be there to lead the company through that difficult period, and I wasn't able to write a letter to his parents. But when I got out of hospital, I went to see them and it was very emotional for all of us and very important, but I could not do that important part of my job. To be in command at whatever level is just absolutely what we joined for as officers. That's what you do.

I still have pains at times. The phantom thing of losing a limb: that goes after time. I still get it now, but it will disappear. My right hand aches, all the time, really. It's not a bad pain, just a dull ache. It's like my hand is in concrete. The tendons are pulling and the joints can ache, and if I do something for a long time, it aches more. My shoulder can ache, too.

Throughout the time of my injury and afterwards, my family were brilliant. It was terrible for them, especially when my wife got that knock on the door. Luckily one of her closest friends, a girlfriend, was staying with her at the time when it happened. She opened the door and found two men in uniform standing there, and of course she expected the worst. They weren't sure that I was going to live for the first night, so the first night she never slept. She was waiting for news, but no news came, which they thought was good, i.e. at least I hadn't died. I was flown into the UK on the Wednesday morning, and she was driven up to meet me.

She had no idea of what my wounds were like. She got dressed up in smart clothes and put makeup on and expected to come in and see me sat up in bed, smiling at her. Of course she walked in and my face was just a mess, I was plugged into machines, I was unconscious and covered in iodine from the field hospital. There was dust and blood in my hair – it was a terrible shock for her, what with my appearance, and the doctor still not sure if I would make it. She was brilliant, though.

It was also tough on my children. They were much younger at the time – three and six – and tough because in their eyes daddy was a big, strong person. They really weren't told what was happening, just that daddy was wounded and he would be okay. They were dropped off at my sister-in-law's, who, with my mother and father, looked after them. But it was strange for them. It was not right because mummy was not there and daddy was not there. They were not old enough to understand, but they were old enough to know that something was wrong. And it all comes back when you don't expect it. It suddenly pops back and they say something and I think, that's affected them more than I realized. They worried when I was in the Army. They were afraid that if I went away again I would never come back. So now that I am out of the Army they are more comfortable.

It is now five years since I was wounded in Iraq. Does it seem like five years? Yes and no. Part of me is frustrated in that I don't want to live my life defined by the actions of one day, and that can be frustrating. I have done some amazing things. You know, with Help for Heroes and the Not Forgotten Association, I have been invited to Buckingham Palace and St James's Palace and done some fantastic things. But you know, I was a soldier and I got blown up. I am not bitter, but at times you do think, I wish it hadn't happened.

You have to be positive. I am not kidding myself that my wounds are not bad and that they nearly killed me. But I am quite lucky to have been that close to death, but actually come out of it relatively unscathed. I am frustrated every day, but it could be a lot worse. I am not a double amputee, or a single amputee, and I am not blind. I have one good eye, so I am bloody lucky. I have two good legs. That is quite important; and as Sergeant Pike reminded me, my family jewels are still there (see page 105). A line that I dismissed at the time, but woke up later in hospital and was incredibly grateful for, knowing that he had come up and said that to me. As a soldier you just like to know that your 'bits' are still there.

I would love to go back to Iraq. I was maimed and nearly killed there, so I have a real interest in seeing it working. The vast majority of people there were incredibly friendly and grateful for what we were doing ... As in all these places, it is a vociferous, violent minority that causes the trouble, and I was very conscious of that. People wanted peace, and they were genuinely grateful for us being there. So I don't hold any animosity towards the people of Iraq at all. I made a couple of good friends with the Iraqi sheikhs that we had to deal with, they were good people. The best one that I met, I later found out, was blown up by the Mahdi Army because they thought he was collaborating. He wasn't collaborating, he was just talking. He just realized that the way for Iraq to go forward was not through the militias, but actually by supporting the Iraqi government and us who were providing security, and they killed him for it. It was very sad.

I'm often asked if I have a desire to find the Iraqi who wounded me and kill him. I must admit I don't, I just don't. It's not something that eats away at me, actually, that anger. I haven't remembered that for awhile, actually. At the time I wanted to go back and kill the fucking bastard, but not since. In hospital you concentrate on getting better when you are that poorly. You haven't got the energy to worry about who did it, and to be honest, knowing the intensity of the fight, he was probably killed anyway. I am not bothered either way. A part of me regrets the fact that I will never be able to go back and meet my enemies. You see World War II Royal Air Force pilots meeting German fighter pilots and having a very emotional reunion, but I know I will never get that opportunity.

I don't understand the desire for revenge. It could eat away at you if you wanted it to. You have to move on. As a soldier, it's not about revenge. It's about a job, and if every time you got sent to war, you had feelings of revenge towards the enemy you are sent to fight, then you are in the wrong job. [4]

Notes

1   Courtesy of the US 2nd Battalion, 7th Marine Regiment

2   *Defence News*, 8 January 2008

3   Courtesy of the *Wounded Warrior Diaries*, US Department of Defense

4   Permission of David Bradley

Appendix

Timelines

Iraq: 1990–2003

1990

2 Aug Iraq Invades Kuwait.

7 Aug Operation Desert Shield begins. First US forces – 15 F-15 Eagle fighters – arrive in Saudi Arabia.

12 Aug First Operation Desert Shield-related US death.

22 Aug US President George H.W. Bush authorizes the first call-up of selected reservists to active duty for 90 days by executive order.

1991

17 Jan Operation Desert Storm begins. United Nations (UN) aircraft launch a devastating air campaign against Iraqi targets in Iraq and Kuwait. Iraq attacks Israel with seven Scud missiles in an attempt to provoke Israel. US Special Operations Forces are the first to receive bio-defence vaccinations.

18 Jan A US Patriot missile intercepts and downs a Scud missile launched at Saudi Arabia.

19 Jan President Bush announces that Israel will not retaliate against Scud attacks.

20 Jan Second attack of three Iraqi Scud missiles kills 17 people in Tel Aviv. First Iraqi prisoners of war captured in a raid on Kuwaiti oil platforms by US troops.

21 Jan Ten Scud missiles are fired at Saudi Arabia; nine are destroyed by Patriot missiles and one falls offshore.

22 Jan Iraq claims to be using Allied POWs as human shields in an attempt to deflect Allied air attacks.

23 Jan Iraq fires six Scud missiles at Saudi Arabia. A Patriot missile destroys one, while the other five fall into lightly populated areas. Iraqi troops set oil tanks and oil wells on fire in Kuwait.

24 Jan Scud missiles are fired at Israel and Saudi Arabia but inflict no casualties.

25 Jan UN air sorties surpass 15,000. Two oil slicks moving south off Kuwait are reported by Saudi officials. Iraq lays blame on the bombing, while the UN says the oil was released by Iraqi troops.

26 Jan Iraqi warplanes land in Iran and are seized by the Iranian military.

27 Jan US F-15 aircraft shoot down three Iraqi MiG-23s in the first major dogfight of the war. Iraq fires more Scud missiles into Israel and Saudi Arabia, with no casualties resulting. More than 75,000 anti-war protestors march in Washington, DC.

28 Jan To stop Iraq from dumping oil into the Persian Gulf, UN aircraft bomb occupied oil facilities in Kuwait.

30 Jan Iraqi troops advance into Saudi Arabia, taking Khafji. A battalion of US Marines fire artillery, mortars and anti-tank missiles at Iraqi bunkers 0.8 km (0.5 miles) away in Kuwait. There are no US casualties. The US and the Soviet Union offer a ceasefire in exchange for an Iraqi withdrawal from Kuwait. Saddam Hussein refuses. US forces in the Gulf now number over 500,000.

1 Feb Khafji is retaken by Saudi and Qatari troops supported by US artillery.

2 Feb A 16 km (10 mile) long Iraqi armoured column advancing into Saudi Arabia is bombed to a halt by Coalition aircraft.

3 Feb Iraq launches two Scuds at Israel, but causes no casualties.

5 Feb The battleship *USS Missouri* fires at Iraqi positions in Kuwait, the first time a ship has fired in combat since the Korean War (1950–53).

6 Feb Heating and transportation problems throughout Iraq worsen as the government suspends fuel sales to civilians.

14 Feb A Baghdad underground bunker, the Amiriyah shelter identified by US military intelligence as a military facility, is destroyed by two bombs dropped by two F-117 Stealth Fighters. Hundreds killed; Iraqi officials claim bunker was a bomb shelter.

15 Feb Pentagon releases figures indicating that more than 1,300 of Iraq's 4,280 tanks have been destroyed, as well as 800 of 2,870 armoured vehicles and 1,100 of 3,110 artillery pieces.

16 Feb Iraq says it will withdraw from Kuwait if certain conditions are met, including Israeli withdrawal from occupied territories, forgiveness of Iraqi debts and UN payment for the rebuilding of Iraq. President Bush dismisses the offer as a 'cruel hoax'.

17 Feb Southern Israel is hit by two Iraqi Scud missiles. There are no casualties.

21 Feb US General Schwarzkopf announces Iraq's military is on the 'verge of collapse'.

22 Feb Soviet spokesman Vitaly Ignatenko announces that the proposed Soviet ceasefire agreement has been accepted by Iraq. The US rejects the agreement, but states it will not attack Iraqi forces that leave Kuwait within 24 hours.

23 Feb President Bush condemns the destruction of Kuwaiti oil wells and demands Iraqi withdrawal by noon on 24 Feb to avoid a ground war. He also rejects the Soviet peace plan.

24 Feb US Army, Marine and Coalition forces begin the ground phase of the war to liberate Kuwait.

25 Feb In a radio speech, Saddam urges his forces 'to kill with all your might'. An Iraqi Scud missile hits a US military barracks in Khobar Towers, Saudi Arabia, killing 28 soldiers and wounding 90. Coalition forces on the outskirts of Kuwait City. 20,000 Iraqis taken prisoner, 270 tanks destroyed.

27 Feb US Marines liberate the US Embassy in Kuwait. Iraqi POWs number 30,000. With Iraqi resistance collapsing and Kuwait free, Bush orders a ceasefire effective at midnight Kuwaiti time.

28 Feb President Bush declares, 'Kuwait is liberated,' and 'Iraq's Army is defeated'.

3 Mar Iraq accepts the terms of a ceasefire.

Mid-Mar/early Apr Iraqi forces suppress rebellions in the south and the north of the country.

8 Apr A plan to establish a UN safe haven in northern Iraq to protect the Kurds is approved at a European Union meeting.

10 Apr The US orders Iraq to end all military activity against the Kurds. A no-fly zone is established over northern Iraq.

1992

26 Aug A no-fly zone, which Iraqi aircraft are not allowed to enter, is set up in southern Iraq, south of latitude 32°N.

1993

27 June US forces launch a cruise missile attack on Iraqi intelligence headquarters in Baghdad in retaliation for the attempted assassination of US President George H.W. Bush in Kuwait in April.

1994

10 Nov Iraqi National Assembly recognizes Kuwait's borders and its independence.

1995

14 Apr UN Security Council Resolution 986 allows partial resumption of Iraq's oil exports to finance purchase of food and medicine.

Aug Saddam Hussein's son-in-law, General Hussein Kamel Hassan al-Majid, his brother and their families flee Iraq and are granted asylum in Jordan.

15 Oct Saddam wins a referendum allowing him to remain president for another 7 years.

1996

20 Feb General Hussein Kamel Hassan al-Majid and his brother, promised a pardon by Saddam Hussein, return to Baghdad and are murdered on 23 Feb.

31 Aug After a call for aid from the Kurdish Democratic Party (KDP), Iraqi forces launch an offensive into the northern no-fly zone and capture Irbil.

3 Sept US extends the northern limit of the southern no-fly zone to latitude 33°N, just south of Baghdad.

12 Dec Saddam Hussein's elder son Uday is seriously wounded in an assassination attempt in Baghdad.

1998

31 Oct Iraq ends cooperation with the UN Special Commission charged with overseeing the disposal of Iraq's weapons of mass destruction.

16–19 Dec After UN staff are evacuated from Baghdad, the US and Britain launch a bombing campaign, Operation Desert Fox, to destroy Iraq's nuclear, biological and chemical (NBC) weapons programmes.

1999

19 Feb Grand Ayatollah Sayyid Muhammad Sadiq al-Sadr, spiritual leader of the Shi'a community, is assassinated in the Iraqi city of Najaf.

Iraq: Operation Iraqi Freedom

2003

19 Mar Coalition forces launch Cruise missiles and bombs at targets in Iraq.

20 Mar Coalition ground forces advance into Iraq. A combined British air- and ground-assault seizes Iraq's al-Faw Peninsula as US Marines assault the port of Umm Qasr.

21 Mar Heavy air attacks are launched against Baghdad as US aircraft unleash 'Shock and Awe' campaign. Iraq's 51st Army Division (8,000 troops), either surrenders or deserts at Iraq's southern border.

22 Mar Coalition troops advance 240 k

(150 miles) into Iraqi territory and cross the River Euphrates. US Air Force and Navy aircraft fly a total of 1,500 sorties thus far.

23 Mar Iraqi troops inflict heavy casualties on US Marines in the southeastern city of An Nasiriyah.

24 Mar US soldiers are now less than 96 km (60 miles) from Baghdad, with Coalition aircraft and helicopters pounding Iraqi positions in front of the capital.

25 Mar Coalition forces kill around 200 Iraqis in a land battle east of Najaf. British troops repulse a counterattack by Iraqi forces southeast of Basra and destroy 20 armoured vehicles. Coalition deaths in the Iraq War now total 43.

26 Mar Around 1,000 US paratroopers from the US Army's 173rd Airborne Brigade land in Kurdish-controlled northern Iraq. They secure an airfield to bring in Coalition troops and armoured vehicles.

27 Mar British forces near Basra face heavy opposition from Iraqi forces.

28 Mar Three US Marine battalions occupy the northern and southern parts of An Nasiriyah.

29 Mar US Marines and Iraqi fighters wage a savage battle for the city of An Nasiriyah.

30 Mar 800 Coalition air sorties are mounted, with more than 60 per cent aimed at Iraqi troops south of Baghdad, especially Republican Guard divisions defending the capital, headquarters of the Fedayeen Saddam paramilitary group and a presidential compound.

1 Apr The beginning of the Battle of Baghdad. US forces engage Medina and Baghdad Republican Guard divisions south of the capital. and in Karbala. US Marines fight close-quarter battles with paramilitary units in An Nasiriyah.

2 Apr The US Army's 3rd Infantry Division engages Republican Guard near Karbala and captures the city with 'little effort'. The US 1st Marine Expeditionary Force attacks Republican Guard's Baghdad Division, capturing a bridge and crossing the Tigris.

3 Apr US forces launch an assault on airport, southwest of Baghdad. Coalition troops heading from southeast are 16 km (10 miles) from Iraqi capital. The US 3rd Infantry Division pushes through Karbala Gap. The 1st Battalion, 7th US Marine Regiment, is on the outskirts of Kut, 64 km (40 miles) south of Baghdad. The US 101st Airborne Division takes control of Najaf. British forces use long-range artillery to shell Iraqi forces around Basra.

4 Apr US forces hold Baghdad's airport. Some 2,500 Iraqi soldiers from the Republican Guard's Baghdad Division surrender to US Marines between Kut and Baghdad. Kurdish forces capture the town of Khazar in northern Iraq.

5 Apr US forces push into Baghdad, encountering only sporadic resistance. The US Army's V Corps moves into the capital from the south, the US 1st Marine Expeditionary Force from the southeast.

6 Apr Coalition forces encircle Baghdad.

7 Apr The US Army's 173rd Airborne Brigade shells Iraqi forces in northern Iraq. British forces make their largest incursion into Basra.

8 Apr British troops are in control of 80 per cent of Basra, where looting has broken out. Troops of the US Army's 101st Airborne Division battle Iraqi forces in Hillah, 80 km (50 miles) south of Baghdad.

9 Apr Hundreds of jubilant Baghdad residents take to the streets, tearing down posters of Saddam and looting government buildings. Iraqi forces dig in at Tikrit.

10 Apr Elements of the US 173rd Airborne Brigade move into Tikrit. The Iraqi Army's V Corps agrees to surrender to US and Kurdish forces outside Mosul. Units of the 101st Airborne mop up remaining pockets of resistance in Hillah.

11 Apr A ceasefire is signed between the commander of the Iraqi Army's V Corps in Mosul and US Special Forces.

12 Apr Elements of the US 1st Marine Expeditionary Force leave Baghdad for Saddam Hussein's hometown of Tikrit.

13 Apr US Marines attack around 2,500 Iraqi fighters loyal to the deposed Iraqi leader inside Tikrit, the last major Iraqi city not under Coalition control.

1 May Just 43 days after announcing the start of the war in Iraq, George W. Bush tells the American people that 'major combat operations in Iraq have ended'.

22 July Uday and Qusay Hussein are killed in a gun battle.

14 Dec Saddam Hussein is captured.

Iraq: Post-war Iraq 2004–10

2004

Feb A suicide bomber kills at least 100 people in Irbil.

Mar Four civilian contractors working for US Army are murdered; their mutilated bodies dragged through the streets of Fallujah.

Apr There is international outrage over photographs showing US guards abusing naked Iraqi prisoners at Abu Ghraib.

May A video is released on the internet showing the beheading of Nick Berg, a US civilian held by militants. Iyad Allawi, a Shi'a politician previously in exile, is unanimously voted in as prime minister of Iraq's interim government.

July A defiant Saddam Hussein makes his first appearance in court on charges of war crimes and genocide.

Dec Nineteen US soldiers are killed when a huge explosion rips apart a mess tent at a base in Mosul.

2005

Jan Millions vote in the first multi-party elections for 50 years. A series of attacks across the country kill at least 36.

Apr Jalal Talabani, a Kurdish politician, former guerrilla leader and co-founder of the Patriotic Union of Kurdistan, is sworn in as president of Iraq.

2006

Jan The Shi'a-led United Iraqi Alliance is announced as the winner of elections.

Feb Famous gold dome at sacred Shia al-Askari shrine in Samarra is blown up, prompting fears of reprisals. Grand Ayatollah Ali al-Sistani, most senior Shi'a cleric in Iraq, forbids his followers from attacking Sunni mosques and calls for seven days of mourning.

June Al-Qaeda leader Abu Musab al-Zarqawi is killed in a US air strike near Baqubah.

Dec Saddam is executed at the Khadamiyah intelligence centre in Baghdad.

2007

Aug More than 400 people are killed as four suicide bombers detonate cars in two villages occupied by Yazidi Kurds in northern Iraq.

Dec British forces formally hand over control of Basra to the Iraqi government in a move paving the way for a major reduction in the number of British troops in Iraq.

2008

Jan A motion is passed by the Iraqi parliament allowing former officials from the Ba'ath Party to return to public life.

Feb Thousands of Turkish troops sent across the border into northern Iraq in a major ground offensive against the Kurdish PKK (Kurdistan Workers' Party) rebel forces.

Mar A roadside bomb followed by a suicide bomb kill 68 people in the centre of Baghdad.

Apr British Defence Secretary Des Browne says final troop withdrawal has been postponed after fierce fighting between Iraqi security forces and Shi'a militia.

2009

Jan The new US Embassy in Baghdad is officially opened amid heavy security.

Mar US President Barack Obama announces the withdrawal of 12,000 US troops from Iraq by the end of August 2010. Up to 50,000 troops will stay on in the country until the end of 2011 to advise Iraqi forces and protect US interests.

Apr The Iraqi parliament appoints Ayad al-Samarrai (Sunni Arab alliance) as speaker.

May Iraqi election authority sets the election date for 30 January 2010.

June US troops withdraw from Iraqi cities, leaving Iraqi forces in control of security.

Oct Prime Minister Al-Maliki announces the formation of a new political grouping of 40 parties called the State of Law, after a split in the broad Shi'a United Iraqi Alliance that won the 2005 elections.

25 Oct Two suicide bombs in Baghdad kill at least 155 people and wound 700 others. Iraqi al-Qaeda claims responsibility.

Dec Iraqi parliament unanimously approves amendment to protect rights of Sunni Muslims and other minorities. Elections to go ahead in February 2010.

8 Dec Five bombs kill 120 people and injure 400 in Baghdad. Iraqi al-Qaeda says it carried out attacks.

30 Dec Al-Qaeda double agent kills 7 CIA agents in a suicide attack on US base in Khost.

30 Dec Suicide bombers kill 27 people in the city of Ramadi

2010

7 Jan Three bombs kill seven people in the town of Hit, Anbar Province.

Afghanistan: Operation Enduring Freedom

2001

12 Sept After 9/11 attacks, Donald Rumsfeld asks US Central Operations Command to prepare military options to deal with the menace to American national security.

21 Sept US Army General Tommy Franks, Commander-in-Chief of CENTCOM, briefs President George W. Bush on plan.

2 Oct Bush approves Operation Enduring Freedom. Its mission is to destroy Taliban in Afghanistan and to eliminate the al-Qaeda network itself.

7 Oct Combat operations in Afghanistan begin with air strikes.

13 Oct Four C-17 transport aircraft begin

dropping more than 68,000 rations per day into Afghanistan.

9 Nov Mazar-i-Sharif is first Afghan city liberated from the Taliban following ground assaults by Northern Alliance forces, plus US Special Forces soldiers supported by US air strikes.

11 Nov Taloqan is liberated from the Taliban.

12 Nov Herat and Shindand are liberated.

13 Nov Afghanistan's capital Kabul is liberated.

14 Nov Jalalabad is liberated.

15 Nov Coalition Joint Forces Land Component Command (CJFLCC) assumes responsibility for land operations in Afghanistan.

25 Nov US Marines of Task Force 58 seize Objective Rhino, a desert airstrip south of Kandahar, establish forward operating base.

26 Nov Konduz, last Taliban stronghold in northern Afghanistan falls to Coalition.

30 Nov Bagram Airfield near Kabul becomes a Coalition forward operating base.

4 Dec The first US Army units deploy to Mazar-i-Sharif.

5 Dec The outlines of an interim Afghan government are developed in a meeting held in Bonn, Germany.

7 Dec Kandahar, the last major Taliban stronghold in Afghanistan, surrenders to forces under the command of Hamid Karzai, an anti-Taliban Afghan politician.

13 Dec Task Force 58 secures Kandahar Airport. US ends humanitarian air-drop missions. More than 2.4 million daily rations have been delivered by air to the Afghans thus far.

22 Dec Hamid Karzai is sworn in as the prime minister of the Afghan interim government. At the same time, the International Security Assistance Force (ISAF) is established in Kabul. ISAF is a NATO-led security and development mission in Afghanistan established by the UN Security Council on 20 December 2001.

2002

3 Jan ISAF consists of 4,500 international troops under the command of British Major-General John McColl.

3–4 Jan Coalition aircraft attack al-Qaeda complex at Zawar Kili, southwest of Khost.

10 Jan The first group of Taliban and al-Qaeda prisoners are flown to the US Navy base at Guantanamo Bay, Cuba.

29 Jan US Marines of Task Force 58 are relieved by elements of the US Army's 101st Airborne Division.

8 Feb Military forces from Spain establish a hospital at Bagram Airfield.

1 Mar Coalition forces join US troops in Operation Anaconda, an assault on al-Qaeda in southeastern Afghanistan.

17 Mar Operation Anaconda concludes. Eight US servicemen killed and 82 wounded.

4 Apr 600 soldiers of the new Afghan National Guard (ANG) graduate after six weeks training by NATO forces.

24 Apr Camp X-Ray holds 295 detainees; less than 24 per cent are native Afghans.

2–17 May 2 Task Force Jacana (British Royal Commandos) initiate Operation Snipe, a sweep in the Gardez region.

15 May The 1st Battalion, Afghan National Army (ANA), commences training under the direction of US Special Forces.

13 June The Loya Jirga ('Grand Assembly') elects Hamid Karzai as the head of the Afghan transitional government.

6 July Haji Abdul Qadir, new Afghan vice-president, is assassinated on his first day.

18–25 Aug Operation Mountain Sweep is conducted, a Coalition effort to locate key enemy personnel and weaponry in the Gardez region.

3 Oct More than 360 soldiers of the 3rd Battalion ANA graduate from Afghan Military Academy in Kabul.

Afghanistan: NATO's War 2001–10

2001

20 Dec The UN issues Security Resolution 1386, authorizing the deployment of a multinational International Security and Assistance Force (ISAF) in and around

Kabul to help stabilize the country and create the conditions for self-sustaining peace, with forces and assets from 18 other countries.

2002

4 Jan ISAF tasks are laid out in a Military Technical Agreement.

10–20 June A national Loya Jirga takes place and gives the transitional authority 18 months in which to hold a second national Loya Jirga in order to adopt a constitution, and 24 months in which to hold national elections.

13 June Hamid Karzai is elected head of the Afghan Transitional Authority.

17 Oct NATO approves a request from Germany and the Netherlands for NATO support in helping them to prepare to take over command of ISAF in early 2003.

27 Nov The Supreme Headquarters Allied Powers Europe (SHAPE) hosts a Force Generation conference for ISAF.

2003

16 Apr The North Atlantic Council agrees to expand NATO's support to the international peacekeeping force in Afghanistan.

5 July The first NATO troops set off for Kabul.

11 Aug NATO takes over command and coordination of ISAF.

13 Oct UN Security Council adopts Resolution 1510 authorizing expansion of ISAF's operations to include operations anywhere in Afghanistan.

19 Dec NATO decides to expand the role of ISAF.

31 Dec NATO assumes command of the Kunduz Provincial Reconstruction Team (PRT), previously led by Germany.

2004

28 June In Istanbul, NATO announces it will expand its Afghan presence through four additional PRTs.

7 Oct First-ever direct Afghan presidential

elections held. Hamid Karzai is declared president two days later.

2005

10 Feb NATO decides to expand ISAF to the western area of Afghanistan.

8 June NATO defence ministers state that the alliance will provide additional support for forthcoming elections and is planning for ISAF expansion in the south of the country.

18 Sept First parliamentary elections in Afghanistan for 30 years.

8 Dec NATO foreign ministers endorse a revised operational plan for the expansion of ISAF to the south and agree to develop an Afghan cooperation programme (defence reform, defence institution building and military aspects of security-sector reform).

2006

31 Jan The London Conference on Afghanistan, co-hosted by UN and Afghanistan, is held, affirming commitment of Afghan government and international community to work towards peace and security under the rule of law, with good governance and human rights protection for all.

8 June The first-ever meeting of defence ministers from NATO and non-NATO ISAF-contributing countries is held. These 37 ministers reconfirm their commitment to expand operations to southern Afghanistan.

31 July ISAF expands its area of operations to six additional provinces in the south of Afghanistan.

12 Sept UN Security Council adopts Resolution 1707 to extend the mandate of ISAF in Afghanistan for a further year.

5 Oct ISAF implements stage four of its expansion by taking on command of the international military forces in eastern Afghanistan from the US-led Coalition.

2008

23 Sept UN Security Council adopts Resolution 1833, extending the ISAF mandate until 13 October 2009.

6 Oct Phase one of the voter-registration process in 14 provinces, including Badakhshan, Nuristan, Ghazni, Kunar and Wardak.

5 Nov Start of phase two of the voter-registration process in ten provinces, including Kabul, Kunduz, Mazar-i-Sharif and Herat.

13 Dec Start of phase three of the voter-registration process in Laghman, Nangarhar, Khost, Paktika, Zabul and Farah provinces.

2009

11 Jan End of phase three of the voter-registration process for the 2009 Afghan presidential elections (ISAF provides security for the nation-wide voter-registration process in support of the Afghan police and the Afghan Army).

20 Jan Start of phase four of the voter-registration process in the provinces of Uruzgan, Kandahar, Helmand and Nimroz.

27 Mar US President Obama announces plans to send a further 4,000 US troops to train Afghan security forces, plus civilians to improve delivery of basic services.

29 Mar President Karzai says he will stay in office after his term ends on 21 May until elections are held in August. He later states he'll run for re-election.

11 May The top US and NATO commander in Afghanistan General David McKiernan, is fired by the Obama Administration. His exit signals a shift from conventional military strategy to a counter-insurgency plan, aimed at reducing civilian deaths.

15 June US General Stanley McChrystal assumes command of international troops in Afghanistan.

2 July US Marines launch assault in lower Helmand in southern Afghanistan.

27 July Britain announces the end of the five-week Operation Panther's Claw, the largest offensive by British forces since mid-2006, saying it has succeeded in driving militants out of population centres ahead of elections.

Aug Presidential and provincial elections are held, marred by Taliban attacks, poor turnout and claims of electoral fraud.

15 Aug Taliban claims responsibility for car bomb that kills seven people and wounds 100 outside the ISAF headquarters in Kabul near the US Embassy.

20 Aug Afghan presidential elections are held.

Sept Leaked report by General McChrystal says the war against the Taliban could be lost within 12 months unless there are significant increases in troop numbers.

2 Sept The number of NATO personnel killed in Afghanistan since the US invasion in 2001 numbers 1,296.

Oct Hamid Karzai is declared winner of August presidential election after opponent Abdullah Abdullah pulls out before the second round. Preliminary results had given Mr Karzai 55 per cent of the vote, but so many ballots are found to be fraudulent that a run-off is called. The British government announces it will send 500 more military personnel to Afghanistan.

Nov Hamid Karzai is sworn in for a second term as president. The Afghan National Army numbers 97,200 troops. Its target strength is 134,000 troops (by Oct 2010). The Afghan National Army Air Corps numbers 2,716 airmen and 47 aircraft. Its target is 8,017 personnel and 154 aircraft.

1 Dec President Obama orders 30,000 more US troops into Afghanistan to increase US troop numbers to 100,000. He says the US will begin withdrawing its forces by 2011.

14 Dec British PM Gordon Brown announces that £150 million will be provided to help counter the improvised explosive device threat in Afghanistan.

19 Dec A total of 240 British forces personnel or MoD civilians have now died while serving in Afghanistan since the start of operations in Oct 2001.

2010

Jan Afghan parliament rejects 17 of Mr Karza's 24 cabinet nominees.

18 Jan Taliban insurgents attack government ministries and other targets in Kabul.

Glossary

82nd Airborne Division Elite US Army paratrooper formation, nicknamed the 'All Am ericans'.

105mm light gun Artillery weapon used by the British Army. Usually crewed by six soldiers, with a maximum range of 17.2 km (10.7 miles).

A-10 Thunderbolt US ground-attack aircraft, also known as the 'Warthog', the 'Flying gun' and the 'Tank-buster'. Its range of weapons includes Maverick air-to-surface missiles, Sidewinder air-to-air missiles, general-purpose bombs, cluster bombs, plus an Avenger 30mm cannon mounted in the nose of the aircraft.

AC-130 Spectre American four-engined close air-support, air interdiction and armed reconnaissance aircraft.

AH-64 Apache American twin-engined attack helicopter with a crew of two.

AHIP Advanced Helicopter Improvement Program (US).

AK-47 Russian 7.62mm assault rifle capable of semi- and full-automatic fire. Has a rate of fire of 600 rounds per minute.

AKM An updated version of the AK-47 assault rifle.

Al-Abbas missile An Iraqi stretched version of the Scud surface-to-surface missile with a range of 750 km (466 miles).

Al-Hussein missile Iraqi improved version of the Scud with a range of 600 km (375 miles).

All Terrain Protected Vehicle (Viking) A fully amphibious, armoured all-terrain vehicle, which consists of two tracked vehicle units linked by a steering mechanism.

Amtrac General term for US armoured amphibious assault vehicles, especially those in US Marine Corps service. The AAVP7A1 used by US Marine Corps service has a crew of three and can carry up to 25 soldiers.

AMX-30 French main battle tank with a crew of four and armed with one 105mm gun, one 20mm gun and one 7.62mm machine gun

AS90 British Army 155mm self-propelled howitzer capable of firing shells up to a range of 40 km (25 miles)

AT-4 A lightweight, self-contained, anti-armour weapon in US service. Capable of penetrating 450mm (17.5in) of armour plate.

AWACS (airborne warning and control system) Aircraft built by Boeing Defense & Space Group. The E-3 AWACS carries out airborne surveillance, and command, control and communications (C3) functions for both tactical and air defence forces.

B-1 bomber US Air Force multi-role, long-range bomber with a crew of four

B-2 bomber US Air Force intercontinental stealth bomber with a crew of two

B-52 Stratofortress US Air Force multi-role long-range bomber with a weapons payload of over 31,818 kg (70,000 lb) and five-man crew.

'Baghdad Biltmore' Nickname given to the place where Allied prisoners were kept during the 1990–91 Gulf War. Located in the basement cells of the Iraqi secret police headquarters in Baghdad.

berm A temporary defensive barrier formed by bulldozing the desert sand into a ridge

BLU-82 A large conventional bomb of weighing 6,818 kg (15,000 lb) that explodes 1 metre (3 ft) off the ground and clears a radius of 300 metres (1,000 ft). Nicknamed the 'Daisy Cutter'.

BMP Russian-built infantry vehicle armed with a 100mm semi-automatic rifled gun/missile launcher. Holds a crew of three and can carry up to seven passengers.

Bradley US Army fighting vehicle with a crew and space for up to seven fully equipped soldiers. Armament comprises a 25mm M242 Bushmaster chain gun, M240C 7.62mm machine and the TOW BGM-71 anti-tank missile system.

Bradley Linebacker Air defence variant of the

Bradley fighting vehicle, equipped with Stinger surface-to-air (SAM) missiles

Bulldog Armoured vehicle of the British Army, built on the same chassis as the FV432 armoured personnel carrier, with a crew of two and space to accommodate up to ten soldiers. Armed with one 7.62mm machine gun.

C-5 Galaxy US four-engined strategic transport aircraft capable of carrying a payload of 130,950 kg (291,000 lb)

C-130 Hercules Four-engine turboprop aircraft that is the workhorse of Western military services. Can transport up to 92 troops or 64 paratroops or 74 litter patients or five standard freight pallets.

CH-47 Chinook twin-engine, tandem rotor transport helicopter in US and British service. Capable of lifting up to 33 fully equipped troops. For medical evacuation, the cabin can accommodate 24 stretchers.

Challenger British Army main battle tank, armed with a 120mm main gun, one 7.62mm chain gun and one 7.62mm anti-aircraft gun.

cluster bomb Air- or ground-launched munition that ejects smaller munitions – a cluster of bomblets

Cobra US attack helicopter with a two-man crew. Armament includes one 20mm cannon, rockets and missiles, including TOW/Hellfire, Sidewinder and Sidearm (anti-radar).

DPCIM (dual-purpose conventional improved munition) An artillery or surface-to-surface missile warhead designed to burst into sub-munitions at an optimum altitude and distance from the desired target for dense area coverage.

Exocet French-built anti-ship missile.

F-1 Mirage French single-seat air-superiority fighter and attack aircraft.

F-15 Eagle American twin-engine, all-weather tactical fighter.

F-16 Fighting Falcon American single-engine multi-role jet fighter aircraft.

F-117 Nighthawk American stealth fighter aircraft.

F/A-18 Hornet American twin-engine, multi-mission, tactical aircraft.

frag The act of wounding or killing a superior officer. The term originally referred to attacking an officer with a fragmentation grenade, but other methods are also used.

Gazelle French light reconnaissance and attack helicopter.

GBU-38 A JDAM (joint direct attack munition) manufactured by Boeing in the US.

George Cross The highest civil decoration of Great Britain.

Ghawar oil field Saudi Arabian oil field, located about 100 km (62 miles) southwest of Dhahran.

GPMG (general-purpose machine gun) British Army 7.62mm machine gun.

Gurkhas Nepalese soldiers traditionally recruited into the British Army.

Hawk American surface-to-air missile system.

Hellfire Air-launched missile capable of knocking out any known tank in the world.

HEMTT (heavy expanded-mobility tactical truck) Heavy truck in US Army service.

HOT (*haut-subsonique optiquement téléguidé* [high subsonic optical guided]) Anti-tank missile system.

HUMMWV (high-mobility multi-purpose wheeled vehicle) US military all-purpose jeep. Also referred to as a Humvee.

Javelin Anti-armour missile.

jihad A Muslim holy war against infidels in defence of the Islamic faith.

LAV (light armoured vehicle) A family of armoured vehicles in service with the US Army and US Marine Corps.

M1A1 Abrams US main battle tank armed with a 120mm gun.

M4 US 5.56mm carbine.

M16 US 5.56mm assault rifle.

M60 US 7.62mm machine gun.

M109 US self-propelled 155mm howitzer.

M113 US armoured personnel carrier.

M114 'Up-Armour' Humvee. A purpose-built version of the Humvee family, intended to provide better protection for crew and systems alike.

M203 grenade launcher Lightweight, single-shot, breech-loaded 40mm weapon designed especially for attachment to the M4 Carbine and the M16 rifle.

M240B machine gun US 7.62mm general-purpose machine gun.

M249 machine gun US 5.56mm air-cooled, belt-fed machine gun.

Merlin helicopter British all-weather, day-and-night, multi-role helicopter.

MH60 Special operations variant of the Black Hawk helicopter.

Mk 19 Belt-fed automatic 40mm grenade launcher.

MLRS (multiple launch rocket system) A rocket artillery system used by a number of countries including Bahrain, Britain, Denmark, France, Germany, Greece, Israel, Italy, Japan, South Korea, Netherlands, Norway, Turkey and the US.

MOP suit (mission-oriented protective posture suit) Protective gear designed to be worn in toxic environments.

mujahedeen Islamic fighters.

Navy Cross The highest medal awarded by the US Department of the Navy and the second-highest award given for valour.

OV-10 Bronco US turbo prop-driven light attack and observation aircraft.

Paladin US 155mm self-propelled howitzer.

Patriot US long-range, all-altitude, all-weather air defence system designed to to counter tactical ballistic missiles, cruise missiles and advanced aircraft.

Pinzgauer High-mobility all-terrain 4x4 and 6x6 military utility vehicles.

PKM Russian 7.62mm heavy machine gun.

POW Prisoner of war.

Puma French-designed four-bladed, twin-engined medium transport/utility helicopter.

Republican Guard Elite formation of the Iraqi Army during the reign of Saddam Hussein.

RPG Rocket-propelled grenade launcher.

Rumaylah oil field An oil field located in Kuwait and southern Iraq.

SA80 British Army 5.56mm assault rifle.

Safaniya oil field The largest offshore oil field in the world, located off Saudi Arabia.

Scud Iraqi surface-to-surface missile.

SH-60 Seahawk Twin turboshaft engine, multi-mission US Navy helicopter.

Silkworm Anti-ship cruise missile.

Squad Automatic Weapon Another term for the M249 machine gun.

T-55 Russian main battle tank armed with a 100mm main gun.

T-62 Russian main battle tank armed with a 115mm main gun.

T-64 Russian main battle tank armed with a 125mm main gun.

T-72 Russian main battle tank armed with a 125mm main gun.

Tomahawk cruise missile US long-range, all-weather, subsonic cruise missile.

TOW (tube-launched, optically tracked, wire-guided) Anti-tank missile.

UAV (unmanned aerial vehicle) Remotely piloted or self-piloted aircraft that can carry cameras, sensors, communications equipment or weapons.

UH-60 Black Hawk US utility tactical transport helicopter.

US National Security Council US President's principal forum for considering national security and foreign policy matters with senior national security advisors and cabinet officials.

Warrior British Army infantry fighting vehicle, armed with a 30mm cannon.

white phosphorous A flare- and smoke-producing agent and an incendiary agent.

List of entries by country

There are 139 entries featured in the book. The following section lists them by their country. The author would like to thank each one for their help in creating this book

Afghanistan
Fariba Ahmadi Kakar
Sameer Ahmad Tahseen

Australia
Dave Bergman
Joe Day
Martin Wallace

Britain
John Allen
David Bradley
Mike Brodie
Rory Bruce
Richard Byrne
Christian Cabaniss
Tom Charles
Tim Collins
Jason Conway
Matthew Croucher
Graham Cushway
Glenn (Dicko) Dixon
Bill Drinkwater
Hugo Farmer
Stephen Grey
Danny Groves
Chris Holmes
Muhammad Khan
Folarin Kuku
Jamie Loden
Jack Lopresti
Jacq McKinnon
Anthony Matthews
Charlie Mayo
Gordon Messenger
Stuart Pearson
John Peters
Duncan Phimister
David Robertson

Patrick Sanders
Eddie Scott
Alli Shields
Al Steele
Alan Strain
Amy Thomas
David 'Tommo'
　　Thompson
Andy Vincent
Kev Walker
Matthew Webb
Christian Wildsmith-
　　Gleave
Brian Wood

Canada
Fraser Clark
Hélène Le Scelleur
Joe McAllister
Kevin Patterson
Barry Pitcher
Ray Wiss

France
Hubert de Laroque la
　　Tour

Iraq
Raad Al-Hamdani
Ismail Hussein Ali
Qais Mizher

Iran
Roshan Khadivi

United States
John Agoglia
Tracy Abernathy-
　　Walden

Ramzy Azar
Chris Bain
Gary Berntsen
Craig Berryman
J. J. Bixby
Charles Blume
Matthew F. Bogdanos
Ken Brown
Todd Brown
Ray G. Brueland
Willard Buhl
Michael Burgoyne
Christopher Campbell
Kim Campbell
Theresa O. Cantrell
Rogelio L. Carrera
Earl J. Catagnus
Lara Yacus Chapman
Jeffrey J. Clark
Rhonda Cornum
Donald Cullison
Greg Darling
Brian Drinkwine
Ladda 'Tammy'
　　Duckworth
Steven Dutch
Brad Z. Edison
Michael Erwin
Doug Feiring
Brandon Friedman
Andrew A. 'Drew' Fuller
Deborah Gilmore
David Haight
Joe Haman
Gerald R. Harkins
Fred L. Hart
Patrick Haygood
Bill Hobbs
James P.L. Holzgrefe

Alex Horton

Andy Hoskinson

Guy L. Hunter

Garrett S. Jones

Dan Kearney

James D. Keeling

Nelson G. Kraft

Drew David Larson

Justin D. LeHew

Robert Lewis

Aubrey McDade Jr.

Billie J. Maddox

Jim L. Manley

Ernest 'Rock' Marcone

David A. Moon

Becky L Morgan

Benjamin Morgan

Dennis G. Morral

Jesse Murphree

John B. Nails

Don Nitti

Jesse G. Odom

Jordan Paquette

John Pettit

Mike Regner

Josue Reyes

Murray Rice

Damon Rooney

James Ross

Paul Samburg

John F. Sattler

Richard D. Schleckser

Ryan 'Doc' Scholl

Donald Shawver

Alvin Shell

Joseph Small

David Swan

Charity Trueblood

Jason Whiteley

David Winkler

Major Zarnik

John G. Zierdt

Index

Abernathy-Walden, Tracy 48–9
Abu Bakr 19
Acharya, Sanjay 177
Afghan National Army (ANA)
    12, 178–9, 189, 191, 197
    casualties 175
Afghanistan 11 *see also*
    hearts and minds;
    Helmand; NATO;
    Operation Enduring
    Freedom
Afghani casualties 175–9
aid programmes 208–9 *see also*
    hearts and minds
    map 156
    nation-building 12–13
    overview 157–8
    Soviet invasion 157–8
Agoglia, John 222–3
al-Qaed Bridge 90–1
al-Qaeda 10–11, 12, 131,
    159, 162–8
al-Sadr, Muqtada 93, 106, 107
Al Sanbouk 29
Allawi. Ayad 118, 121
Allen, John 190
Ambush Alley 79–80
Amin, Hafizullah 157
An Nasiriyah 76–83, 87–92
Anbar Province 137–8
Australian Forces 98–9,
    169–70, 175
Azar, Ramzy 86–7

Ba'ath Party 20
Baghdad 87–92
Baghdad Biltmore 58–61
Bain, Chris 97
Baqubah 139–44
Basra 105–13, 145–7
Basra Palace 144–5
Battle of 73 Easting 41–2
Battle of Basra 145–7
Battle of Danny Boy 104–5
Battle of Fallujah 228–30
    first entry to city account
        123–4
    Gator Battery account 125–6
    guerrilla warfare account
        119–21
    Navy Cross account 126–7
    ordnance disposal account
        124
    overview 118–19
    repatriation account 127–9
    second battle account 121–3

street-wise account 125
strike fighter account 124–5
Task Force Fury account 126
Battle of Khafji 41
Bayan Palace 25
Bergman, Dave 219–20
Berntsen, Gary 160–2
Berryman, Craig 65
bin Laden, Osama 10–11,
    159, 161–2
Bixby, J. J. 137–8
Black Hawk helicopters 114
Blackbird fighters 89
Blair, Tony 68
Blount, Buford 70
Blume, Charles 77–8
Bogdanos, Matthew F. 171–2
Bradley, David 105–13, 230–8
British casualties 13–14, 224
British Forces 23
    1st Armoured Division 37,
        69
    2nd Field Regiment 47–8
    4 Rifles Battle Group 144–5
    7th Armoured Brigade 37
    16th Air Assault Brigade
        173, 185, 227–8
    40 Commando Regiment
        194–5
    Aeromedical Evacuation
        Team 198–9
    Black Watch Regiment 204
    Cheshire Regiment 105–13,
        230
    Combat Support Logistic
        Corps 205–6
    Exeter, HMS 34–5
    Grenadier Guards 190–1
    Gurkhas 193, 196–7
    Household Cavalry
        Regiment 180
    Light Dragoons 203–4
    No IV (Army Cooperation)
        Squadron 196–7
    Parachute Regiment 186–8
    Princess of Wales's Royal
        Regiment 104–5, 201–2,
        230
    Royal Anglian Regiment
        191–3
    Royal Artillery 47–8, 190
    Royal Electrical &
        Mechanical Engineers
        193–4
    Royal Irish Regiment 72
    Royal Logistic Corps 198
    Royal Marine Commandos
        180, 200, 201–2
    Royal Marines Reserve 188

Royal Military Police
    199–200
Royal Naval Reserve 218–19
Royal Navy 34–5
Royal Regiment of
    Scotland 197, 206
Royal Welsh Fusiliers 193–4
Territorial Army 201, 202–3,
    205–6
United Kingdom Task
    Force (UKTF) 188
Welsh Guards 195–6
Brodie, Mike 34–5
Brown, Ken 86
Brown, Todd 73–4
Bruce, Rory 188
Buhl, Willard 124
Burgoyne, Michael 125–6
Bush, George H.W. 10, 22, 38
Bush, George W. 10, 11, 68,
    130
Byrne, Richard 218–19

Cabaniss, Christian 204–5
Camp Bastion 178, 186, 201,
    202–3
Camp Blackjack 100
Camp Fallujah 99
Camp Pennsylvania, Kuwait 71
Camp Taji 138
Campbell, Christopher 220–1
Campbell, Kim 85–6
Canadian Forces 173, 175–9,
    211–14
Cantrell, Theresa O. 26–7
Carrera, Rogelio L. 61–3
Casey, George W. 118–19
casualties
    Afghani 175–9
    ANA 175
    booby trap account 225–7
    British 13–14, 224
    Iraqi 38, 119
    landmine account 227–8
    overview 224–5
    Taliban 173
    UK treatment account
        230–8
    US 38, 119, 224
    women 176
Catagnus, Earl J. 119–21
Chapman, Lara Yacus 138
Charles, Tom 195–6
Clark, Fraser 214–16
Clinton, Bill 172
Collins, Tim 72–3
Combat Stress 15
Comfort, USS 86–7
compensation 14

Conway, James 69
Conway, Jason 187
Cornum, Rhonda 57–8
Croucher, Matthew 194–5
Cullison, Donald 217–18
Cushway, Graham 147–53

Daoud Khan, Muhammed 157
Darling, Greg 170–1
Day, Joe 98–9
de Laroque la Tour, Hubert
  40–1
Dixon, Glen 'Dicko' 47–8
Diyala 140–1
Drinkwater, Bill 192
Drinkwine, Brian 126
Duckworth, Ladda 'Tammy'
  114
Dutch Forces 173
Dutch, Steven 52–3

Edison, Brad Z. 119–21
Erwin, Michael 123–4

Fahd, King 22
Faisal II 20
Fallujah 98–9 *see also* Battle
  of Fallujah
Farmer, Hugo 188
Feiring, Doug 78–83
First Gulf War *see also*
  Operation Desert Sabre;
  Operation Desert Shield;
  Operation Desert Storm
  casualties 38
  map 18
  overview 9
Forward Operating Base
  Gardez 217–18
Forward Operating Base
  Lynx 181–2
Forward Operating Base
  Robinson 190
French Forces 23, 37, 40–1
friendly fire 178–9
Fuller, Andrew A. 'Drew'
  138–9

Geneva Convention 54
German Forces 173
Ghawar oil field 22
Gilmore, Deborah 32–3
Glaspie, April 22
Gleave, Christian Wildsmith-
  196–7
Goddard, Nicola 176
Grey, Stephen 179–81
Groves, Danny 186–7

Guerrillas 120

Haditha 91, 131–3
Haight, David 183–4
Hall, Lundy 49–51
Haman, Joe 131–3
Hamdani, Raad Al- 87–92
Harkins, Gerald R. 30–2
Hart, Fred L. 24–6
Haygood, Patrick 38–9
  hearts and minds
    agricultural development
      account 218–19
    civilian casualties account
      221–2
    effectiveness 222–3
  Health Services account
    213–14
  Helmand account 192
    mine clearance accounts
      219–21
    Provincial Reconstruction
      Teams 210–13
    reconstruction accounts
      214–18
    UNICEF account 209–10
  Helmand 178
    Alamo Base account 186–7
    Camp Bastion account
      193–4
    Camp Bastion field hospital
      account 202–3
    Diesel account 202
    drugs account 201–2
    Forward Operating Base
      Inkerman account 200
    George Cross account 194–5
    Gereshk account 191
    green zone account 195–6
    Harrier account 196–7
    hearts-and-minds account
      192
    Khanjar account 204–5
    logistics accounts 205–6
    MERT account 201
    mobile outreach groups
      account 190
    Nawzad account 191–2
    nurse's account 198–9
    overview 185–6
    Panther's Claw accounts
      203–4
    RMP account 199–200
    Sangin base accounts 187–8
    spokesmen accounts 188–9
    women in combat accounts
      198–200
  Help for Heroes 6–7, 14–15
  Hobbs, Bill 42

Holmes, Chris 191–2
Holzgrefe, James P. L. 71
Horton, Alex 139–44
Hoskinson, Andy 51–2
Hunter, Guy L. Jr. 60–1

IDF (indirect fire) attacks
  151–3
IEDs (improvised explosive
  devices) 13, 181–2
'Infantry Squad Tactics in
  Military Operations' 119
insurgency *see also* Battle of
  Fallujah
  air ambulance account
    113–14
  Al Taji base camp account 97
  ambush account 96–7,
    100–4
  Baqubah account 139–44
  Basra account 105–13
  Basra Palace account 144–5
  Bronze Star account 133
  casualties 119
  checkpoint account 104–5
  Fallujah 98–9
  Haditha account 131–3
  helicopter account 114
  living conditions account 94
  officer protection account
    116
  overview 93
  police account 95–6
  private security account
    147–53
  reality of life accounts 115,
    116–17
  Special Forces account
    138–9
  Task Force Saber accounts
    134–8
  terrain account 94–5
  troop surge 130–1, 149–50
  women in combat accounts
    138
International Security
  Assistance Forces (IASF)
  178–9, 208
Iran 20, 21, 92
Iraq 9–10 *see also* First Gulf
  War; insurgency
  Iran war 20, 21, 92
  Islam 19–20
  map 68
  occupation *see* Operation
    Iraqi Freedom
  oil revenues 19–20, 21
  police stations 95–6
  politics 20

territorial disputes 21–2
trade embargoes 22
weather account 94
Iraq, invasion and occupation
  11–12
Iraqi casualties 38, 119
Iraqi Forces
  10th Brigade 84–5
  Fedayeen Saddam 69, 70
  Mahdi Army 93, 105–13,
    145–7
  Medina Division 84–5
  Republican Army 87–92
  Republican Guard 25, 38
  Security Forces 118
  Tawakalna Division 41–2
Islam 19
Ismail Hussein, Ali 95–6
Istiqlal 29

Jones, Garrett S. 225–7
Jordanian Forces 175–6

Kabul 157, 158, 159, 161
Kajaki Dam 178
Kakar, Fariba Ahmadi 174
Kandahar 159, 211–13
Kandahar Field Hospital
  175–9
Kandahar Provincial
  Reconstruction Team
  214–16
Karmal, Babrak 157
Karzai, Hamid 173
Kassem, Abd al-Karim 20
Kearney, Dan 183
Keeling, James D. 119–21
Kellogg Brown & Root 175
Khadivi, Roshan 209–10
Khan, Muhammad 192–3
Khatoon 143
Khobar Towers 9
Korengal River Valley 183
Kraft, Nelson G. 162–7
Kuku, Folarin 190–1
Kurds 70
Kuwait 9
  air campaign *see* Operation
    Desert Storm
  ground campaign *see*
    Operation Desert Sabre
  invasion of *see* Operation
    Desert Shield
  Iraqi debts 21
  liberation of 37–8
  prisoners of war 61–3
  territorial disputes 21–2
Kuwaiti Forces 24

Larson, Drew David 113–14
Le Scelleur, Hélène 213–14
LeHew, Justin D. 76–7
Lewis, Robert 46–7
Loden, Jamie 188
Lopresti, Jack 201
Lukowiak, Ken 15
Lynch, Jessica 69

McAllister, Joe 216–17
McDade, Aubrey Jr. 126–7
McKiernan, David 68
McKinnon, Jacq 198–9
Maddox, Billie J. 63
Mahdi Army 93, 105–13,
  145–7
Manley, Jim L. 64
Marcone, Ernest 'Rock' 83–5
Martyrs 120
Matthews, Anthony 203–4
Mayo, Charlie 189
Mazar-i-Sharif 159, 160–2
Messenger, Gordon 201–2
Middle East map 8
Mine Action Centre 219–20
Mirwais Hospital 178
Mizher, Qais 145–7
Moon, David A. 119–21
Morgan, Becky L. 32–3
Morgan, Benjamin 116
Morral, Dennis G. 28–30
Muhammad 19
Murphree, Jesse 182
Musa Qala 177–8, 179–81,
  186–7

Nails, John B. 94–5
Najaf 106
Najibullah, Mohammad 158
NATO (North Atlantic
  Treaty Organization)
  12–13, 173–4 *see also*
  Helmand
  Afghan account 174
  economic war account 183–4
  physicians' accounts 175–9,
    181–2
  Purple Heart account 182
  reporter account 179–81
  role of 208
  village account 183
New Zealand Forces 175
9/11 terrorist attacks 10, 11,
  159
Nitti, Don 94
Northern Alliance 159

Obama, Barack 13, 174, 204
Odom, Jesse G. 74–6

Operation Achilles 189
Operation Anaconda
  air strikes account 169
  B-52s account 169–70
  overview 159–60
  rifle platoon account 168–9
  Task Force account 164–7
  tea invitation account 171–2
  Whaleback account 170–1
Operation Arrowhead Ripper
  140–4
Operation Bawwabatu
  Annaher 131–3
Operation Desert Sabre 9–10,
  37–8
  artillery account 47–8
  Bradley fighting vehicle
    account 38–9
  chemical warfare accounts
    42–3
  logistics account 49–51
  Maintenance Platoon
    account 41–2
  transport account 43–6
Operation Desert Shield
  air defence ship account
    34–5
  Corps Support account 27–8
  invasion account 24–6
  logistics account 30–2
  map 36
  overview 9, 22–4
  Scud account 26–7
  search and rescue account
    28–30
  weather account 33–4
  women in combat accounts
    32–3, 48–9
Operation Desert Storm
  10–11, 37–8
  Abrams tank account 39–40
  helicopter account 40–1
  remotely controlled vehicle
    account 46–7
Operation Diesel 201–2
Operation Enduring Freedom
  11
  CIA account 160–2
  overview 158, 159–60
  Shah-i-Kot Valley accounts
    162–8
Operation Glacier 4 188
Operation Herrick 185
Operation Iraqi Freedom
  chaplain's account 86
  civil affairs account 52–3
  close-air-support mission
    account 85–6
  cross border account 71

eve-of-invasion speech 72–3
first company in account
74–6
Iraqi account 87–92
minefield account 51–2
An Nasiriyah accounts
76–83
overview 11–12, 69–71
prisoners of war 86–7
reception account 73–4
Saddam International
Airport account 83–5
Operation Khanjar 204–5
Operation Kryptonite 178
Operation Medusa 173
Operation Mountain Thrust
173
Operation Panther's Claw
203–4
Operation Phantom Fury 118

Pakistan 185–6
Paquette, Jordan 136–7
Patterson, Kevin 175–9
Pearson, Stuart 227–8
Perkins, David 70
Peters, John 58–60
Petraeus, David 70
Petraeus, David H. 131
Pettit, John 42–3
Phimister, Duncan 202–3
Pitcher, Barry 210–13
prisoners of war
British prisoners 58–60
Iraqi abuses 54–5
Iraqi prisoners 55, 63–4,
86–7
Kuwaiti prisoners 61–3
long-term effects 65
US prisoners 55–6, 60–1
women prisoners 57–8
private security companies
147–53

Qusay Saddam Hussein 90–1

Ramadi 134
Ray G. Brueland 33–4
Red Cross 56, 178
Regner, Mike 125
Reid, John 13
Reyes, Josue 116–17
Rice, Murray 96–7
Robertson, David 197
Romanian Forces 175–6
Rooney, Damon 135–6
Ross, James 100–4
Rumaylah oil field 21
Russell, Andrew 126–7

Saddam Hussein
chemical attacks 23–4
in custody 11–12
fall of Baghdad 88, 89–90,
91–2
Iran war 20
Kuwait and 9, 21–2
statue toppled 70
WMD 10
Saddam International Airport
83–5
Sadr City 93
Safaniya oil field 22
Samarra 93
Samburg, Paul 39–40
Sanders, Patrick 144–5
Sattler, John F. 121–3
Saudi Arabia 9, 10, 22, 33–4
Schleckser, Richard D. 169
Scholl, Ryan 'Doc' 124–5
Schwarzkopf, Norman 22–3
Scott, Eddie 206
Shah-i-Kot Valley 159–60,
162–7, 168–9
Shatt al-Arab waterway dispute
20
Shawver, Donald 41–2
Shell, Alvin 228–30
Shi'a Muslims 19, 93
Shields, Alli 198
Shir Zai Hospital 178
Small, Joseph 55–6
Steele, Al 204
Strain, Alan 205–6
suicide bombers 95–6
Sunni Muslims 19, 93
Swan, David 134

Tahseen, Sameer Ahmad
221–2
Taliban *see also* Helmand;
NATO; Operation
Enduring Freedom
defeat 2001 11, 12
overview 158
politican's account 174
Taliban casualties 173
Taraki, Noor Muhammad 157
Thomas, Amy 199–200
Thompson, David 'Tommo'
200
Tikrit 94
Tora Bora cave complex 159,
161–2
Trueblood, Charity 133
Turkey 70

UN Security Council 22
United Nations 208

United Nations Children's
Fund (UNICEF) 209–10
US casualties
Afghanistan 224
First Gulf War 38
insurgency 119
Iraq 224
US Forces 23
1 Marine Expeditionary
Force 121–3
1st Armored Division 37,
38, 70
1st Cavalry Division 51–2,
100–4, 123–4, 125, 141
1st Cavalry Regiment 37
1st Corps Support
Command 27–8
1st Infantry Division 37, 38
1st Marine Division 37, 38,
42, 42–3, 77–8, 225–7
1st Marine Expeditionary
Force 69, 74–6, 125
1st Marine Regiment 124,
131
1st SRIG 46–7
2nd Armored Cavalry
Regiment 37, 41–2
2nd Assault Amphibious
Battalion 76–7
2nd Brigade Combat Team
125
2nd Infantry Division
139–44
2nd Marine Division 37, 38,
131–3
2nd Marine Expeditionary
Brigade 204–5
2nd Marine Regiment 76–7
3rd Armored Cavalry
Regiment 37, 96–7
3rd Armored Division 37,
39–40
3rd Battalion 119
3rd Brigade Combat Team
183–4
3rd Infantry Division 70,
83–5
3rd Stryker Brigade 139–44
4th Brigade Combat Team
126
4th Infantry Division 70,
73–4
5th Air Defense Artillery
Regiment 100–4
5th Marine Regiment 42–3,
119
7th Cavalry Regiment 123–4
8th Cavalry Regiment
115–17

8th Marine Regiment 126
10th Mountain Infantry
Division 170–1
15th Infantry Regiment
38–9
16th Military Police Brigade
(Airborne) 228–30
17th Air Cavalry Regiment
71
19th Air Support Operations
Squadron 169
24th Infantry Division 38–9
24th Mechanized Infantry
Division 37, 38–9
32nd Medical Supply 26–7
32nd MEDSOM 33–4
44th Medical Brigade 63
69th Armor Regiment 83–5
82nd Airborne Division 23,
30–2, 126, 180–1
82nd Field Artillery 51–2,
125
82nd Medical Company
113–14
87th Infantry Regiment
162–7
101st Airborne Division 37,
38, 70, 71, 86, 168–9
173rd Airborne Brigade 70
173rd Airborne Brigade
Combat Team 183
327 Infantry Regiment 71
332rd Air Expeditionary
Wing 85–6
404th Aviation Support
Battalion 94
432nd Civil Affairs Company
52–3

503rd Infantry Regiment 182
507th Maintenance
Company 69
732nd Expeditionary
Logistics Squadron 133
1485th Transport Company
43–6
Air Force Reserve 127–9
Army Reserve 32–3
Combined Forces Land
Component Command 69
Corps Support Group 49–51
Dog Company 115–17
Dragon Brigade 30–2
Joint Special Operations
Command 161
Marine Air Control Group 1
32–3
Marine Corps 32–3, 46–7,
55–6, 78–83, 98–9, 151
Marine Wing Support
Squadron 273 48–9
Nicholas, USS 28–30
Optical and Maintenance
Battalion 26–7
Special Forces 138–9
Strike Fighter Squadron 81
124–5
Task Force 1-87th Infantry
162–7
Task Force Fury 126, 180
Task Force Saber 134–8
Task Force Tarawa 76–7
USS *Comfort* 86–7
V Corps 69, 70, 88–9
VII Corps 37, 38
XVIII Airborne Corps 23,
30–2, 38, 38–9, 220–1

Walker, Kev 193–4
Wallace, Martin 169–70
Wallace, William Scott 69
War on Terror 11, 185
Warrior tanks 108
Webb, Matthew 202
Whiteley, Jason 115
Winkler, David 43–6
Wiss, Ray 181–2
WMD 10
women in combat accounts
casualties 176
Helmand account 198–200
insurgency accounts 114,
138
Operation Desert Shield
32–3, 48–9
Operation Iraqi Freedom
85–6
POWs 57–8
Wood, Brian 104–5
Wootton Bassett 14

Zahir Shah, Muhammad 157
Zarnik, Major 127–9
Zierdt, John G. 27–8

Acknowledgements

The author would like to thank
the following individuals for
their invaluable help in making
this book possible: Gary
Berntsen, David Bradley, Mike
Brodie, Richard Byrne, Lara
Chapman, Rhonda Cornum,
Graham Cushway, Steve Dent,
William Deveneau, Kathy M.
Doyle, Steven Dutch, Tonya S.
Goforth, Danny Groves, Lundy
W. Hall, Nat Helms, Bill
Hobbs, Alex Horton, Roshan

Khadivi, Edward Marek, Chad
Pagel, John Pettit, Tim Relf,
Donald Shawver, Jenifer Stepp,
Aruna Vasudevan.

Picture credits
Getty Images Cover image,
Plate section I: Pages 1, 2, 3, 4,
5, 6b, 7, 8b.
Press Association Plate section
II: Pages 3, 4, 5, 7b, 8.
Others Plate section I: Pages
6t, 8t, Plate section II: Pages

2, 6. Each of these belongs to
the individual depicted.
Plate II, page 1 photograph
is from the US Department
of Defense.

Map credits Stephen Dew